# The Early Martyr Narratives

DIVINATIONS: REREADING LATE ANCIENT RELIGION

Series Editors: Daniel Boyarin, Virginia Burrus, Derek Krueger

A complete list of books in the series
is available from the publisher.

# THE
# EARLY MARTYR
# NARRATIVES

Neither Authentic Accounts
nor Forgeries

Éric Rebillard

**PENN**

UNIVERSITY OF PENNSYLVANIA PRESS

PHILADELPHIA

Published by
University of Pennsylvania Press
Philadelphia, Pennsylvania 19104-4112
www.upenn.edu/pennpress

Printed in the United States of America on acid-free paper

10 9 8 7 6 5 4 3 2 1

Library of Congress Cataloging-in-Publication Data

Names: Rebillard, Éric, author.
Title: The early martyr narratives : neither authentic accounts
    nor forgeries / Éric Rebillard.
Other titles: Divinations.
Description: 1st edition. | Philadelphia : University of
    Pennsylvania Press, [2020] | Series: Divinations :
    rereading late ancient religion | Includes bibliographical
    references and index.
Identifiers: LCCN 2020004966 | ISBN 978-0-8122-5260-6
    (hardcover)
Subjects: LCSH: Martyrologies—History and criticism. |
    Christian martyrs—Biography—Early works to 1800—
    History and criticism. | Christian literature, Early—
    Criticism, Textual.
Classification: LCC BR1609 .R43 2020 | DDC 272/.1—dc23
LC record available at https://lccn.loc.gov/2020004966

# CONTENTS

# ABBREVIATIONS

AASS      *Acta Sanctorum quotquot toto orbe coluntur.* Paris: Victor
              Palmé, 1863–1940.
AAgap     *Acts of Agape, Irene, Chione, and Companions*
ACypr     *Acts of Cyprian*
APerp     *Acts of Perpetua and Felicity*
AScil      *Acts of the Scilitan Martyrs*
BHG      Halkin, François. *Bibliotheca hagiographica Graeca.* Subsidia
              Hagiographica 8. 3rd ed. Brussels: Société des Bollandistes,
              1957; Halkin, François. *Novum Auctarium Bibliothecae*
              *hagiographicae Graecae.* Subsidia Hagiographica 65. Brussels:
              Société des Bollandistes, 1984.
BHL      *Bibliotheca hagiographica Latina antiquae et mediae aetatis.*
              Subsidia Hagiographica 6. Brussels: Société des Bollandistes,
              1898–1901; *Bibliotheca hagiographica Latina antiquae et mediae*
              *aetatis. Novum Supplementum.* Subsidia Hagiographica 70.
              Brussels: Société des Bollandistes, 1986.
BHO      Peeters, Paul. *Bibliotheca hagiographica Orientalis.* Subsidia
              Hagiographica 10. 3rd ed. Brussels: Société des Bollandistes,
              1970.
CPL      *Clavis patrum Latinorum.* Corpus Christianorum. Series
              Latina. Turnhout: Brepols, 1995.
MCarp     *Martyrdom of Carpus, Papylus, and Agathonice*
MPion     *Martyrdom of Pionius*
MPol      *Martyrdom of Polycarp*
PCrispin   *Acts of Crispina*
PDon      *Passion of Donatus*
PIR[2]      *Prosopographia Imperii Romani Saec. I. II. III. Editio altera.*
              Berlin: 1933–.
PLuc      *Passion of Lucius, Montanus, and Their Companions*

PMar            *Passion of Marian and James*
PMax            *Passion of Maxima, Secunda, and Donatilla*
PPerp           *Passion of Perpetua, Felicity, and Their Companions*
PSaturnDat      *Passion of Saturninus, Dativus, and Their Companions* (or *Acts of the Abitinian Martyrs*)
VCypr           *Life of Cyprian*

In addition to the abbreviations listed above, I use the following lists of abbreviations for ancient authors and texts:

| | |
|---|---|
| Greek texts | List I. Authors and Works, *Diccionario Griego-Español* (http://dge.cchs.csic.es/lst/2lst1.htm). |
| Latin texts | Index of Sources, *Thesaurus Linguae Latinae* (http://www.thesaurus.badw.de/en/tll-digital/index/). |
| Old Testament and New Testament | *The SBL Handbook of Style* (Peabody, MA, 1999). |
| Papyri | *Checklist of Greek, Latin, Demotic, and Coptic Papyri, Ostraca, and Tablets* (http://scriptorium.lib.duke.edu/papyrus/texts/clist.html). |

# NOTE ON TEXTS AND TRANSLATIONS

Unless otherwise noted, Greek and Latin texts are respectively those of the digital editions of the *Thesaurus Linguae Graecae* (stephanus.tlg.uci.edu) and the *Library of Latin Texts* (clt.brepolis.net).

Translations are mine unless otherwise noted.

# Introduction

## Collecting Martyr Texts: A Short History

Between Eusebius of Caesarea, who first compiled a collection of martyr narratives around 300,[1] and Thierry Ruinart, whose *Acta primorum martyrum sincera et selecta* was published in 1689 and remained the collection of reference until the beginning of the twentieth century,[2] the project of collecting martyr narratives seems to come full circle.[3] Like Eusebius, Ruinart collected martyr narratives with a view to writing a history of the persecutions and he arranged the texts in chronological order of the events they describe. There is, however, a new dimension to Ruinart's collection: criteria of selection.

Since the Humanists, scholars had been troubled by the dubious historical reliability of many of the anonymous texts included in the medieval collections.[4] With the Reformation, attacks against the fables and lies found in the vitae of the medieval saints intensified. The Reformers promoted a new, "purified" hagiography, one that would focus on reliable texts written by authors who were reputed historians, if not eyewitnesses to the events they described.[5] Thus, the *Farrago* of Hermann Bonnus (1539) and the *Magnifice consolatoria exempla* of Georg Spalatin (1544) included only those martyr narratives found in Rufinus's translation of the *Ecclesiastical History* of Eusebius.[6] Anonymous martyr narratives such as those copied in the medieval legendaries were considered particularly suspicious.[7] These attacks on the cult of the saints and its textual support incited a reaction that has been aptly labeled a Catholic "militant hagiography."[8] This culminated in the ambitious project of Jean Bolland (1596–1665), who undertook to collect all available testimonies, independently of their historical value and regardless of whether they might distress Catholics or provoke heretics to mockery.[9]

It seemed, as Thierry Ruinart explained in his preface, just as fruitless to collect all available texts as it was to limit the collection of martyr narratives to authored texts. Following the impetus of Jean Mabillon (1632–1707), Ruinart sought to distinguish the authentic or genuine texts from the dubious and the false ones.[10] The authentic, he called "acts" (*acta*), a term that remains in use today: "However, those who have undertaken to present these ancient monuments as they are in the antique manuscripts, since their goal was to collect all together the lives of every and all martyrs and confessors, dubious or false, as well as genuine, they were forced to proceed in such a way that they needed many and also huge volumes and that few acts were included and these were mixed with the dubious and false texts so that even the most learned scholars could not identify them without a lot of work."[11] Ruinart did not in his preface describe the criteria he employed when selecting texts for the *Acta primorum martyrum sincera et selecta*. However, after consulting Ruinart's correspondence with the historian Le Nain de Tillemont (1637–98), François Dolbeau lists the following grounds on which Ruinart excluded texts: "Some are historical: inaccurate data about the emperors, chronological inconsistencies, anachronisms about administrative realities, lies unmasked by better sources, false details about the trial procedure, the liturgy, or geography. Other grounds for rejection are more literary, related to the narrative or the language: incoherent texts, too many scriptural quotations, too many miracles, late vocabulary."[12] These criteria have since been refined, and the number of texts accepted as authentic has shrunk considerably over time. In particular, the Bollandist scholar Hippolyte Delehaye (1859–1941) divided hagiographical texts into six classes: official reports, eyewitness accounts, texts whose main source belongs to the first two classes, historical romances, imaginative romances, and forgeries,[13] and wrote: "The new Ruinart that we should like to undertake would contain only the historical documents that belong to the first three categories."[14] Delehaye himself never published his ideal collection, but he did produce a list of eighteen texts he deemed authentic.[15]

Timothy D. Barnes has since resubmitted the texts to fierce historical criticism and created a subcategory of pre-Decian acts.[16] His explicitly stated goal was to find reliable documents for understanding the legal basis of persecutions before the edict of Decius (250). He reviewed nine texts and concluded that six of them "preserve as accurate a report of what happened as may be expected from a contemporary."[17] Recently, however, even these texts have been declared forgeries or frauds.[18]

Thus, despite the progress of historical criticism since Ruinart, the pendulum continues to swing back and forth. The reason why it does is that the search for authenticity and the assumption that there were documents written at the time of martyrdom or very close to it continue to haunt scholarship on martyr narratives.

## The Specter of Authenticity

I borrow the concept of hauntology from Derrida's *Specters of Marx*.[19] That scholars inherit issues from previous scholarship is obvious, and we do not need French theory to help us understand it. However, the notion of haunting "offers a powerful way to speak about forces that affect us profoundly while remaining invisible or elusive."[20]

A concern with authenticity is central even in the context of today's secular scholarship. The objective is no longer to provide concrete evidence of the persecutions of Christians in the Roman empire as it was for Eusebius or Ruinart, nor is it to establish the legitimacy of the cult of the saints as it was for the Catholic "militant" hagiography (and negatively for the Protestant "purified" one). However, the assumption remains that a document was composed at the time of the martyrdom or very soon thereafter, either by an eyewitness or by someone who had access to the official records of the trial, and that this document is the model to which available texts ought to be compared in order to determine whether they contain authentic elements.[21]

This assumption is present when Eusebius refers his readers to the documents he collected, it is present in the apocryphal letter of Jerome that prefaces the *Martyrologium Hieronymianum* and describes the search for trial records through the whole Roman empire, and it is present in the debate between Protestants and Catholics when the former rejected narratives on the basis of their anonymity while the latter strove to seek out the most ancient witnesses. Ruinart made the assumption quite explicit when he attempted to establish criteria for selecting authentic texts.[22]

The extent to which authenticity is a specter that haunts martyr narratives studies is well illustrated by Bart D. Ehrman's and Candida R. Moss's recent attempts to argue that *all* martyr narratives are forgeries or frauds. Indeed, they each base their claims on the fact that "no early Christian account has been preserved without emendation."[23] Such a statement presupposes, if not that actual nonemendated accounts could exist, at least that existing accounts should be compared to what these nonemendated accounts would possibly be, and evaluated against them. Thus, these claims are also a by-product of the search for authenticity.

## A New Approach

We inevitably inherit assumptions about authenticity when we work with a corpus that has been collected—and even edited, as we will see in Chapter 3—in a search for authentic texts. Thus, when scholars such as Ehrman and Moss start with a small group of accounts that previous researchers have selected for their historical reliability, only to reject them as not being "precise historical reports of what actually happened," they presume that these texts were intended to be or claimed to be historical reports.[24] It is another matter altogether that later Christian tradition would consider them as such.

The alternative, to set aside entirely the question of the historical reliability of martyr narratives, is not satisfactory. Indeed, when scholars such as Elizabeth Castelli and Lucy Grig suggest we understand that these texts themselves constructed, if not invented, the memory of the martyrs, they neglect two issues.[25] First, an indirect result is that the date of composition of the texts becomes largely irrelevant: the focus is on the use, reuse, and abuse of these texts in the ecclesiastical tradition rather than on the context of their original production. Second, a paradoxical consequence is that the corpus of texts submitted to scrutiny is, as in the case of Ehrman and Moss, a corpus constituted on the basis of the very same assumptions that have been rejected.

In order to escape the impasse into which either approach leads us, I suggest that the first necessary step is to reject the traditional corpus of texts, and to start afresh by establishing which texts can safely be considered the earliest extant narratives. I will dispense with the issue of authenticity and I will resist dating the texts on the basis of internal elements. Instead, in Chapter 1, I consider only texts concerned with Christians executed before 260, the ancient martyrs, and only those attested to in external evidence before 300. I then attempt to close the gap between their *terminus ante quem*—when the texts are attested in external evidence—and their date of composition by examining their first context of use. In each case, we find that it is a context of intra-ecclesiastical conflict during a period free of persecution. Rather than deduce from this that they are forgeries written for the sake of polemic or apologetics, as does Ehrman, I emphasize that these texts were not produced simply in response to the events they report. We ought therefore to question the traditional generic categorization of martyr narratives and seek a better understanding of exactly what kind of texts we are dealing with.

Another long-standing hindrance to the study of martyr narratives has been the assumption of their derivation from the court protocols of the trials that preceded the executions. It has been established beyond discussion that no martyr text simply reproduces such protocols, yet it is still commonly held that these protocols are constitutive of the character and development of martyrdom accounts.

Very few martyr texts assume the protocol form, and I suggest in Chapter 2 that the format was adopted only after the Great Persecution and only for a brief time. I maintain that we ought to consider the significance and impact of the format rather than argue about whether or not actual protocols have been used, and that we also pay attention to the topoi associated with court protocols as they appear in martyr texts. It then becomes clear that these elements work as authenticating devices, and thus that it is the textuality of martyr narratives that demands further scrutiny.

Chapter 3 pursues this line of inquiry first by analyzing Ehrman's arguments about the *Martyrdom of Polycarp*. This illustrative case study raises important questions about the textual characteristics of martyr narratives. I suggest that they are "living texts," which, in addition to being anonymous, present in the manuscript traditions a textual fluidity. This has been largely ignored in the editing process, which is for the most part interested in reconstructing the original, authentic text underlying the manuscript variations. The example of the so-called Donatist recensions of African martyr narratives and a close study of the many versions of the *Acts of the Scilitan Martyrs* demonstrate the advantages of treating these as living texts. This discussion also paves the way for the next chapter by emphasizing that it is crucial to understand the audience's horizon of expectations when confronting such texts.

Indeed, Chapter 4 builds on the idea that the intended audience did not expect a precise historical report and was prepared to hear or read a *version* of the story.[26] I try, first, to repurpose the now common discourse about the blurring of boundaries between fiction and history in ancient texts, and to show how ancient texts challenge modern definitions of fiction. The resultant picture is that of an audience who readily accepts the historicity of the martyr but does not expect to hear or read a truthful story.

The second part of Chapter 4 begins with a close study of the narration in the earliest martyr texts. The tension between a narration that both refers to its own textuality and appears to cite documents generates a type of fictional complicity with the audience. The use of documents is itself a major device in many martyr narratives, and I suggest that, through the fictional complicity it institutes, the ultimate impossibility of testimony is challenged.

It is my hope that these four chapters successfully argue the case that martyrdom narratives should not be studied with traditional criteria applied in favor of or against their authenticity, and that the question of what kind of texts we are studying is here addressed more satisfactorily than it has been thus far.

## CHAPTER I

# The Earliest Narratives
# and Their Reception

In order to study the production of martyr narratives at its inception, I establish which texts may securely be considered the earliest extant narratives. It is not my intention that this initial group of texts be viewed as a "canon," nor even as a closed list; it is simply a group of texts that both deal with martyrs executed before 260 and are attested before 300.[1] (Although other martyr narratives were very likely composed before 300, comments regarding these are necessarily speculative.) Accordingly, in the first section of this chapter I describe and apply new criteria of selection. In the second, I examine the earliest known contexts of reception of these texts in an attempt to close the gap between their first external attestation and their production.[2] I find that these contexts are all located within the period that opens with the edict of Decius (250) or in that which follows the persecution of Valerian (258–60). In each case, it is a period of peace insofar as the traditional narrative of the persecutions is concerned. This finding suggests that we should consider whether the production of the texts was motivated by factors extrinsic to the persecution and execution of the martyrs whose stories are told.

## The Earliest Narratives

I will treat only narratives concerning those whom Eusebius calls the "ancient martyrs," that is, martyrs executed before 260, when Gallienus repealed Valerian's edict of persecution.[3] The reason for this initial limitation is that texts concerned with the victims of the Great Persecution—there are no records of

executions of Christians between 260 and 303[4]—were written in a very different context. Indeed, even if we are careful not to overemphasize the effects of
the "Constantinian revolution," the number of victims executed and the freedom of cult granted to the Christians by Constantine, not to mention the privi-
leges he accorded to the Christian clergy, significantly transformed the nature
of the memory work on Christian martyrs.[5]

Our criteria should not permit assumptions about authenticity and date of
composition. I use a two-step process: first, there needs to be external evidence
for the existence of a narrative; second, there needs to be sufficient evidence that
one of the extant texts could be the narrative attested in the external evidence.
For the reasons stated above, the external evidence of composition must predate
300.[6] As all narratives about the "ancient martyrs" written in other languages
are translations of an earlier Greek or Latin original, I therefore consider only
Greek and Latin narratives.

## Greek Narratives

No external evidence attests to a Greek narrative before Eusebius does in the
*Collection of Ancient Martyrdoms* that he compiled for the writing of his *Ecclesiastical History*.[7] Eusebius's collection is now lost, but references to it in the
*Ecclesiastical History* allow us to reconstruct its content. Eusebius's *Collection*
included narratives for Apollonius, Carpus and his companions, Pionius, Polycarp, and the martyrs of Lyon and Vienne.[8]

The only extant Greek narrative about Apollonius (BHG 49) presents
details that belong to a tradition different from that known to Eusebius, and the
same is true of the Armenian version (BHO 79), which is a translation of a
different, lost Greek text.[9] Neither BHG 49 nor BHO 79 can, therefore, be
included among the earliest narratives.

Until the discovery of BHG 293 by Aubé in 1881, the text known to Eusebius about Carpus and his companions was assumed to be lost. While Aubé
himself was quite cautious about the identification of BHG 293 as the text
known to Eusebius,[10] Harnack affirmed that BHG 293 was both the original
version and the text Eusebius used.[11] In 1920, Franchi de' Cavalieri discovered a
narrative in Latin, BHL 1622m, which he thought to be a translation of a Greek
text that was closer to the original than BHG 293.[12] Lietzmann presented a
series of arguments against Cavalieri's appraisal of BHL 1622m, and, when
Delehaye revisited the dossier in 1940, he concluded that the narrative known to

Eusebius was lost.[13] A conservative approach, therefore, does not include BHG 293 among the earliest narratives.[14]

In the case of Pionius the situation is relatively straightforward. Eusebius included in his *Collection of Ancient Martyrdoms* a text whose content matches that of the only Greek narrative known to us (BHG 1546).[15] There is, however, a discrepancy in the dating of the martyrdom: Eusebius seems to date the martyrdom to the reign of Marcus Aurelius while BHG 1546 dates it to the persecution of Decius.[16] There are other inconsistencies in this section of Eusebius, such as the mention of Metrodorus, but these may be due to the dossier—Eusebius found the text in a collection of material related to Smyrna.[17] Thus, this is no solid ground for rejecting BHG 1546, and I count it among the earliest narratives.

For Polycarp, Boudewijn Dehandschutter has established that the text excerpted by Eusebius is the text known through the menologia tradition and not an independent, earlier version.[18] As four of the six manuscripts within this tradition also contain the colophon (as well as two other manuscripts that represent two different traditions), there is no reason to postulate that the colophon is a later addition.[19] Hence, I consider BHG 1556–59 to be the text known to Eusebius.[20]

No text concerning the martyrs of Lyon and Vienne has been preserved except the *Letter of the Churches of Lyon and Vienne* that is found in Eusebius's *Ecclesiastical History*.[21] Though he included the whole text and a small dossier of other documents in his *Collection of Ancient Martyrdoms*, Eusebius supplied only excerpts of the *Letter* in the *Ecclesiastical History*.[22] This narrative will, therefore, receive only cursory treatment.

## Latin Narratives

Augustine provides us with a *terminus ante quem* for several Latin texts just as Eusebius does for Greek texts.[23] Indeed, in some of his sermons, he refers to the practice of reading martyr narratives before preaching on the day of their feast, and he sometimes inserts short quotes from them into the body of his sermons.[24] Such a *terminus ante quem*, however, is more than a century later than the *terminus ante quem* for the texts known to Eusebius. As noted above, between 300 and 430 crucial changes occurred that affected the memory work dealing with Christian martyrs. We must, therefore, seek an earlier *terminus ante quem*.

Tertullian, who gathered much information about executions of Christians in his writings,[25] is sometimes said to have known both the *Acts of the Scilitan Martyrs* (BHL 7527) and the *Passion of Perpetua and Felicity* (BHL 6633). In the *Ad Scapulam*, Tertullian reports that Vigellius Saturninus was to his knowledge the first proconsul to put Christians to death in North Africa.[26] Saturninus is in fact the name of the proconsul responsible for the execution of the Scilitan martyrs in BHL 7527, but Tertullian names neither the martyrs nor their city, and as a consequence, his reference to Saturninus is insufficient to guarantee his knowledge of the *Acts*.[27] In the *De anima*, Tertullian mentions Perpetua and refers to one of her visions.[28] We can conclude that he had access to the account she wrote, but not necessarily to the *Passion* (BHL 6633) in which it was included.[29]

The first testimony of BHL 6633 is provided by the *Life of Cyprian*, composed by Pontius, a deacon of the Carthaginian church, soon after Cyprian's execution in 258.[30] It has long been noted that Pontius alludes to Perpetua and her companions in his preface.[31] His text also evinces knowledge of BHL 6633. Indeed, Pontius anticipates his reference to Perpetua and her companions with echoes of the preface to BHL 6633: "It is proper to briefly record a few things, not because the life of so great a man could remain obscure from anyone, even of the pagans, but so that he be offered to those who come after us also, as a great and incomparable model in eternal memory, and thus that he be set forth in writing as an example to be imitated."[32] *Documenta, litteris digerere, exemplum, posteri* are words and expressions that appear at the very beginning of the preface to BHL 6633: "If the ancient examples of faith that bear witness to God's grace and accomplish man's edification have been set forth in writing so that by reading them aloud, by performing the deeds, so to speak, God might be honored and man strengthened, why should not new models equally suited to these goals be set forth? Indeed, these examples will eventually be ancient and indispensable for those who come after us, if they are reckoned of a lesser authority in the present time because of a prejudiced reverence for antiquity."[33] It is clear that Pontius knew BHL 6633, and he therefore provides a *terminus ante quem* of 260 for this text.

It is usually thought that Pontius also knew and used a version of the *Acts of Cyprian*.[34] In his preface, however, Pontius clearly implies that it is not the case: he states that he writes the *Life* so that Cyprian's martyrdom be known too, and when he mentions precedents for writing martyr narratives, he refers only to the *Passion of Perpetua*, and not to any narrative about Cyprian.[35] On the one hand, none of the passages presented as borrowings by Pontius from the *Acts* is conclusive.[36] On the other hand, the passing reference to Cyprian's vision in the *Acts*, which assumes that it is well known, must point to the *Life*, which is the only actual record of the vision.[37] Thus, the *Acts* were composed after the *Life*, and there is no *terminus ante quem* for them other than Augustine.[38]

## Conclusion

The list of extant martyr narratives for which a secure *terminus ante quem* before 300 can be established is short. There are two Greek texts: BHG 1546, the *Martyrdom of Pionius* (MPion) and BHG 1556–59, the *Martyrdom of Polycarp* (MPol). To these we can add the fragments of a third text preserved by Eusebius in the *Ecclesiastical History* 5.1–4: the *Letter of the Churches of Lyon and Vienne* (BHG 1573). There also are two Latin texts: BHL 2041, the *Life of Cyprian* by Pontius (VCypr) and BHL 6633, the *Passion of Perpetua, Felicity, and Their Companions* (PPerp).

# Earlier Contexts of Use

Is it possible to narrow the gap between the year of execution of the martyrs and that of the external attestation to the existence of a narrative? Few modern scholars would propose that the time of composition is simply that of the execution. Instead, since the seventeenth century at least, internal evidence has been used for dating individual texts, but this seems only to lead into an impasse. Understanding how and why will help us to conceive an alternative approach.

## On Dating Martyr Narratives

In "On the Dating of Polycarp," Candida Moss describes well the difficulties encountered by scholars when they use the content of the narrative to determine its date.[39] She reviews old arguments regarding the integrity and authenticity of the account and convincingly argues that a dating in the second century, close to the time of the execution, is unsustainable. She then tries to determine when the text was likely composed by considering both "the texts, ideas, and practices with which MPol is familiar and the reception history of the account."[40]

Among the "texts, ideas, and practices with which MPol is familiar," I comment only on MPol 17–18, usually described as a passage on relics.[41] Though such an interpretation has been contested, Moss seems to concede that MPol 17–18 "presupposes a situation in which the cult of the saints is well established."[42] If MPol is from the second century, it would be the only text to describe the practice of collecting and venerating relics. There are, however, several testimonies from the third century.[43] This passage would thus join the other passages about ideas and practices that better fit into a third-century context. There is more to the passage, however: "What seems most out of place in MPol is the anachronistic (or, perhaps better, prochronistic) *apologia* for the absence of relics."[44] Such an apologia would reflect the concern of ecclesiastical authorities with the status of the martyrs, a concern that better fits a fourth-century context.[45] Because this element points to a period later than the other elements she analyses—all of which are appropriate to a third-century context—she concludes that we should "treat MPol as a third-century composition that may have been redacted in the fourth century."[46] Not only is it quite surprising to see Moss fall back on the same type of arguments—referring to the integrity of the text—as those that she has so convincingly refuted earlier in her paper, but it is clear that our actual knowledge of the "prehistory" of the cult of the martyrs is not sufficiently grounded to reach any such definitive conclusion.[47]

When she examines the reception history of MPol, Moss establishes that there is no evidence that it circulated before the third century.[48] She further notes that, although MPion contains evidence that its producer knew about the story of Polycarp, no element "necessarily refers to a literary account of the death of Polycarp."[49] It is only because she assumes that the commemoration of Polycarp necessitated an "act of memorialization" in the form of a literary text that she can conclude that MPol circulated before the middle of the third century, when MPion attests to his commemoration. Her wording deserves attention: "If Polycarp's death was commemorated on a certain day then it seems likely that there were literary acts to accompany this act of memorialization."[50] However, nothing in the extant third-century evidence associates commemoration with a textual account.[51] When Cyprian gives instruction to ensure that information is collected for the commemoration of those executed in Carthage during his absence, he requires nothing more than that the day of their execution be recorded.[52] Moss's interpretation of this element of the reception history of MPol therefore rests on a baseless assumption.

Moss's careful attempt to date MPol illustrates well the impasse arrived at when the content of the account is used for dating. Inevitably such attempts rest on assumptions that are either left implicit or unprovable. To get closer to the date of composition, I suggest, therefore, that we consider the earliest contexts in which we know the texts were used. I do not mean to reconstruct the reception history of the texts, as Moss does, nor to study their intertextuality,[53] but to investigate the function or role the texts performed in the earliest context in which they were used. This should also provide us with a sense of what early Christians expected from these narratives.

### MPol and MPion

Eusebius indicates that he found the texts about Polycarp and Pionius in an existing collection of material concerned with martyrs from Smyrna. Following his extracts from the narrative about Polycarp, he adds: "Of such an end was the admirable and apostolic Polycarp deemed worthy, as set down by the brethren of the church of Smyrna in their epistle, which we have made known. In the same writing about him, there are also other narratives of martyrdoms that took place in the same city of Smyrna and at the same time as the martyrdom of Polycarp. Among them was Metrodorus who seems to have been a presbyter of the error of Marcion and was put to death by fire. One of the best-known and most celebrated martyrs of that time was Pionius."[54] The letter (ἡ ἐπιστολὴ) from the church of Smyrna and the writing (ἡ γραφὴ) seem to be two different texts, the latter being a compilation of martyr narratives from Smyrna. Eusebius mentions two such narratives in addition to Polycarp's: one about a Marcionite named Metrodorus and one about Pionius. The way he introduces the narrative about Pionius seems to imply that there were also other narratives. There is no preserved narrative about Metrodorus, who is also mentioned in MPion and described there also as a Marcionite presbyter, executed at the same time as Pionius.[55] Whether the information given by Eusebius derives from MPion or from a narrative he found in the Smyrnaean compilation is impossible to determine.[56] In any case, Eusebius chose to include in his own collection only the narratives about Polycarp and Pionius.

Because Pionius was a victim of the edict of Decius, the Smyrnaean compilation must date to after 250. Moreover, Walter Ameling has convincingly argued that MPion was published "as part of an ongoing debate" in Smyrna about the Christians who had sacrificed (the lapsi) and that it used "the authority of the martyr Pionios to broadcast and underpin a certain position in the Smyrnaean church."[57] Such a debate points to the period following the end of

the enforcement of the edict. It is therefore most likely the context in which the
Smyrnaean compilation was composed.[58] This does not necessarily mean that
the compiled texts were all composed at the same time, but it does provide us
with the earliest known context in which they were used.

The epilogue of MPol attributes a major role in its transmission to one
Pionius.[59] Though this Pionius is sometimes dubbed "Pseudo-Pionius" and dis-
tinguished from the Smyrnaean martyr, it seems inescapable that the name
Pionius is intended to convey that he is the well-known third-century martyr.[60]
The mention of Pionius establishes an association between Polycarp and Pionius, an association that is emphasized in MPion,[61] and thus it reinforces the
authority of Pionius himself. MPol does not seem to have much potential utility
in the debate over the status of the lapsi. It touches on the correct attitude
toward martyrdom and briefly addresses the status of the martyrs—they ought
to be cherished, not worshipped.[62] Thus, the main function of MPol in the
Smyrnaean compilation could well have been to lend authority to Pionius
through that of Polycarp, an authority needed by those in the Smyrnaean
church who supported the readmission of the lapsi.[63]

The Smyrnaean compilation, which was available to Eusebius, might well
have been composed in the aftermath of the edict of Decius in order to
strengthen the positions of those Christians who supported the readmission of
the lapsi. It thus provides us with the first context in which we can see how
MPol and MPion were used. The goal of the compilation was not to encourage
Christians to face persecution, at least not primarily, but to weigh in on ecclesiastical controversies by citing the authority of the martyrs. The same seems to
be the case with the other earliest narratives.

## Letter of the Churches of Lyon and Vienne

After quoting several extracts from the *Letter*, Eusebius refers to a few documents associated with the same churches. The first is a judgment of the Gallic
brothers against the followers of Montanus, followed by a dossier of letters written by some of the Gallic martyrs and addressed to the churches of Asia and
Phrygia and to Eleutherus of Rome.[64] There then follows a short extract of a
letter recommending Irenaeus to the same Eleutherus.[65] The fact that Eusebius
concludes this catalogue of documents with a reference to a list of all the martyrs that are mentioned in the *Letter* suggests that all these texts were compiled
in a unique dossier.[66]

According to Pierre Nautin, the dossier was a single compilation by Irenaeus (whom Nautin also believes to be the author of the *Letter*) in the context of his fight against the rigorist tendencies of some of the churches of Asia Minor.[67] The hypothesis of Irenaeus's authorship has been largely ignored by modern scholars and should be abandoned. Winrich A. Löhr has argued that the *Letter* itself did not have a polemical tone, but was included in a polemical dossier at a date posterior to its composition.[68] Whatever the case, certain episodes in the *Letter*'s narrative could easily have been wielded against the New Prophecy.[69] The first context of reception of the *Letter of the Churches of Lyon and Vienne* is again as part of a compilation of documents used in a polemical context. The references to Irenaeus and Eleutherus locate this context in the last quarter of the second century at the earliest. However, given our fragmentary knowledge of the dossier, we cannot exclude that it was compiled later.

## Earliest African Martyr Narratives

In the case of the earliest African martyr narratives there is no evidence that they have been compiled in a dossier.[70] There is, however, evidence that they were used and/or composed in a polemical context.

I established earlier that VCypr, which was composed by Pontius within the years immediately following the end of the persecution of Valerian, provides a *terminus ante quem* for PPerp.[71] I now go a step further and suggest that Pontius's preface points us to the first context, as far as we can know, in which PPerp was used.[72]

Pontius's reference to PPerp presents the characteristics of a generic definition: "Our ancestors, out of admiration for martyrdom itself, have granted such honor even to lay people and catechumens who obtained martyrdom that they have written much—or should I say, almost everything—about their sufferings, and so those martyrs came to our knowledge too, we, who were not yet born. It would, therefore, be unfortunate that the suffering of so great a bishop and so great a martyr as Cyprian be omitted, a man who, even without his martyrdom, had much to teach."[73] Anyone familiar with PPerp would have identified Perpetua, Felicity, and their companions as the laypeople and catechumens targeted here by Pontius.[74] This is more than an allusion to the martyrs. Not only does Pontius claim that his hero is superior (he is a bishop, not a layperson or a catechumen) but he also adds that his narrative is of higher quality (brief, not prolix). In other words, he points to a predecessor over whom he claims superiority. This means that he has the narrative itself in mind, not just its characters.

The contrast that Pontius draws between the figure of the bishop-martyr Cyprian and the lay martyrs evokes the conflicts between the bishop and some members of the Carthaginian clergy that arose during Cyprian's episcopacy, and the role that martyrs and confessors played in these conflicts.[75] Because of the special authority accorded to them, Cyprian and his opponents used martyrs and confessors to weigh in on conflicts that were personal and political as well as theological.[76] Though Cyprian does not mention his rival bishops in Carthage after the dispute over the reconciliation of the lapsi was resolved, the conflict over rebaptism followed the same lines of fracture within the church.[77] Dissent between members of the Carthaginian clergy seems to have continued, if less publicly, and even the death of Cyprian did not bring it to an end. Pontius clearly writes at a time of tensions, probably over Cyprian's replacement, and his portrait of Cyprian is strongly apologetic.[78] The focus on the authority of the bishop, the lengthy defense of his exile, the silence about internal conflicts—whether over the reconciliation of the lapsi or the rebaptism of the schismatics—all this points to serious tensions among Christians in Carthage and in North Africa more generally in the aftermath of Cyprian's death. The authority of the bishop that Cyprian strove to assert during his episcopacy is not as uncontested as his carefully crafted dossier of letters would have us believe. Thus, there is strong evidence that an intra-ecclesial conflict over the source of authority lingered in Carthage, and that whatever equilibrium Cyprian was able to establish was weakened after his death.

Pontius attests that PPerp was used in this context, and there are some elements that suggest that the redactor of PPerp, taking a stand in this conflict, might have reused earlier material related to the martyrs. Indeed, he proclaims at the end of his preface: "For this reason, we too proclaim to you, brothers and young sons, what we have heard and touched, so that you too, who are present, might be reminded of the glory of the Lord, and so that you, who now know by hearing, might have fellowship with the holy martyrs and, through them, with our Lord Jesus Christ, to whom is glory and honor forever and ever."[79] The statement of fellowship with Christ through the martyrs is already a strong endorsement of the authority of the martyrs.

The whole passage, however, is also intertwined with allusions to 1 John 1:1–3: "We declare to you what was from the beginning, what we have heard, what we have seen with our eyes, what we have looked at and touched with our hands ... we declare to you what we have seen and heard <u>so that you also may have fellowship</u> with us; and truly our fellowship is with the Father and with his Son Jesus Christ." Though the redactor does not allude directly to what follows in 1 John, in particular 1 John 1:7 concerning the cleansing of sins,[80] the association between fellowship and cleansing of sins would have resonated strongly in the context of the debate over the reconciliation of the lapsi.[81]

Many other elements of the passion would have resonated similarly. The visions of both Perpetua and Saturus confirm the great authority of the soon-to-be martyrs; the role Perpetua played in the healing and salvation of her brother could be an indirect reference to the power of the confessors in matters of absolution;[82] a curious episode in the vision of Saturus, where a bishop and a priest cast themselves before the feet of the two martyrs and ask them to help resolve their dispute, clearly affirms the superiority of the confessors/martyrs over the clergy.[83] Thus, all these elements, though they belong to accounts probably written at the beginning of the third century,[84] seem to acquire an additional layer of meaning in the context of the mid-third-century crisis. The redactor might well have seen in them opportunities for strengthening the authority of confessors and martyrs, and some episodes for which he is responsible play the same role. The episode of Felicity, an addition by the redactor, demonstrates the power of the confessors when their prayers are granted and she delivers her baby in time to suffer martyrdom with them.[85] The account of the sufferings and steadfastness of the martyrs also serve to further exalt their example.[86]

Neither Pontius's reference to "our ancestors" nor his comment that he was not yet born at the time of the suffering of Perpetua and her companions should necessarily be taken as indications of the time of composition of PPerp; Pontius simply alludes to the time of their martyrdom. Pontius's claim to superiority would be all the stronger if PPerp were a relatively recent text, not one composed half a century earlier. A redaction of the passion in the years following the persecution of Valerian and Gallienus can be presented only as a plausible hypothesis, but it should nonetheless be noted that both the Greek translation of the passion and the two versions of APerp date the martyrdom of Perpetua and her companions to the persecution of Valerian and Gallienus.[87] There seems to have been a lot of interest in Perpetua, Felicity, and their companions in the period following the persecution.[88]

Two other African martyr narratives confirm that this was indeed the case. The first concerns Marian and James, who were executed in Lambaesis in 259 along with two bishops and a host of laypeople.[89] Their hagiographical dossier comprises a unique text: BHL 131 (PMar). Their feast was regularly celebrated in Hippo during the episcopacy of Augustine, though only one of his preserved sermons was preached for it. Augustine does not explicitly mention the reading of a narrative about their martyrdom, but it is commonly accepted that he paraphrases a passage of PMar.[90] The second text is about Lucius, Montanus, and their companions, who were arrested and executed in Carthage not long after the execution of Cyprian, probably in 259.[91] Their hagiographical dossier also comprises a unique text: BHL 6009 (PLuc). There is no evidence that Augustine knew of PLuc, but a Donatist text, transmitted in some of the same manuscripts, borrowed from it and thus provides a *terminus ante quem* in the fifth century.[92]

Though a *terminus ante quem* prior to the fifth century cannot be established for both texts, they present so many affinities with PPerp on one hand and with the works of Cyprian on the other that a composition in the aftermath of the persecution of Valerian and Gallienus seems highly plausible. Indeed, the influence of PPerp on these texts, at both a structural and a thematic level, has long been noticed. While Harris and Gifford thought it proved their inauthenticity,[93] Franchi de' Cavalieri suggested that PPerp simply provided a schema that was followed by all martyr narratives in North Africa.[94] More recently Valeria Lomanto has shown how many features of PPerp were interpreted rather than simply imitated in PMar and PLuc.[95] The dependence of both texts on the works of Cyprian has also been demonstrated by the careful studies of Franchi de' Cavalieri,[96] and François Dolbeau's recent critical edition of PLuc has established that the text of its scriptural citations conforms to that of Cyprian.[97] Finally, Claudia Lucca shows that many elements of the narratives, especially the visions and their contents but also the speeches of the main characters, are contextually appropriate to the aftermath of the persecution of Valerian and Gallienus.[98] Lucca is mainly interested in showing how the texts promote prophetic and charismatic powers against older thinking about the waning of prophecy in early Christianity. However, she also convincingly argues that PLuc takes a stand against an anti-Cyprianic party in Carthage and goes so far as to promote a successor to Cyprian in the person of Lucianus.[99]

Indeed, the importance of episcopal mediation and ecclesiastical ordination in both texts, often in clear opposition to PPerp, suggests that these issues continued to be debated after the death of Cyprian, and that the redactor of PPerp and the redactors of PLuc and PMar were in opposition.[100] Thus, the three martyr narratives establish a very different hierarchy between clergy and martyrs.[101] Whereas in PPerp Perpetua and Saturus are presented as arbiters between a bishop and a presbyter because of their status,[102] in PMar the bishop

Cyprian welcomes Marian into heaven and is thus promoted to the position of intermediary between the martyrs and God.[103] In PLuc two of the three visions of Flavianus feature a bishop, Cyprian in the first and Successus in the second.[104] In both texts, the main beneficiaries of visions are also members of the clergy. In PMar, Aemilianus is the only lay beneficiary, but his vision establishes the superiority of the reward granted to martyrs who belong to the clergy.[105] In PLuc, the visions of Renus and Quartillosia, both laypersons, also enhance the role of the clergy. The vision of Renus serves to announce that he will not endure martyrdom as opposed to his companions who are all clerics.[106] The vision of Quartillosia presents a young man of wondrous size as an intermediary between the martyrs and the grace of Christ. Her companions, when Quartillosia reports her vision, identify the youth as Lucianus, a presbyter.[107]

There is thus strong evidence that PLuc and PMar, like PPerp and VCypr, were used at a time when Carthaginian Christians were divided into multiple factions, each claiming the authority of the martyrs whose memory, whether their death was recent or not, they mobilized in their polemics. It is likely that PMar and PLuc were composed at this time. I suggested that it could be the case also of PPerp as a whole, which would attest to how earlier martyrs and material related to them could be put to use in a new narrative.[108]

## Conclusion

The dossier of narratives that we can ascertain were composed before 300 is small: four texts, two in Greek and two in Latin. They contain an account of the martyrdoms of Polycarp, Pionius, Perpetua and her companions, and Cyprian. As mentioned at the beginning of the chapter, I am fully aware that other texts were likely composed before 300. However, unless we fall back on criteria of authenticity or on a dating that is based on the content of the accounts—with all the shortcomings attendant on these tactics—it is not possible to enlarge the corpus. The question arises, however, of what we can learn about the production of the earliest martyr narratives given the small sample available.

The paltry number of narratives should not be thought to correlate to the number of actual executions. Current discussion of the history of the persecutions openly downplays the severity and frequency of executions before 250.[109] Nevertheless, if we take the case of North Africa, which is exceptionally well documented, there is no doubt that there were more executions of Christians than those attested in PPerp and VCypr.[110]

Moreover, what we learn about the production of the earliest martyr narratives cannot be used for writing (or unwriting for that matter) the history of the persecutions. In the *Ecclesiastical History*, Eusebius used martyr narratives, among other documents, to write a history of the early persecutions, and he himself wrote the *Martyrs of Palestine* as a contribution to the history of the Great Persecution. Modern historians have done the same. The earliest attested usage of martyr narratives, however, was different. The small group of texts that I can determine to be produced before 300 were exploited to promote agendas unrelated to the martyrdoms themselves. Their utility lay in the authority that was granted to the martyrs and could be put to the service of a cause or a party. In the case of the African narratives, it even seems that such utility could have motivated the production of the texts. Thus, it does not seem that their primary aim was to document the persecutions.

Similarly, it does not seem to be the case that the earliest martyr narratives were produced in order to foster conversions. On the basis of a few isolated comments—the most famous one by Tertullian: "The blood of Christians is seed"[111]—many scholars used to surmise that the example of the martyrs was a primary motivation for conversion.[112] Danny Praet has definitively disproved this conclusion.[113] I would add that in any case narratives per se did not seem to have played a role in conversion; no references to martyr narratives appear even in the few prescriptive texts that advise Christians facing persecution.[114]

Were the earliest martyr narratives the spontaneous products of the circumstances, as Hippolyte Delehaye believed?[115] The findings above strongly suggest that this was not the case. However, before I inquire further into exactly what kind of texts martyr narratives are, and before I enlarge the list of texts under consideration beyond the earliest narratives, I must first address the relationship between martyr narratives and the actual records of the trials that preceded the executions. For too long the view that martyr narratives are largely derivative of official recordings—even in the case of texts that do not adopt the protocol form—has distracted scholars from a full understanding of their textuality. Only once this issue is addressed will I be able to return to the central task of this book.

## CHAPTER 2

# Martyr Narratives and Court Recordings

The cryptic confessions of Christians as they survive in contemporary passions closely derived from court records.

—Nicholson 2009

Only around a dozen cases have been singled out as preserving the essence of the close to verbatim protocols of the hearings of Christians before a Roman magistrate.

—Huebner 2019

These are two typical statements about the relationship between court protocols and martyrdom accounts. They diverge in their appreciation of the nature of the relationship, but they both assume that there is one, and that it is constitutive of the character and development of martyrdom accounts. In this chapter, I revisit this assumption and its consequences for our understanding of these texts. First, I define what a martyr text in protocol form is and review the texts that match this definition. This is a crucial step because a good case can be made that this textual form was used only after the Great Persecution and only for a rather brief period. Second, I look into the possibility that the producers of martyr texts used court protocols, and what their claim to have done so implies. If we examine what role this claim performs in the texts rather than focusing on its veracity, we start to appreciate the meaning of a widespread set of commonplaces found in many martyr narratives. Finally, I review whether my findings affect Glen W. Bowersock's claim that the centrality of the interrogation scenes in Christian martyr texts can be used as evidence that they are not derivative of the Jewish tradition of martyrdom.[1]

## Martyr Texts in the Protocol Form

I start by defining what is a text written in the protocol form.[2] According to Barnes, a text qualifies as written in the protocol form if it seems to derive from the minutes of actual judicial proceedings. He uses criteria of authenticity rather than criteria of composition.

Two examples will illustrate his method. First, he includes in his list BHG 197b, a Greek version of the *Passion of Athenogenes of Pedachthoe*, or rather what he called the "genuine documents embedded" in it.[3] The final redactor of BHG 197b, Anysius, used a version of the *Passion* that dates to before the end of the sixth century, BHG 197.[4] The modern editor of the text, Pierre Maraval, also dates the version composed by Anysius to around the end of the sixth century.[5] He argues, however, that the two interrogation scenes depend closely on the official court protocols, especially when compared to those same scenes in BHG 197.[6] Second, Barnes also includes BHL 2037a, the long version of the *Acts of Cyprian*, though he believes that only the first part is based on an official document, while the second, despite including an interrogation scene in the protocol style, contains too many narrative elements to have derived from an official document.[7]

I suggest that we leave aside, at least temporarily, the question of the relationships between these texts and official documents and focus instead on compositional criteria. To qualify as written in the protocol form a text must be composed primarily of a dialogue between a judge and the accused Christians, that is, one or more interrogation scenes, with an introductory formula and a concluding section.[8] I do not consider as written in the protocol form texts in which an interrogation scene in the protocol style is introduced as an element of the greater narrative.

Two examples will clarify this definition. In the Greek version of the *Acts of Agape, Irene, Chione, and Companions* (BHG 34), after a lengthy introduction detailing the arrest of the martyrs, the narrator writes: "What follows is a report of the case against them."[9] A typical interrogation scene then follows before the narrative resumes. Similarly, in MPion 19.1, the narrator writes: "After this, the proconsul came to Smyrna. Pionius was brought before him and he became a martyr three days before the Ides of March. The following report of the proceedings was made."[10] The inclusion of protocol-form documents within a narrative is a different, if not historically unrelated, compositional feature.[11] It does not qualify a text as written in the protocol form. If we apply the criterion that the main body of the text is a judicial dialogue, we will obtain a corpus of texts that share the same format and the same focus on the trials of martyrs.

A good starting point for assembling the texts is Barnes's list.[12] It comprises ten texts once we eliminate the *Passion of Athenogenes of Pedachthoe*.[13] A few more should be eliminated and a few others can be added, as we will see below.

## Ancient Martyrs

Barnes lists three texts about ancient martyrs as written in the protocol form: the *Acts of Justin*, the *Acts of the Scilitan Martyrs*, and the *Acts of Cyprian*.

The hagiographical dossier of Justin comprises the following texts in Greek:[14]

—BHG 972z, the shorter recension, known as text A or α;[15]

—BHG 973, the longer or middle recension, known as text B or β;[16]

—BHG 974, the version of the "Imperial Menologion," known as text C or γ;[17]

—BHG 974e, an early Byzantine epitome.[18]

Though Justin is well known to Eusebius, who quotes extracts from the *Apology* and mentions the circumstances of his martyrdom,[19] it is clear that he is not familiar with any version of the *Acts of Justin*.[20] The execution of Justin, in Rome, is traditionally dated to 165 after the *Chronicon Paschale*.[21] This date is compatible with that of the urban prefecture of Rusticus, who in all versions of the *Acts* is the judge who tries Justin and his companions.[22] As Peter Lampe writes, "nothing stands in the way of identifying the entire group which was arrested with Justin and Euelpistus as Justin's circle of students."[23] The introductions to BHG 972z and BHG 973 respectively refer to "the time of the lawless commands" and to "defenders of idolatry," and BHG 973 adds that commands were posted publicly against the Christians.[24] Clearly, both versions were composed at a time when the exact circumstances of the arrest and execution were not known. Despite Gary Bisbee's attempt to date BHG 972z to the first part of the third century, most scholars date both versions to the fourth century at the earliest.[25] The absence of an external *terminus ante quem* forces us to leave the question open.

I have already argued that Tertullian does not provide a *terminus ante quem* for the *Acts of the Scilitan Martyrs*.[26] Scholars have pointed to elements in the account that do not fit a second-century context, but as we have seen above, there is much uncertainty surrounding such evidence. One much-discussed issue is the statement that the trial is held *in secretario*.[27] It now seems that trial *in secretario* is not a post-Diocletian practice; nevertheless, the first attestation of such a trial is that of the Scilitan martyrs and the next is that of Cyprian. Any dating based on this element is, therefore, bound to be a case of circular reasoning.[28] The discrepancy between the list of the Christians who were arrested and that of those who were executed could be used as an argument against dating the composition to the time of the execution, unless one allows for a later interpolation.[29] Finally, it has recently been pointed out that the role played by books in the account is quite unusual for the second century.[30] In sum, however, no definitive arguments can be made regarding dating, and there is no *terminus ante quem* for a composition before Augustine.[31]

None of the versions of the *Acts of Cyprian* matches my definition of a text in the protocol form as they all include the interrogation scene in a broader narrative.[32]

To Barnes's list, we could add the *Acts of Carpus, Papylus, and Agathonice*. Both the Greek version (BHG 293) and the Latin one (BHL 1622m) present the compositional characteristics of a protocol-form text. Neither, as I have already pointed out, can be definitively identified as the version known to Eusebius.[33]

## Military Martyrs

Three texts about Christian soldiers executed at the end of the third century adopt the protocol form.[34] Barnes includes in his list only the martyrdom of Marcellus, who was executed in 298 at Tingi (modern Tangier).[35] It is known through at least three versions of a passion preserved in Latin. There is no external evidence for dating its composition.[36] Barnes rejects the other two texts because he deems them inauthentic: the martyrdoms of Maximilianus and Julius. Maximilianus, the son of a *temonarius* named Fabius Victor, was executed in 295 at Theveste when his father presented him for enlistment. The Latin narrative (BHL 5813) follows the protocol form. There is no external evidence for dating its composition; attempts to date it on the basis of internal elements produce results that range from the period of Constantine to the late fourth or early fifth century, and even to the eighth and ninth centuries.[37] Julius was a veteran who refused to sacrifice and was executed at Durostorum in 304. The Latin narrative (BHL 4555) follows the protocol form.[38] There is no external evidence for dating its composition.[39]

## Martyrs of the Great Persecution

The majority of texts in protocol form concern martyrs of the Great Persecution. Of these, three texts relate to African martyrs. Barnes accepts in his canon the *Acts of Felix*, bishop of Thibiuca, a small city near Carthage, executed in 303.[40] He refers, however, to a text that has not been preserved but only hypothetically reconstituted by Delehaye.[41] The extant versions are clearly of a late composition, at a time when the two Italian cities of Venusia and Nola held rival claims to be the place of Felix's execution.[42] The discovery in 1996 of the *Acts of Gallonius* has often been described as the addition of a precious ancient testimony.[43] Gallonius was executed in 303 at Uthina.[44] Like the *Acts of Cyprian*, the text reports two successive trials and includes some narrative elements that cannot derive from an official document. There is no external evidence that enables us to date its composition.[45] Finally, the *Acts of Crispina*, who was executed in 304 at Theveste (modern Tébessa, Algeria), is known in two Latin versions that follow the protocol form.[46] This martyr was known to Augustine, but he provides information about her that is not attested in either of the versions of the *Acts*, and he cannot, therefore, serve as a *terminus ante quem* for their composition.[47]

One text concerns a Sicilian martyr, Euplus, who was executed in 304.[48] There are several versions of the martyrdom of Euplus in both Greek and Latin, and three of the Greek versions are written in the protocol form.[49] There is no external evidence for the date of their composition.[50]

The last three cases, from Egypt, can be dated to the fourth century. The first concerns Stephanus, a priest from a village in the Antinoite nome, executed in 305.[51] A papyrus that can be dated to the second half of the fourth century preserves a Coptic fragment that is a translation of a Greek text in the protocol form.[52] The second text is about Phileas, bishop of Thmuis, executed in 307.[53] Eusebius, who mentions his martyrdom alongside that of Philoramus, does not refer to any text on the topic.[54] However, two Greek versions of the *Acts of Phileas*, both in the protocol form, are known from papyri dated respectively to 310–50 and 320–50.[55] Barnes does not mention the third text, about Dioscorus, who was executed in 307 in Egypt, likely because, until recently, it was known only through later Syriac and Latin versions.[56] The dossier of his martyrdom has, however, been enriched by the publication of a small fragment of a Greek version, known through a fourth-century papyrus from Oxyrhynchus, which confirms that the text follows the protocol form.[57]

## Conclusion

Of the eleven texts that adopt the protocol form, few can be dated with external evidence, but the papyrus fragments of the *Acts of Dioscorus*, the *Acts of Phileas*, and the *Acts of Stephanus* are all dated to the fourth century, and in the case of the *Acts of Phileas* even to the first half of it. The martyrs commemorated in these texts are victims of the Great Persecution, as are the majority of the martyrs whose martyrdom is told in a protocol-form text, especially if we include the "military martyrs" executed in the last few years of the third century. However, none of the texts in the protocol form for martyrs executed before 260 can be dated with any certainty before the fourth century.

I would like to suggest that it is only in the aftermath of the Great Persecution that the protocol form became the format par excellence for martyr texts. It also seems that this situation pertained for only a brief period; later martyr texts included one or more interrogation scenes in the protocol style, but within a larger narrative frame.[58] As the taste for interrogation scenes developed starting in the fourth century, producers may have been led to compose texts that conformed to this new model, even when writing about the ancient martyrs.

A good case can be made for such a process with the two versions of the *Acts of Perpetua and Felicity* (BHL 6634–35 and BHL 6636), which were composed in North Africa in the fifth century.[59] Indeed, the two versions share a conspicuous addition when compared to the *Passion of Perpetua and Felicity* (BHL 6633): a developed interrogation scene.[60] I would like to suggest that the *Acts of Cyprian* (BHL 2037a) were similarly composed in the fourth century, once the interrogation scenes, which do not feature in Pontius's *Life of Cyprian*, became a generic marker of martyr texts. The same, I contend, could well be the case with the *Acts of the Scilitan Martyrs* and the *Acts of Justin*.

The claim that texts in the protocol format are a late development in the writing of martyr narratives suggests that the format should not be used as an infallible test of authenticity but considered instead for what it does in the texts. I will come back to this in the light of the many topoi attached to protocols in martyr narratives.

## Martyr Texts and Official Protocols

Martyr texts in protocol form have often been compared to actual protocols.[61] Indeed, it is well attested independently of the acts of the Christian martyrs, both in anecdotal evidence and in many papyri from Egypt, that trials were recorded and the minutes archived.[62]

## Official Protocols: Format and Access

Since at least the second century and probably since the reforms of Augustus, a governor's archives were retained in the provinces and available to his successors.[63] The criminal cases that governors tried, as well as all their other cases, were recorded in shorthand during the trial and subsequently transcribed.[64] Trials were recorded not as single documents but as entries in the official journals of the governors. These were called *commentarii* or *hypomnêmatismoi*.[65] It was possible to have excerpts drawn up from the *commentarii*. Authorization from the magistrate was required and a fee was charged for the service.[66]

The practice of drawing up excerpts from *commentarii* stops at the end of the third century. It does not seem, however, that the practice of maintaining an official journal was discontinued and the hypothesis of a shift in the recording system from journals to single transcripts (*acta* and *gesta*, *hypomnêmata* and *pepragmena*) does not convince the specialists.[67]

What probably changed for Christians after 260 were the conditions under which they could access the protocols. As I have noted, there is evidence that a magistrate's authorization was required for access to protocols, and it is quite unlikely that Christians, or their lawyers, could have formulated a legitimate, legal request for accessing the records of prior trials.[68] The need to use an official record for writing a martyrdom account would definitely not have been receivable. After 260, once Gallienus put an end to the persecution of Valerian,[69] and most surely after 313 and after 324, once Constantine granted freedom to Christians in both the West and the East, access to official documents involving Christians and the local churches became easier for Christians, and there is ample evidence that they used judicial documents in courts.[70]

## P.Mil.Vogl. 6.287: An Actual Protocol?

Until very recently it was commonly held that no official protocol of the trial of a Christian had been preserved. Sabine Huebner now claims to have identified one in a second-century papyrus preserved in the library of the Università degli

Studi of Milan.[71] I quote her translation of the very fragmentary text so that we can briefly assess the strength of the case:[72]

1   [Extract of the minutes of the governor XXX, in the year X
of the Emperor XX] on 12th Pharmouthi (April 7),
        [at the court in XXX. XXX came and stated] through their
        lawyers, as I learned
        . . . ] with regard to what I said,
        . . . ] I do not acquit of the charges, I will decide/examine/
        determine
5   . . . ] and concerning the congregation, if anyone
        . . . ] owing to the suspicion I do not
        . . . ] I cannot: everything though
        . . . ] of the nome where he is serving as strategos
        . . . ] the conspiracy of which he reproached
10  . . . ] the delegates/representatives, however,
        . . . , son of . . . ]ros, Soter, Son of Sotas, Sotas, son of
        . . . ] Dioscorus, son of Origenes
        . . . ] ever in Tekmei to
        . . . ] being present and not
15  . . . ] stand (?) before the tribunal
        . . . ] they are . . . and for these
        . . . ] they remained silent
        . . . ] every one of the town of the (?)eites

Vandoni, the first editor of the papyrus, deemed that the text was too fragmentary for a reconstruction of the nature of the trial.[73] Gallazzi mentions the possibility that the συνωμοσία (l. 9) is a Jewish conspiracy though he acknowledges that nothing in the text corroborates the hypothesis.[74] Huebner states: "A considerably more obvious religious faction, who in the second and third centuries were regularly charged with conspiracy, were Christians."[75] The word συνωμοσία, however, is never used in connection with a charge against the Christians. Huebner argues from the use of what she presents as the Latin equivalents of συνωμοσία, *coniuratio*, *conspiratio*, and *factio*, in less than a handful of passages that conspiracy "entered the canon of charges laid against Christians."[76] Before examining these passages, I must emphasize that that conspiracy alone could not be a legal basis for the repression of Christians; it would need to have been specifically conspiracy for treason or for damage to *maiestas*.[77] This was, believed Mommsen, the reason why Christians were persecuted.[78] The word συνωμοσία in itself, however, is insufficient to determine the charge that is leveled against Christians. Mommsen's theory, to which Huebner does not appear to refer, has been criticized many times and is not currently in favor among Roman historians.[79] As Huebner does not engage with the scholarly discussion on the topic, it is difficult to determine her exact position.

Let us turn, therefore, to the passages that Huebner discusses. The first comes from the famous letter of Pliny to the emperor Trajan wherein he reports that repentant Christians have told him that they were bound by an oath.[80] The mention of the oath leads Huebner to bring up the accusation of conspiracy, likely because the provision of an oath is characteristic of a *coniuratio*.[81] However, given that the letter is a juridical consultation with the emperor, we can assume that if Pliny had in mind a crime of conspiracy he would say so explicitly. In any case, James Corke-Webster has now shown that the rescript that Trajan sent in response to Pliny has not been used in later treatment of Christians.[82]

Then, Huebner cites three texts that partly derive from each other. The first is an extract of the speech of the pagan Caecilius in the *Octavius* of Minucius Felix: "In view of this, is it not an absolute scandal—you will allow me, I hope, to be rather forthright about the strong feelings I have for my case—is it not scandalous that the gods should be mobbed by a deplorable, illegal, and desperate faction? They have collected from the lowest possible dregs of society the more ignorant fools together with gullible women (readily persuaded, as is their weak sex); they have thus formed a mob associated in a blasphemous conspiracy, who with nocturnal assemblies, periodic fasts, and inhuman feasts seal their pact not with some religious ritual but with desecrating profanation."[83] Three keywords—*factio, conspiratio, congregationes*—are again found in the two texts that Huebner quotes from Tertullian. In the *Ad Nationes*, Tertullian briefly addresses the following objection: "You are of us, and yet you conspire against us!" His answer is short: "We acknowledge the Roman loyalty to the Caesars: no conspiracy has ever broken out from us."[84] The example of the provinces that supported the rivals of Septimius Severus shows that the crime that Tertullian denounces here is that of *maiestas*, an accusation that he develops at length in the *Apology*.[85] The third extract comes from the conclusion to a lengthy development in the *Apology* on Christian sects and *illicitae factiones*: "This gathering of Christians may properly be called illegal, if it is like illegal gatherings; it may properly be condemned, if any complain of it on the score on which complaint is made of factions. To whose hurt have we ever met? We are when assembled just what we are when apart; taken together the same as singly; we injure none;

we grieve none. When decent people, when good men, gather, when the pious and when the chaste assemble, that is not to be called a faction, but a council."[86] In addition to their common use of *factio*, both Tertullian and Minucius Felix use cognates of the English "congregation" for describing the Christian meetings, and Huebner then argues that the word συνοικίον from line 5 of the papyrus should be translated as "congregation," a word that she suggests has a special Christian connotation.[87] Unfortunately, this not the case, and without any context it is difficult to provide an accurate translation for συνοικίον.[88]

The accusation of conspiracy and the crime of *maiestas* are not found in the Greek apologists.[89] These are new elements introduced by Tertullian, from whom Minucius Felix likely borrowed.[90] Indeed, Tertullian likes to pepper his writing with legal terms, but he generally employs them in their broader popular senses rather than with their technical meanings.[91] This has been established long ago for *sacrilegium* and *maiestas*; the accusations listed by Tertullian under these crimes do not correspond to their legal definitions.[92] More recently, James Corke-Webster has shown how Tertullian misleadingly uses the letters of Pliny and Trajan to critique the Roman legal system.[93] If the charge of conspiracy entered a "canon," as Huebner claims, it was likely only the canon of Christian apologetics.

The last text mentioned by Huebner is the sentence pronounced against Cyprian and supposedly reported verbatim in the *Acts of Cyprian*.[94] Cyprian was condemned to death in the context of the edicts of Valerian, a context in which Christian assemblies were explicitly forbidden, and in which no crime of conspiracy needed to be leveled against the Christians.[95]

The papyrus is dated to the second century by its editors, a dating that Huebner does not dispute;[96] she even uses a report of legal proceedings from the mid-second century for her reconstruction.[97] She concludes, however, that the trial took place during the persecution of Decius or that of Valerian, a context in which the crime of the Christians was not conspiracy for treason or *maiestas*, but disobedience to imperial edicts.[98] This quite unexpected conclusion seems to be driven by her desire to identify the Dioscorus, son of Origenes, mentioned on l.12, with the Antonius Dioscorus, son of Origenes, a citizen of Alexandria, designated as a Christian in a papyrus from the first half of the third century.[99] Though the combination of Dioscorus and Origenes seems to be unique to the Milan papyrus, both names are quite common, and the identification is at best fragile.[100]

To sum up, it is quite unlikely that P.Mil.Vogl. 6.287 is "the first authentic court record of a Roman trial of Christians," and it is to be expected that further study will provide us with alternative, more convincing interpretations. In any case, P.Mil.Vogl. 6.287 will not bring new light onto the use of court records for the production of martyr narratives.

## The Use of Court Protocols

The existence of court protocols is alluded to in several martyr texts.[101] Geffcken has rightly warned that these passages cannot be taken as proof that an official document was used in composing these texts.[102] Nevertheless, a letter of Augustine, included among those published by Johannes Divjak in 1981, shows that their use should not be discounted too hastily.[103]

The letter is addressed to Paulinus, deacon of the church of Milan and secretary of Ambrose.[104] Its date cannot be established, and the text of the letter as transmitted in its two manuscripts is unfortunately corrupted and lacunary; furthermore, the letter of Paulinus to which Augustine responds is lost. It seems clear, however, that Paulinus had asked Augustine to write martyr narratives in his own language and thus to follow Ambrose's model, which had been evoked in a prior discussion.[105]

It also appears that Paulinus had sent Augustine materials to use in such an endeavor. Among the materials sent to Augustine were two types of texts: narratives, that is, texts written by authors in their own words, and extracts from judicial proceedings.[106] Augustine rejects Paulinus's request because, as he says, unlike Ambrose, he could not contribute any material beyond that which appeared in the judicial protocols.[107] Interestingly, Augustine compares Ambrose's practice to that of the redactor of the *Acts of Cyprian*. The passages he mentions are found in the longer version of the *Acts of Cyprian* (BHL 2037a).[108] According to Augustine, the text is "an account composed by someone or other" that recalls the "narratives in the language of others," and he explicitly says that these details could not be found in the court protocols.[109]

Whether the redactor of the *Acts of Cyprian* actually used official proceedings and added details to them is impossible to establish. What is relevant is that Augustine thought so, likely because it was common practice in his own time. The redactor of the *Acts of the Abitinian Martyrs* (BHL 7492), a fifth-century Donatist text,[110] claims to have done just this. He thus writes in his preface: "Therefore, I begin a narrative of the celestial battles and the new struggles undertaken by the bravest soldiers of Christ, the unconquered warriors and the glorious martyrs. I begin, then, to write my narrative using the public records."[111]

The practice that Augustine ascribes to Ambrose or to the anonymous author of the *Acts of Cyprian* does not seem any different from what the author of the *Acts of the Abitinian Martyrs* claims to do when he states that he writes his narrative using court protocols.

Indeed, it seems that official proceedings from the trials of Christians during the persecution of Diocletian were readily available. Thus, the Council of Arles, summoned by Constantine in 314 in order to address the controversy that had developed in Africa after the end of the persecution, requires that accusations against *traditores*, those clerics who had surrendered the Scriptures, be based on *acta publica* and not on mere denunciations.[112] Extracts of official proceedings are preserved among the documents compiled in the so-called Appendix to Optatus, *Against the Donatists*: the records of the trial of Silvanus of Cirta before Zenophilus and those of the trial of Felix of Abthugni.[113] During both trials, municipal records were read and used contradictorily by the opponents.[114] Similarly, at the Conference of Carthage in 411, both Catholics and Donatists produced official documents, some of which were concerned with the trials of martyrs.[115]

Thus, it is not unlikely that in the fourth century and later, Christians procured court protocols and used them to write martyr narratives. Using court protocols, however, is a very different practice from reproducing them. Indeed, it is now generally accepted that no martyr text constitutes an unedited copy of an official document, even with an introduction and an epilogue added.[116] For the producers of martyr texts, however, court protocols seem to have played a much more important role than providing raw data about the trials. I now turn to a few topoi associated with court protocols.

## *The Topoi of Court Protocols*

A first topos are stories about prosecutors destroying these official documents. This is how Prudentius explains that he does not know much about the two martyrs from Calagurris, whom he celebrates in the first hymn of the *Peristephanon*: "Alas for what is forgotten and lost to knowledge in the silence of the olden time! We are denied the facts about these matters, the very tradition is destroyed, for long ago a reviling soldier of the guard took away the records, lest generations taught by documents that held the memory fast should make public the details, the time and manner of their martyrdom, and spread them abroad in sweet speech for posterity to hear."[117] The absence of tradition can only be explained by the malignant destruction of the court protocols.

In the first half of the fifth century, the redactor of the *Passion of Victor Maurus* (BHL 8580) imagines a similar scenario: the judge had ordered all the notes taken by the *notarii* to be burned at the end of the trial.[118] However, one of them, Maximianus, secretly wrote down from memory what he saw, as he explains in a first-person epilogue to the text.[119] A similar scenario is presented in the mid-sixth-century version of the *Passion of Vincentius* (BHL 8631): the judge forbids notes to be taken during the trial.[120]

This first topos confirms that Christians of the fourth century and later believed that the court protocols of martyr trials played a vital role in the traditions about the martyrs.

Another, similar topos is attached to the *excerptores* or *notarii*. These are both quite common characters in martyr narratives. An early testimony of their importance comes from Asterius, bishop of Amasea in Asia Minor around 400, who wrote an *Ecphrasis on the Holy Martyr Euphemia* (BHG 623), a description of a painting of the martyrdom of Euphemia that he must have seen in a church in Chalcedon.[121] First he describes the judge, then the attendants: "Then the guards of the office and many soldiers, the secretaries with their tablets and styluses; one of them has lifted up his hand from the wax and observes intensely the condemned, his face turned towards her as if he was ordering her to speak louder so that he, struggling to hear, should not write down any manifest mistake."[122] As the emphasis on the gesture of one of the *notarii* shows, their presence assures the accuracy of the report. It is not surprising, then, that some writers of martyr narratives claim to have obtained copies of these notes and based their narratives upon them.

The *Passion of Tarachus, Probus, and Andronicus* (BHG 1574) is followed in the manuscripts by a letter written by eleven Christians who present themselves as witnesses and claim to have purchased the protocols of the trial, which they call "the martyrs' written confessions," for two hundred denarii.[123] The text, long considered "authentic" and then ascribed by Delehaye to the category of the "passions épiques," cannot be dated with any certainty.[124] This is also the case with the *Passion of Pontius of Cimiez* (BHL 6896), in which one Valerius purchases the *gesta martyris* from the *excerptores*.[125]

Several martyrs supposedly belonged themselves to the ranks of the *excerptores*.[126] A fifth-century sermon describes how Genesius, as he was taking notes during the trial of Christians in Arles, revealed that he was Christian by throwing aside his writing tablets.[127] In the *Passion of Speusippus, Elasippus, and Melesippus, notarii* appear in an epilogue that provides a genealogy for the text.[128] Neon, the *notarius* who was recording the trial of the three martyrs, when he can no longer tolerate the injustice of the trial, closes his tablets and gives them to his colleague Turbon. He runs to a temple and smashes all its statues before being executed. Turbon then writes down the whole account and is in turn martyred.[129]

The figure of the *notarius/excerptor* martyr is familiar enough that the redactor of the *Passion of Cassianus of Tangiers* (BHL 1636) uses it to invent a story for Cassianus.[130] He makes him the *excerptor* at the trial of another martyr from Tangiers, the centurion Marcellus. As the sentence is pronounced, Cassianus throws his stylus and his codex to the ground.[131] With the version of the *Passion of Theodore the General* (BHG 1750), whose redactor, the *notarius* Augarus, also threw down his tablets before continuing his job at the request of the martyr himself,[132] we reach a period that is too late for our purpose.[133]

What is interesting in these various topoi is not that late antique Christians "*thought* that *excerptores* and *notarii* helped to compile the *acta martyrum* during the trials of the Christians."[134] As we will see in Chapter 4, the audience of martyr texts knew how to recognize topoi and understood that the producers of the texts did not attach any truth claims to them. These topoi were used by the producers of martyr texts as authenticating devices.[135] As Cliff Ando has pointed out, a common trust in authenticated documents developed "as the bureaucracy of Rome invaded the mechanics of daily life."[136] By adopting the protocol form, the text producers extend, so to speak, the accuracy of the court transcripts to the martyr texts. This observation provides incentive for further study of the textuality of martyrdom accounts.

## Conclusion

I have made several claims in this chapter, the consequences of which demand further consideration. First, I suggest that the protocol form was not adopted until the fourth century and that only then or later were accounts written in this format for earlier martyrs, such as Perpetua or the Scilitan martyrs. A prior account was sometimes available, but it was one in which the interrogation scene did not receive a lot of emphasis.[137] This format seems well adapted for the liturgical reading of an account during the service for a martyr commemoration, as the vivid dialogue, short and dramatic, between the judge and the martyr provided the preacher with engaging material for a homily.[138] Though the practice developed slowly and was not universal, it could, nevertheless, have provided the impetus for the production of texts in this format.[139]

Second, I show that the use of official protocols for writing martyrdom accounts could not have been common before a time when Christians received some form of official recognition, therefore after 260, or even more likely after 313/324. Augustine, however, seems to consider it a normal practice, and there is plenty evidence for the use of official protocols, including Christian trials, in other contexts. On the other hand, official protocols were not expected simply to be copied and inserted into a larger narrative. As with the use of all documents in ancient texts, the use of official protocols provided a point of departure, elements of content to be elaborated.[140]

Thus, while many historians have viewed the protocol format as a warranty of authenticity or reliability, I conclude that we should consider the role it performs in the text; when use of this format is considered alongside the various topoi attached to the official recording of the trials, it is the textuality of these accounts that is emphasized. I will return to this point in my fourth and last chapter.

Finally, the claim that court protocols are not the prototype of the earliest accounts, nor one of the forms they adopt—which debunks one of the most common assumptions about early martyr texts—raises some questions about Bowersock's position on the origin of martyrdom. For Bowersock, martyrdom appears in the second century as "something entirely new" in the ancient world with no precedent among the Greeks or the Jews.[141] Among the evidence he brings to bear is that legal documentation of the trials is embedded in the written records of martyrdom, so that "martyrdoms form a cohesive part of the structure of the Roman empire."[142] With the exception of the *Martyrdom of Pionius*, none of the texts that Bowersock presents as embedding court protocols has a *terminus ante quem* prior to the fourth century. His argument is at least weakened, and I would like to suggest that the use of official protocols is not relevant to the question of the origin of martyrdom.

Bowersock also claims that no Jewish martyr text includes interrogations and that this can be adduced as evidence that a Jewish tradition is not the source for Christian martyrdom narratives.[143] Daniel Boyarin rightly objected to this last claim.[144] When Saul Lieberman compares material on Roman legal institutions in rabbinic texts and in the acts of the Christian martyrs, he mentions several interrogation scenes but notes that the standard questions are usually omitted and only the incriminating questions preserved.[145] The same is true in the texts collected by Jan Willem van Henten and Friedrich Avemarie, whether it is the martyrdom of Miriam bat Tanhum and her seven sons, that of Rabbi Aquiva, or that of Rabbi Hanina ben Teradion.[146] Henten and Avemarie note that "the rabbinic concern for martyrdom was not so much with individual cases and with historical details as it was with theology and ethics."[147]

There is, therefore, some difference in the way the interrogation scene is treated in both traditions. However, when we consider the role played by these elements in the texts rather than their relation to actual proceedings, we come to realize that both traditions share in the universal belief "in the truth value of imperial documents" that I mentioned earlier.[148]

## CHAPTER 3

# From Forgeries to Living Texts

In this chapter, I start looking into the textual characteristics of martyr narratives by reviewing the arguments used by Bart D. Ehrman for qualifying the *Martyrdom of Polycarp* as a forgery. His thesis raises important questions not only about authorship but also about the audience's horizon of expectations. Thus, the case study of the *Martyrdom of Polycarp* will lead me to suggest that forgery is a classification that should pertain only when dealing with texts that "represent a single 'symbolic act' by a single (postulated) agent or author,"[1] and then to argue that martyr texts should instead be viewed as "living texts."[2]

## The *Martyrdom of Polycarp* as Forgery

In *Forgery and Counterforgery*, Bart D. Ehrman engages in a polemic against the "Neutestamentlers" who interpret the pseudepigrapha of the New Testament as "transparent fictions."[3] For Ehrman, forgery and deceit are committed every time an author makes a false authorial claim.[4] He distinguishes "normal" cases of forgery, in which "an author falsely claims to be a well-known person," from special cases such as embedded forgeries, redactional forgeries, and non-pseudepigraphic forgeries.[5] Embedded forgeries are writings that "embed first-person narratives—or other self-identifying devices—in their discourse, without differentiating the first person from the author."[6] Forgeries are non-pseudepigraphic when there is a false authorial claim without naming an author.[7] What is crucial for Ehrman is the question of intent; disregarding many of the possible authorial motivations, he believes that there is only one intention: deceit.[8] He rejects, therefore, the numerous attempts of New Testament scholars—since all ancient sources, including early Christian sources, unanimously condemned forgeries—to redeem texts that have been judged forgeries.[9]

The *Martyrdom of Polycarp* (MPol) is categorized by Ehrman as a pseudepigraphic forgery. What makes MPol a forgery, according to Ehrman, is that the account was written by someone living later but posing as an eyewitness. He begins his argument with a review of all the objections raised against the authenticity of the text, from Lipsius and Keim in the nineteenth century to Sylvia Ronchey and Candida R. Moss in the twentieth and twenty-first centuries.[10] He accepts the conclusion that the text was composed in the late third century at the earliest.[11] Then, Ehrman examines what he presents as the claims of the author of MPol to be an eyewitness.[12] He isolates, in essence, three passages in which first-person statements are found.

In MPol 2.2, the author, emphasizing the extraordinary endurance of torments by the martyrs, writes that they were "showing to us all that, in the very hour of their torture, the most noble martyrs of Christ were absent from their flesh, or rather, that the Lord was standing by and conversing with them."[13] According to Ehrman, the author here claims to have observed the endurance of the martyrs.[14] We could, however, also understand that the lesson is addressed to a more general "us," that is, "all Christians."

In MPol 9.1, as Polycarp enters the stadium where he will be tried and martyred, a voice is heard saying: "Be strong Polycarp, and be a man." The author writes: "No one saw who had spoken, but those among our people who were there heard the voice."[15] The reference to "our people" does indeed assure the authenticity of the miracle, as Ehrman suggests, but we should note that the author does not actually claim to have been among those present.

Finally, in MPol 15.1–2, when Polycarp is on the pyre and the fire is lit, the author writes: "As a great flame blazed forth, we, to whom it was granted to see it, saw a miracle; we were also preserved to announce what happened to the rest of the world. For the fire made the form of a vault, like the sail of a ship when it is filled out by the wind, and it formed a wall around the body of the martyr. And in the middle, he was not like flesh that is burnt, but like bread that is baked or like gold and silver that are tested in a furnace. For we also perceived a very pleasant scent, as of wafting frankincense or some other of the precious aromas."[16] This case is clear-cut; the "we" claims to be both eyewitness and responsible for the account.

There is one other first-person passage, at the beginning of MPol: "We write to you, brothers, about those who suffered martyrdom and about the blessed Polycarp."[17] Though it is not an eyewitness statement, it is curious that

Ehrman fails to mention this passage, which establishes the first-person narrative at the very beginning of the account.

All these passages appear in what is presented as a letter from the church of Smyrna, clearly delineated within the larger text by its inscription and by its farewell. Indeed, after a long doxology, the letter ends with the following greetings: "Greet all the saints. Those who are with us greet you, and so does Evarestus, the scribe, with all his household."[18] The text of MPol, however, does not end with the letter.

First, there is a brief paragraph providing information about the date of the execution: "The blessed Polycarp was martyred on the second day at the beginning of the month of Xanthicus, seven days before the Kalends of March, on a great Sabbath, at the eighth hour. He was apprehended by Herod, when Philip of Tralles was high-priest and Statius Quadratus proconsul, while Jesus Christ reigns through the ages, to whom be glory, honor, power, majesty, and eternal throne from generation to generation. Amen."[19] On this Ehrman writes: "In chapter 21, the author gives us a precise indication of when the martyrdom took place."[20] He then points out that the different dating elements cannot be reconciled and that the mistake betrays a later author. There are two problems with Ehrman's argument here: first, new evidence now shows that there is no mistake on the date;[21] second, "the author" of this paragraph is not "the author" of what precedes, as the following section makes clear.

In six of the eight manuscripts that contain MPol, there then follows a colophon that provides a history of the transmission of the letter. It appears as follows in the text of the menologia tradition:[22]

> We pray that you fare well, brothers, as you walk by the word of Jesus Christ according to the gospel, with whom is glory to God, Father and Holy Spirit, for the salvation of the holy elect, as the blessed Polycarp was martyred, in whose footsteps may we be found in the kingdom of Jesus Christ. Gaius copied these writings from those of Irenaeus, a disciple of Polycarp; he lived with Irenaeus. I, Socrates, wrote them in Corinth from Gaius's copy. Grace be with all. I, Pionius, again wrote them down from the aforementioned written copy, having searched out these writings after the blessed Polycarp manifested them to me in a revelation, as I will explain later. I gathered them together, now almost worn away by time, so that the Lord Jesus Christ might bring me also to his heavenly kingdom, together with

his elect. Glory to him, with the Father and Holy Spirit for ages upon ages. Amen.[23]

This section, after a few words of commendation, recounts the transmission history of the letter. A statement in the third person describes the role of Gaius, a familiar of Irenaeus, whose connection with Polycarp is well attested.[24] Irenaeus had a copy of the letter and Gaius was able to make a copy of it. Then, in a statement in the first person, Socrates says that he made a copy from Gaius's copy in Corinth. A second statement in the first person stages Pionius, who found Socrates's aged copy after Polycarp had appeared to him in a vision. Though no identification is provided, the most likely hypothesis is that Pionius is the presbyter from Smyrna who was executed in 250. Indeed, the *Martyrdom of Pionius* emphasizes the parallel between Pionius and Polycarp.[25] I would suggest that for the colophon to make sense to the reader as supporting the authenticity of the letter, this section has to have been written at a time when readers would know of the association, and therefore between the execution of Pionius (250) and Eusebius's attestation of the text of MPol (c. 300).[26]

Though many scholars consider sections 21 and 22 to be later additions, Ehrman rightly views them as integral to the larger text.[27] They add, however, several levels to the narration that he fails to analyze in their consequences for the audience. The "we" of the eyewitness statements does refer to the collective author of the letter, the church of Smyrna, not to the narrator who presents himself as the copyist of MPol. It means that the "we" in the letter is not the level at which forgery should be detected. I think the distinction is important as the audience of the text would know what to make of the letter included in it.[28]

Should we then regard the colophon as evidence of forgery? Indeed, Ehrman writes: "The narrative functions, in fact, like the eyewitness reports generally in this account, to make believable that which, on the surface, defies belief."[29] For Ehrman, "discovery narratives" such as MPol 22 are one of the techniques forgers use "to cover up the traces of their deceit."[30] He describes similar discovery narratives as a "ploy used by some forgers in order to explain why it is that a writing by an ancient author was not widely known by earlier readers."[31] He thus writes about MPol that the colophon "functions here as it does in other places, such as the *Apocalypse of Paul*, to explain why the account has now surfaced in the middle to late third century (after the days of Pionius) when it was previously unknown to interested Christian readers."[32]

The *Apocalypse of Paul* is a fifth-century text that points to a different context, that of the invention of a Christian tradition on the model of the invention of relics.[33] Ehrman also compares the preface to *A Journal of the Trojan War* and the story, reported by Livy and Pliny, of the discovery of Pythagorean writings written by Numa Pompilius.[34] Though they share some elements, these "discovery narratives" are of a different nature and belong to different literary contexts. Furthermore, Ehrman does not consider the impact of these stories on the audience nor the audience's potential response to them, but only the perspective of the forger. Thus, Ehrman rejects the possibility that such narratives could signal fiction. We will see in Chapter 4 that the notion of fiction requires a lot more discussion than Ehrman grants it.[35]

Another issue that Ehrman does not address fully is that of the anonymity of MPol. Anonymity is, like fiction, grouped by Ehrman among other phenomena related to forgery. His discussion of anonymity, however, is confined to New Testament texts,[36] and the phenomenon is disregarded with the comment that "all of New Testament anonymata and almost all other anonymous writings of the early Christian centuries came to be attributed eventually."[37] To my knowledge this is not the case with MPol nor with most other martyr texts, but Ehrman nevertheless claims that these texts as well as all the other texts he considers are authored, that is, "represent a single 'symbolic act' by a single (postulated) agent or author."[38] Indeed, in his own edition of MPol, Ehrman assumes that the text "was produced by Pionius."[39]

Not only has MPol never been attributed, even falsely, but its text in the manuscript tradition lacks the stability that characterizes most authored texts. Some of the variants between manuscripts are patently more than scribal errors.[40] Two manuscripts stand out: the first, M, a twelfth-century manuscript from Moscow, has long been known;[41] the second manuscript, K, only recently rediscovered, is a twelfth-century manuscript from the former library of the monastery of Kosinitza at Drama (Greece) that had disappeared after the Balkan wars of 1912–13.[42] In addition to many other specific textual variants, both manuscripts present a colophon that is significantly different from that of the menologia tradition.

In M, the section on the transmission history of the letter reads as follows:

Gaius, who was a fellow citizen of Irenaeus, copied these writings from the papers of Irenaeus, a student of holy Polycarp. For this man Irenaeus, being in Rome at the time of the testimony of the bishop Polycarp, taught many men, and many of his excellent and very accurate writings are published, in which he mentions Polycarp and that he studied under him. He both capably refuted all heresies and transmitted the ecclesiastic and Catholic rule as he received them from the holy man. He says this too: "Once when Marcion (from whom are named the Marcionites) met with holy Polycarp and said, 'Recognize us, Polycarp,' Polycarp said to Marcion, 'I recognize, I recognize the firstborn of Satan.'" And this is also recorded in the writings of Irenaeus, that on the hour and day that Polycarp bore witness in Smyrna, Irenaeus, who was in the city of the Romans, heard a voice like the sound of a trumpet, saying, "Polycarp has born witness." So from these writings of Irenaeus, as stated previously, Gaius made a copy, and so did Isocrates from Gaius' transcripts in Corinth. And I Pionus wrote them again from the transcripts of Isocrates, having searched for these writings in accordance with a revelation from holy Polycarp. And I gathered them together, now almost worn away with time, so that the Lord Jesus Christ might bring me also to his heavenly kingdom, together with his elect. Glory to him, with the Father and the Son and the Holy Spirit for ages upon ages. Amen.[43]

M names the second intermediary Isocrates, instead of Socrates, though he still locates him in Corinth. The variant does not seem particularly significant.[44] The main new element of M is the development of the reference to Irenaeus. Indeed, M adds first some biographical information about Irenaeus, and then two anecdotes about Polycarp that M says come from the works of Irenaeus. The first one is about an encounter between Polycarp and the heretic Marcion. This is from an identifiable text of Irenaeus; the passage is also quoted by Eusebius.[45] The second anecdote, however, is known only through M: the trumpet call that announced to Irenaeus in Rome that Polycarp was martyred in Smyrna.[46] The addition of the anecdote about Marcion gives an antiheretical and more specifically anti-Marcionite flavor to the colophon.[47] In turn, the colophon invites us to read the whole text through an anti-Marcionite lens.[48]

The colophon in K is similar to that found in the menologia tradition until it adds, after the note by Pionius, several distinct elements.[49] First, K gives material about three figures who are called φιλομάρτυρες: Alce, with a reference to her appearance in the writing of Ignatius;[50] Irenaeus, with the same material as M, but with an additional anecdote reported by Polycarp about John and Cerinthus in the bathhouse;[51] and Isocrates, with a wholly new story that Dehandschutter summarizes as follows: "This man was devoted to the Greek ψευδοπαιδεία, and visited all the philosophical schools (Pythagoras, Plato, Aristotle, Epicurus), but he got not convinced, neither by the ποιητικὴ ψευδολογία nor the ῥητορικὴ κακοτεχνία. Then sounds a voice: 'Isocrates, the truth is in Christianity.' When somewhat later the heavenly voice speaks again: 'Isocrates, the truth is in the Catholic church,' Isocrates decides to go to Smyrna and due to the blessed martyrs, has fellowship with the holy and Catholic church."[52] The version K seems to shift the emphasis onto another dimension of Polycarp: opponent to pagan wisdom and herald of the truth of Christianity.[53]

Some scholars have responded to the differences between the colophons in the different manuscripts by arguing that the colophon itself was a secondary addition. There is no evidence to support this claim as most manuscripts contain a version of it.[54] The fact that it is precisely the colophon that is so considerably modified in the different versions of MPol strengthens my earlier point about its importance for our understanding of the whole text. The colophon is the passage of the text to which the audience would look for cues on how to understand the text, albeit retrospectively. As the intended message changed over time or in different contexts, MPol was adapted or partly rewritten. This points to a fluidity of the text, for which we must account.

Thus, the notion that forgery is evidenced by false authorial claims should be abandoned when dealing with martyr narratives.[55] The combination of anonymity and textual fluidity better fits with what Christine T. Thomas has called "stories without authors and without texts."[56] Thomas uses this phrase or the label "open texts" to describe works such as the *Alexander Romance, Joseph and Aseneth*, and the Apocryphal Acts of the Apostles.[57] The category can also be applied for a better understanding of the textual characteristics of martyr narratives.

## "Stories Without Authors and Without Texts"

According to Thomas, textual fluidity is expressed by "multiple recensions that cannot be reduced to a typical stemmatic relationship," excerpts and epitomes, and early translations. As she writes: "Although these characteristics of 'fluidity' are not sufficient to define a genre, precisely this lack of an original text is significant in assessing the type of writing these works were considered to be by their ancient audience."[58]

I will use the case of Polycarp again as an example of a martyrdom story that fits the description of a fluid text. Of the nine manuscripts of MPol, six belong to a family called the menologia tradition (g), and two stand apart,

M and K. No stemmatic relationship has been established between g, M, and K.[59] The eleventh-century Byzantine "Imperial Menologion" contains an epitome of the life and death of Polycarp.[60] Moreover, this abridgment, a typical βίος ἐν συντόμῳ,[61] seems to present enough narrative variants that Dehandschutter supposes it derives from a version of the martyrdom that is independent of g.[62] Another independent Greek version is attested through fragments written in Sahidic, the so-called Harris fragments.[63] In this version, Polycarp is closely associated with the apostle John, and his death is presented as a requisite for John's peaceful death.[64] This would bring the number of versions of the martyrdom of Polycarp up to five.[65] All these versions use elements of the same story material but arrange them into different narrative discourses.[66]

Finally, there are several ancient translations of the *Martyrdom of Polycarp*.[67] Traditionally these have not received much attention beyond their potential contribution to the critical edition of the "authentic" Greek text.[68] Thus, when he published the text of the Latin version (BHL 6870), Zahn thought it derived from a Greek version unknown to us.[69] Soon afterward, however, the Latin text was disregarded by Lightfoot since its variants, resulting from a very loose and paraphrastic version, do not affect the establishment of the Greek text.[70] A recent study of the translation technique concludes that this Latin version, dated to the end of the fourth or the early fifth century, alternates between actual translations and free improvisations.[71] The goal of the translator is not to provide access to an authoritative text but to serve the needs of a Christian Latin readership.[72] Syriac, Coptic, and Armenian versions that can be dated to the beginning of the fifth century are also usually disregarded because they are viewed as being composed of excerpts that derive from Eusebius and therefore of no value in establishing the Greek text.[73] The Coptic version, however, is not just an abridged extract of Eusebius. It presents, for instance, a proper prologue and a conclusion.[74] The Church Slavonic translation does not seem to date from before the tenth century and is therefore too late for consideration here.[75]

Multiple recensions, abridgments, translations, all these versions seem to be independent "performances" of a story rather than versions of an authoritative text.[76] Before exploring further how textual fluidity characterizes martyr narratives and how this should affect our understanding of these texts, I will first elaborate on the concept of "open text."

Thomas borrows the concept of "open text" from David Konstan, who uses it to describe texts such as the *Alexander Romance*, the *Life of Aesop*, or the *History of Apollonius of Tyre* "that admit a degree of variation or indeterminacy that is incompatible with authorial control."[77] Konstan goes further and suggests that "the aim in editing an open text is not to prune away ostensible supplements or to reduce the multiple recensions to an initial or genuine original."[78] Obviously such a view is incompatible with the categorization of martyr narratives either as authentic or as forged. The label of "open text," however, is ambiguous as it has been used for several different notions. First, it competes with a key concept in Umberto Eco's semiotics, that of "open work" or "open text," as it came to be familiar to his readers in English.[79] For Eco, an open text is a text that is written with an active reader as its intended audience.[80] The notion is clearly not relevant to our discussion. Second, "open" is also used in textual criticism to describe texts for which an archetype cannot be constructed.[81] As we have seen, this is only one of the characteristics of the texts Thomas identifies as "open texts."

An alternative to "open texts" is "living texts." The expression seems to have been coined by Henri Quentin for describing texts such as the Vulgate; he was compelled to devise a new method when he composed an edition of this text. In a severe critique of Lachmann, Quentin not only urges textual critics to keep separate their quest for the original and their reconstruction of the archetype, but also points out that for some texts the manuscript tradition does not allow the textual critic to reconstruct an archetype.[82] For Quentin, however, this characteristic is due not only to the nature of the textual tradition, as is the case with the notion of "open recension," but also to the nature of the text itself: "on les sait par cœur et ils se déforment au cours de traditions orales parallèles, comme cela a dû être le cas pour les chansons des trouvères, ou bien on en considère les moindres détails avec une attention intense et on les corrige sans cesse au cours des âges comme cela a été le cas de la Bible."[83] The characterization of some texts (rather than their tradition) as "living," that is, not fixed, proved to outlive the method devised by Quentin and is now quite common among medievalists.[84]

There is a risk, however, in extending the use of the label to texts of a very different nature. It is one thing to say that manuscript variations deserve attention, another altogether to claim that manuscript variations reveal an attitude toward the text that sets it in a special category. The label "living text," which I prefer to "open text,"[85] should be reserved for texts that are attested through multiple versions each of which constitutes a performance of the story it tells.[86] In the remainder of this chapter I will offer two examples that illustrate how martyr narratives are "living texts" in this sense.

## "Donatist" and "Catholic" Versions of African Martyrdoms

First, I revisit the dossier of the so-called Donatist and Catholic versions of African martyr texts. In his fundamental study of Donatist martyrs, Monceaux distinguishes between martyrs who died before the beginning of the schism and those who died as victims of the imperial and Catholic repression.[87] The first category of martyrs is common to all North African Christians. For the commemoration of the martyrs of the first category, the Donatists, according to Monceaux, interpolated existing Catholic versions of their martyrdom.[88] His example of choice is the *Passion of Saturninus, Dativus, and Their Companions*, also known as the *Acts of the Abitinian Martyrs* (BHL 7492, PSaturnDat). It relates the execution of a group of Christians in Abitina during the Great Persecution. According to Monceaux, the Donatists added to it an "appendix," a hateful pamphlet directed against the Catholics Mensurius and Caecilianus.[89] Such an approach still dominates the approach to the dossier. Similar Donatist interpolations would, thus, be attested in the *Acts of Crispina* (BHL 1989) and in the *Passion of Maxima, Secunda, and Donatilla* (BHL 5809, PMax).[90] Since its discovery in a manuscript from Würzburg by Reitzenstein in 1913, another text is added to the dossier: a version of the *Acts of Cyprian* (BHL 2039d).[91]

Too often scholars do not distinguish between the attestation of an actual Donatist version in the manuscript tradition and the hypothesis that a version is Donatist compared to a supposed non-Donatist original.[92] Only the first category is relevant to our discussion; it includes a version of the *Acts of Cyprian*, a version of the *Acts of Crispina*, and, possibly, a version of the *Passion of Lucius and Montanus*.[93] As we will see, it is in most cases impossible to decide whether the original is Catholic or Donatist. Ultimately, I suggest that we abandon the pursuit of an alleged original and recognize all versions as independent performances.

### ACypr

The Donatist version of the *Acts of Cyprian* (BHL 2039d) is known through a unique ninth-century manuscript from Würzburg.[94] The manuscript contains a small dossier of texts that includes works of Cyprian and some attributed to him.[95] Because BHL 2039d is identified as Donatist, Reitzenstein suggests that this dossier was compiled by the Donatists. The inclusion of Cyprian's *Letter 67*, in which the intervention of Stephen, bishop of Rome, in the matter of the excommunication of two Spanish bishops is contested, could indicate that the dossier was compiled when Constantine involved Miltiades, the bishop of Rome, in the resolution of the Donatist conflict.[96] This version, like the shorter recension of the *Acts* (BHL 2039), does not include the trial of 257 (1) but does includes the execution (4), which is present only in one group of manuscripts for the shorter recension; its text is close to that of the longer recension (BHL 2037a).[97]

BHL 2039d presents several divergences from the versions attested in the other manuscripts. Maureen A. Tilley, and Alden Bass after her, note as a first variant Cyprian's dress at his arraignment: the officers "disguised him."[98] The variant *uelauerunt*, however, as has been clearly noted by both Reitzenstein and Franchi de' Cavalieri, simply betrays a misunderstanding of the *texerunt* present in other manuscripts, where it means "escorted" or "guarded" and not, as in the first meaning of *texerunt*, "covered."[99] More significant is the insertion, after the proconsul's speech and before the reading of the sentence, of the phrase *Laudes Deo*:

| BHL 2039d | BHL 2039 | BHL 2037a |
|---|---|---|
| And Cyprian: "Praise be to God!" Together with him the believers: "Praise be to God." And the proconsul and vir clarissimus Galerius Maximus read the sentence from a tablet: "It is resolved that Tascius Cyprian along with his people be executed by the sword."[100] | And he read the sentence from a tablet: "It is resolved that Tascius Cyprian be executed by the sword."[101] | And he read the sentence from a tablet: "It is resolved that Tascius Cyprian be executed by the sword." The bishop Cyprian said: "Thanks be to God."[102] |

As is well known, Augustine identifies the phrase *Laudes Deo* as the cri de guerre of the Donatists while the Catholics preferred the phrase *Gratias Deo*.[103] Though the opposition should not be forced, the phrase *Laudes Deo* seems to be a clear index of Donatism, especially in texts that precede 411.[104]

The focus on the Donatist *signum* should not lead us to overlook the emphasis that BHL 2039d places on the participation of Cyprian's Christian brothers: they praise God with him and they are included in the death sentence. BHL 2039d is the only version to mention that other Christians were condemned along with Cyprian. BHL 2037a indicates only that the brothers wished to have been executed with him.[105]

Commentators have noted that in BHL 2039d Cyprian asks for twenty instead of twenty-five gold coins to be given to the executioner.[106] More interesting is an addition describing a gesture Cyprian makes while he awaits the executioner:

| BHL 2039d | BHL 2037a |
|---|---|
| While waiting for the executioner, he raised his eyes to heaven in prayer and when the raging executioner had come, he moved his eyes from heaven to earth and he bid the executioner be given twenty gold coins.[107] | And he began to await the executioner. And when the executioner had come, he bid his people to give that same executioner twenty-five gold coins.[108] |

The contrast between the rage of the executioner and the peaceful and forgiving state of mind of Cyprian is all the greater.

It is difficult to interpret the fact that the deacon who helps Cyprian is named Donatus in BHL 2039d instead of Julianus as in the rest of the tradition. According to Franchi de' Cavalieri and Delehaye, this is another hint from the interpolator, using the namesake of his sect as a *signum*.[109] Jean-Louis Maier and Francesco Scorza Barcellona suggest that Donatus could be the name of the deacon and that the Julianus of the tradition results from a copyist's mistake, as it is also the name of the presbyter who helps Cyprian.[110] We are clearly in the realm of gratuitous and misguided speculations prompted by the search for an authentic text!

The final difference worth mentioning is the addition in BHL 2039d of a comment on the death of the proconsul: "Galerius Maximus died racked with guilt and consumed by his disease."[111] At least one other manuscript adds a comment on the death of Galerius Maximus: "he died, strangled by the devil."[112]

The misguided variant *uelauerunt* for *texerunt* strongly suggests the textual dependence of BHL 2039d on a written text similar to that of the manuscripts of BHL 2039, which include the execution narrative. However, to present the redactor of the text as a mere interpolator is to miss the point.[113] BHL 2039d presents some narrative choices that go beyond mere "donatization." Both the executioner and the proconsul are presented in a darker light. The participation of Cyprian's Christian brothers is emphasized. Thus, BHL 2039d is a good example of how a redactor would rework a text that he regarded as "living."

## PCrispin

The *Acts of Crispina* are extant in four manuscripts that have been divided into two versions (PCrispin; BHL 1989a and 1989b).[114] When Monceaux examined the textual tradition regarding Crispina, he knew only BHL 1989a as edited by Ruinart on the basis of two manuscripts from Reims. He concluded that there were two versions of the narrative about Crispina: a Catholic version, known to Augustine but not preserved, and a Donatist version, contained in one of the manuscripts collated by Ruinart, later corrected by the Catholic copyist responsible for the second manuscript.[115] After Franchi de' Cavalieri discovered a first and then a second manuscript containing a different version of PCrispin (BHL 1989b), Delehaye thought that this version was the original and that it was Catholic, while the Donatist version of Monceaux was the mere product of sectarian interpolations.[116]

Monceaux noted two clear Donatist interpolations in BHL 1989a.[117] In 4.2, after the sentence is read, Crispina says: *Christi laudes ago*, in which Monceaux recognized the cri de guerre of the Donatists.[118] In 4.3, the final doxology refers to the unity of the Holy Spirit, a Donatist theologoumenon according to Monceaux.[119] BHL 1989a also mentions the martyrs Maxima, Secunda, and Donatilla.[120] As Monceaux considered their passion (BHL 5809) as Donatist, he deemed this mention to be another Donatist interpolation.[121] The other version, BHL 1989b, does not contain any of these elements. The first two are only present in one manuscript of the version BHL 1989a.[122] The case for a Catholic and a Donatist version seems difficult to make.[123]

There is no room here for a full comparison of the four transmitted texts, but other differences between BHL 1989a and BHL 1989b merit attention. BHL 1989b includes a short description of the execution at the end of the narrative: "And making the sign of the cross on her forehead and putting out her neck, she was beheaded for the name of the Lord Jesus Christ, to whom is honor for ever. Amen."[124] This element, which is missing in BHL 1989a, emphasizes Crispina's willingness to die. The responses of Crispina to Anullinus's interrogation also present notable variants:

| BHL 1989a | BHL 1989b |
|---|---|
| What do you want? That I be sacrilegious against God and not against the emperor? No way. God is great, who made the sea, the green grass, and the dry earth. But what can men offer me who are the creatures of his hands.[125] | Perish *the gods who have not made heaven and earth*! I offer sacrifice to the eternal God who abides forever. He is the true God who is to be feared; he has made the sea, the green grass, and the dry earth. But what can men offer me who are the creatures of his hands.[127] |

| BHL 1989a | BHL 1989b |
|---|---|
| I lose my head at once, but only if I offer incense to idols.[126] | I should be very happy to lose my head for the sake of my God. For I refuse to sacrifice to these ridiculous deaf and dumb idols.[128] |

These variants cannot be reduced to scribal errors, but it seems hazardous to decide which were original. Again, the four known texts are better considered as four "performances" of the martyrdom of Crispina.

## PLuc

The last text I want to consider briefly has not yet been included in the dossier of the Donatist martyr texts.[129] It is the *Passion of Lucius, Montanus and Their Companions* (PLuc; BHL 6009), which is preserved in eighteen manuscripts that François Dolbeau has divided into two distinct families.[130] The first family (α), attested in three manuscripts, commemorates the feast of the martyrs on May 23, as does the sixth-century, Catholic, Calendar of Carthage (CPL 2030). The second family (β) generally commemorates the martyrs on February 24. Dolbeau has established that six out of the thirteen preserved manuscripts from the β family also include the *Passion of Donatus* (PDon; BHL 2303b) and that the latter is transmitted only in these six manuscripts.[131] Such a transmission history suggests that the β-family text belonged to a Donatist dossier that also included PDon. Considering two omissions in the text of the α family, Dolbeau further suggests that PLuc, as transmitted by the β family, is a Donatist version and that the α family transmits a Catholic rewriting.

The first omission is in PLuc 14.4:

| β family | α family |
|---|---|
| Then he put off the inconsiderate haste of the lapsed, a denial of peace, until full penance and the judgment of Christ.[132] | Then he put off the inconsiderate haste of the lapsed, a denial of peace.[133] |

The haste of the lapsi is in both texts described as a refusal to seek the peace of reconciliation. The α family omits to identify precisely until when reconciliation should be delayed.

The second omission is in PLuc 23.3–5:

| β family | α family |
|---|---|
| "This is my commandment, that you love each other as I have loved you." He added these last words and in the manner of a testament he sealed with his faith the end of his speech: he honored the priest Lucianus with the most generous recommendation and, to the extent that he could, destined him for the episcopate. Nor did he do so without cause. For it was not difficult to have knowledge when his spirit was near to heaven and to Christ.[134] | "This is my commandment, that you love each other as I have loved you." He added these last words and in the manner of a testament he sealed with his faith the end of his speech. Nor did he do so without cause. For it was not difficult to have knowledge when his spirit was near to heaven and to Christ.[135] |

The α family omits the recommendation by Montanus that Lucianus succeed Cyprian as bishop of Carthage. According to Dolbeau, the two statements were omitted by the α family in order to mitigate what they implied about the charismatic authority of martyrs and confessors, authority with which the Catholic church was not very comfortable.[136] Jean-Paul Bouhot objects to Dolbeau's interpretation that PLuc was composed before the beginning of the Donatist schism and suggests that the omissions can better be explained simply as a sixth-century revision.[137] I would like to suggest that both families transmit a third-century version and that the missing elements from the α family point to a performance of the text that tries to downplay the authority of Montanus in the context of the tensions that I described in Chapter 1 as characteristics of the few years following the death of Cyprian.[138]

It is impossible, however, to further explore the version of the α family, as Dolbeau did not include in his apparatus the variants that were specific to individual manuscripts when the tradition was stable.[139] Only a new collation of the two preserved manuscripts from the family would allow us to determine more precisely the particulars of the "performance" they represent.

*   *   *

The case of the so-called Donatist versions shows well the limits of the principles of critical editions when they are applied to "living texts." Should we push our approach to its logical extreme and advocate for the publication of a synopsis of the different manuscripts rather than editing the manuscripts into a single text?[140] A short text, the *Acts of the Scilitan Martyrs* (AScil), presents an opportunity to explore this option.

## A Synoptic Edition of AScil

The *Bibliotheca Hagiographica Latina* lists eight versions of AScil (BHL 7527–34), to which can be added a translation in Greek (BHG 1645). I include the following six texts in the synoptic:

—Text 1 is BHL 7527 discovered by Robinson in 1891 in a ninth-century manuscript, London, British Library, Add. 11880.[141]

—Text 2 is BHL 7529 published in 1889 from a manuscript from Chartres, Bibliothèque municipale, 0500 (0190).[142]

—Text 3 is BHL 7531 published in 1597 by Baronius in the *Annales* from a manuscript of the Biblioteca Vallicelliana, Tomus X.[143]

—Text 4 is BHL 7532 published by Ruinart in 1689 from a manuscript he found in the Bibliothèque Colbert.[144]

—Text 5 is BHL 7533 that Aubé found in two manuscripts of the *Passionarium Mozarabicum*.[145]

—Text 6 is BHG 1645, a Greek translation that Usener found in a manuscript copied in 890 by a monk named Anastasius, who himself found it in a collection of hagiographical texts compiled by Methodius, future Patriarch of Constantinople, during his exile in Rome (815 and 821).[146]

I do not include in the synoptic:

—BHL 7528, a fragment published by Mabillon that agrees with BHL 7527;[147]

—BHL 7530, a text found in a manuscript from Brussels; only a few variants have been published;[148]

—BHL 7534, which locates the martyrdom of the Scilitans in Rome at the time of Julian the Apostate; it was composed in the twelfth century in order to explain the presence of relics of the Scilitans in the Santi Giovanni e Paolo basilica.[149]

A consensus has been reached regarding the relationships between the six texts I include in the synoptic and their relative chronology.

The first family comprises Texts 1 (BHL 7527), 2 (BHL 7529), and 6 (BHG 1645). Text 1 is considered to be the original, or the closest to it. The main argument in favor of its originality seems to be its brevity. Thus, Robinson writes: "It is brief, almost to obscurity; and we can readily understand that it would need to be paraphrased and enlarged for Church purposes, so as to provide a somewhat longer and less difficult lection for the commemoration of the Martyrs."[150] Brevity is then implicitly associated with authenticity.[151] It is the fact that this text appears as close as possible to the actual court protocol that seems to support the scholarly opinion that it is the original.[152] Presenting its modifications as mostly additions, scholars judge that Text 2 belongs to the same family and is posterior to Text 1.[153] The modifications it presents are a good indication of what we lose when the principles of textual criticism are used to produce a single text. Text 6, the Greek version, which was once thought to be the original text, is now presented as a translation of a text close to Text 1 though it presents amplifications and significant variants.[154] It should be noted that the "original text" is not as stable as modern editions would let us believe. In his edition of

BHL 7527, Robinson used two other manuscripts that already offer a number of variants and additions.[155]

The second family has only one known member, Text 3 (BHL 7531), so that it is impossible to evaluate the stability of the text.[156] In this case, the modifications go well beyond additions; they affect the very structure of the narrative. The trial is divided in two days, and male and female martyrs are treated in two distinct groups. This is the version used by Bede in his *Martyrology*, which thus provides a *terminus ante quem* of 735 for Text 3.[157]

The third family includes Texts 4 (BHL 7532) and 5 (BHL 7533).[158] Despite many similarities, these two texts also present significant variants.

The relative chronology of the second and third families is difficult to establish, as there is no indication of their dates beyond the *terminus ante quem* of Bede for Text 3 (BHL 7531).[159] In any case, the line between texts that supposedly contain only additions and texts that belong to a different family is thin. The perspective adopted here, in which each text is a singular performance of the story, makes better sense of these differences. It is impossible to reach any conclusion concerning how far apart in time all these texts were initially composed.

I proceed now to a selective examination of the synoptic texts. There is no need to comment on the variations of the date of the execution or the different forms of the names. These elements regularly suffer during transmission, and the differences might not stem from different versions. The first words of the proconsul (1) in Texts 1 and 6 contain only the order: "return to your senses."[160] Texts 2, 4, and 5 also contain the order to sacrifice with a wording that varies. It seems reasonable to consider that the order to sacrifice is an addition that makes the text clearer.[161] However, when we consider Speratus's reply (2), there is a parallel addition about sacrificing to God in Text 2 and the other manuscripts of Text 1. This raises the possibility that the mention of sacrifice is not a clarification brought to Text 1 but a deliberate decision to emphasize one of the most sensitive points of opposition between Christians and their persecutors.

The reply of Speratus (2) is much longer and very similar in its wording in both Texts 4 and 5. Both these texts are interested in the precepts the Christians have received from their God and in their reactions when confronted with injustice. This seems to be more than a simple amplification of what appears in Text 1. Instead of a simple opposition between service to the Roman emperor and service to God, these texts create a contrast between the moral conduct of Christians and pagans: not only do Christians not do evil to anyone, but when evil is done to them, they do not respond with evil. Instead they pray for those who do them harm.

When the proconsul addresses all the martyrs (8), the first to reply is Cittinus, then speak Donata, Vestia, and Secunda (9). In Texts 1, 4, 5, and 6, there is no intervention from the proconsul until all the martyrs have answered one by one. In Text 2, Donata's reply is missing, and the replies of the other martyrs are each preceded by a brief question from the proconsul.[162] Text 3 introduces elements of narrative that create a second interrogative session: after the reply of Cittinus the martyrs are sent back to prison, and when they are called back the following day, Saturninus proceeds with two separate interrogations, first questioning the women individually, then addressing the men collectively before the interrogation again returns to Speratus specifically. The result of this is that the women and their replies are highlighted. A similar organization of the trial is found in APerp 1–2, as noted by Aubé.[163] There is no point in wondering whether the organization of one text is more authentic than that of the other. The variety in the tradition shows that the actual trial procedure, if it was at all known, is of less interest than the possibilities its staging offered for conveying a given message.

When Delehaye proceeds to a comparison of the different versions of AScil, he does so exclusively from a perspective of textual transmission, pointing to errors, corrections, paraphrases, etc. made by different copyists whom he considers to have had not much respect for the original.[164] There is no reason, however, to assume that all the modifications were made through the copying process itself. The performance of the martyrdom account that we know through a specific manuscript precedes the copy that transmits it to us.[165] Though it is difficult to pinpoint the precise meaning of every modification that has been made and to locate the contexts of all these performances, the modifications are, nevertheless, revealing of an attitude toward martyrdom accounts that is incompatible with the notion of an authored text.

I find indirect confirmation of this attitude to martyr texts in the very way Augustine "quotes" from the version of AScil that was read in church before he preaches for the feast of the martyrs. Four sermons for the feast of the Scilitan martyrs are preserved.[166] Augustine explicitly mentions that a martyrdom account has been read before the sermon in three of the four texts.[167] In two of his sermons he quotes the answer of Donata to the proconsul: "Honor to Caesar as Caesar, but fear to God."[168] The quote appears to be a verbatim quote of the answer as found in BHL 7527.[169] It can thus be assumed that the version he had in his library was a copy of BHL 7527.[170]

In another sermon, however, Augustine seems to quote much more freely from the text: "Recall, dearly beloved, how the judge who was trying them called their confession 'a persuasion of vanity,' to which one of them replied, 'The persuasion of vanity is to commit murder, to bear false witness.'"[171] Augustine must here refer to Speratus's answer to the proconsul Saturninus calling all of them to "cease to be of this persuasion." The answer in BHL 7527 reads as follows: "It is an evil persuasion to commit murder, to give false testimony."[172] There is no mention of "vanity" in BHL 7527 or in any other version of AScil for that matter. We might suppose that Augustine's version of AScil presented a different reading and that it left no trace in the manuscript tradition, or we might suppose that Augustine is misremembering the text that was read a few minutes before he started to preach. But the better explanation is that Augustine introduced the idea of vanity because it fitted the lesson he wanted to draw from the example of the martyrs.

Indeed, a little later in the same sermon, he seems to imagine another fragment of dialogue between the judge and the martyr: "This is what true witnesses held on to; with their minds they could perceive his gifts to come. That's why they made light of all things that pass away: *Vain is salvation from man* (Ps. 60:11). The reason he wasn't frightened when he was told, 'If you confess Christ, you will be punished,' is that he had in mind, *A false witness will not go unpunished* (Prov. 19:5). These blessed saints spoke the truth, and were put to death."[173] Edmund Hill, the translator, rightly notes that the third sentence is "suddenly in the singular."[174] The interpretation of the audience could only have been that Augustine had again quoted from the martyrdom account. Here Augustine goes as far as reading the thoughts of the martyr.

This example shows well how both the preacher, who had read a martyrdom account, and the audience, who had listened to it, had no problem with changing the text according to the performance of it that would be meaningful in their present context.[175] No one would have assumed that the words of martyrs reported in a martyrdom account or in a sermon that celebrated their anniversary were the exact words the martyrs had actually uttered.

## Conclusion

I have offered just a few examples in support of my contention that martyrdom accounts are best viewed as "living texts." The manuscript traditions of these texts reveal many variants that are not interpretable as scribal errors, and efforts to edit them out into a single text—especially when criteria of textual criticism are combined with the criterion of authenticity—result in a fundamental misunderstanding of their nature. What is needed at this point is a different model, one that can more accurately describe the relationships between different versions of a single martyrdom account and that escapes the constraints and the pitfalls of traditional textual criticism and of the search for authenticity.

The Functional Requirements for Bibliographic Records, known as FRBR, is a data model that was first published in 1998.[176] Though it was designed as a model for organizing library holdings, it proposes a foundational taxonomy of entities that is useful for our purposes. These entities are Work, Expression, Manifestation, and Item (WEMI).[177] A Work is an abstract entity that can be recognized through its different realizations, or Expressions. In turn, each Expression can be embodied in different Manifestations. Finally, an Item is a single exemplar of a Manifestation. The following example illustrates the taxonomy:

Work: Ronald Hayman's Playback
    Expression: the author's text edited for publication
        Manifestation: the book published in 1973 by Davis-Poynter
            Item: copy autographed by the author.[178]

When a traditional critical edition reduces all the different versions present in the manuscript tradition to one text, it runs the risk of confusing Work, Expression, Manifestation, and Item. I propose that we view a specific martyrdom account as a Work that is realized through different Expressions that are embodied in Manifestations. It is important to keep the last two entities, Manifestations and Items, separate, at least theoretically. Admittedly, Manifestations are often undistinguishable from Items in our case, but this does not mean that the Items, that is, the texts as we found them in the different manuscripts, should be viewed only as the products of the manuscript copyists: they embody a Manifestation that is not directly accessible and of which they provide a copy.[179]

In the case of Polycarp, the Work is the story of the martyrdom of Polycarp. The Greek text of MPol is an Expression of it and so is, for instance, the Latin translation BHL 6870. The menologia tradition represents a different Manifestation of the Greek text of MPol than the two Manifestations contained in the manuscripts M and K. In the case of M and K, Manifestation and Item are the same. For the Manifestation known as the menologia tradition, there are six Items of it.

The main benefit of this model is that it helps us to understand that the "original text" of many modern editions is just another Expression of the Work, and not the Work itself. It also provides us with an entity, the Manifestation, that sits in between the Expression of the Work and the Item, which is the text found in the manuscripts. I do not intend, however, to negate centuries of philological work and to claim that each Manifestation as embodied in the different manuscripts is a Manifestation of a different Expression.[180]

I am also well aware of the impracticality of the printing of synoptic editions. Even with such a short text as AScil we have reached the limits of what can be done. On the other hand, as Franz Fischer writes: "The digital medium supports an egalitarian presentation of text versions."[181] After an initial enthusiasm for the raw publication of many or all witnesses of a text, digital scholarly editions are now working on solutions that enable readers to apprehend a multiplicity of extant texts and their relationships, whether or not a single text is proposed.[182]

In any case, I hope I have succeeded in conveying that martyrdom accounts are not the kind of texts that are reducible to an "original" form, and in showing what can be gained when we think about manuscripts as evidence for different performances of the text rather than as a source for variant readings. I am not denying the value of textual criticism, especially insofar as it can help determine the earliest available text. This project, however, should not lead us to neglect or disregard variant texts because they have been deemed late or, worse, inauthentic.

CHAPTER 4

# History, Fiction, Document, Testimony

In his 1991 Sather Lectures, Glen W. Bowersock calls attention to what he terms "fiction as history."[1] For Bowersock, fiction is fabrication, falsehood as opposed to truth, and history is a story about the past.[2] Thus, he groups under the paradoxical label of "fiction as history" texts that rewrite the past by introducing fictions in the midst of facts. He includes martyr narratives in this category of "instructive fiction," though he does believe that the earliest are derived from court protocols.[3] For Bowersock, the reign of Nero is when this type of fiction begins to proliferate.[4] His insightful lectures have provided the starting point for many attempts to define a category of texts or identify a literary genre that could accommodate Christian narratives that are often described as blending fact and fiction, such as the Gospels, Luke-Acts, or the Apocryphal Acts of the Apostles.

One such attempt is the work of Christine M. Thomas on the *Acts of Peter*.[5] We saw in Chapter 3 that martyrdom narratives and the Apocryphal Acts of the Apostles share the important characteristic of textual fluidity. As some of the Apocryphal Acts of the Apostles also include a martyrdom account, which sometimes has its own independent transmission history,[6] it is worth examining why Thomas defines the *Acts of Peter* as a "historical novel."[7] She proceeds to a comparison between the *Acts of Peter* and the ancient novels. By "novels" she does not mean only, or even primarily, the five well-known imperial romances,[8] which have so often been compared to the Apocryphal Acts of the Apostles,[9] but an array of texts that include earlier novelistic fragments as well as, for instance, the *Alexander Romance*. These narratives focus on "figures of great public significance," at least within their tradition, and on the noteworthy events in which they were involved.[10] She emphasizes that "the individual figure, rather than any specific version of the story of his life . . . functions as the fabric of the narrative,"[11] and she suggests that we understand "historical" as "referential to events outside the text itself," as did ancient grammarians and rhetoricians in their typology of narrative.[12]

Thomas rejects the classification of such texts as biographies, because they do not focus on the character of their main figure, and she then addresses what she calls, following Reitzenstein, the "historical monograph" as a possible *comparandum*.[13] For Reitzenstein, the monograph was characteristic of the so-called tragic history that developed during the Hellenistic period and that Polybius so fiercely attacked.[14] Such monographs centered on a leading figure in a short and entertaining account of his public exploits.[15] Despite many similarities, Thomas objects that the fluidity of the Apocryphal Acts prevents a definitive identification with any form of historiography.

Her next step is to find texts that share with the Apocryphal Acts two essential features that seem contradictory: historical content and the absence of any formal relationship to ancient historiography. She suggests that we leave aside the notion of fiction that is usually associated with novels, as it is irrelevant to ancient texts: "By ancient standards, literary works that told of real events, no matter how novelistically, were histories."[16] She rejects the label of fiction all the more because it is associated with the imperial romances, which she considers to belong to a very different kind of text. Thomas concludes that the *Acts of Peter* are "best described as historical novels," texts that "fall between novel and history."[17]

Thomas has succeeded in shifting scholarly discussion away from the all-encompassing comparison between ancient novels and Apocryphal Acts of the Apostles. However, her definition of a genre for these texts, neither novel nor history, but historical novel, is ultimately disappointing. This is because she has attempted to answer two questions: "how ancient readers would have classified [the *Acts of Peter*], and how they would have responded to its implicit claim to narrate events."[18] There is no need to assume that an ancient audience would have sought to classify a text in order to determine their response to its claim to narrate events. As has been stated recently by Alan J. Bale, "Yes, genre dictates a reader's expectations, but no, this does not mean that a reader identifies a genre and then ceases to modify those expectations."[19] In other words, Thomas's assumptions foreclose the possibility of intertextual dialogue.[20]

In this chapter I will not propose a new genre that can adequately encompass martyrdom narratives, but I will explore how generic cues in these texts might have been perceived by their audience. First, however, I need to address a few issues regarding the way historiography, truth, fiction, and storytelling were conceived at the time martyrdom narratives were first composed.

## Historiography, Truth, and Fiction

Though Thomas ultimately rejects any comparison with historiography, I need to address the role of fiction in the genre of historiography. The first misconception that must be dismissed is a widespread perception among scholars, especially those dealing with early Christian narratives, that historiography, starting in the Hellenistic period, blurs the distinction between fact and fiction in a marked and characteristic manner.[21] Thus, a persistent account holds that in the Hellenistic age a new type of historiography emerged, conveniently called tragic history. Tragic history, by this account, aimed primarily to stir the reader's emotions and to this end was prone to use sensational elements. It also tended to be satisfied with plausibility over factuality. It is thought to have ultimately derived from Aristotle and the Peripatetics as an attempt to make historiography more universal by borrowing the manner and method of tragedy.[22] As very little Hellenistic historiography actually survives, this account has been developed out of the judgments of later historians, in particular Polybius's critique of Phylarchus.[23] Most elements of this account have, however, been criticized. John Marincola's rereading of the passage of Polybius shows that he does not attack Phylarchus for writing a different type of historiography, but because he is a bad historian.[24] Emotions, in particular, are not rejected from historiography, only their misuse.[25] Thus, specialists of ancient historiography now agree that there is nothing like "tragic history" as "a significant mode of Hellenistic historiography."[26]

Cicero's letter to Lucceius, which has been adduced in discussions of tragic history,[27] and a crucial passage of his *De oratore* have been at the center of a similar debate on rhetoric and ancient historiography.[28] In 1988, Anthony J. Woodman proposed "a radically new interpretation" of these two passages.[29] He argued that for Cicero historiographical truth was not about factuality but about impartiality, and that *inventio* was as crucial to historiography as it was to rhetoric. In other words, while "the Romans required the hard core of history to be true," it was necessary only for "its elaboration to be plausible."[30] He concluded his study with a general claim that raised the delicate and sensitive question of the reliability of ancient historiography: "Classical historiography . . . is primarily a rhetorical genre and is to be classified (in modern terms) as literature rather than as history."[31] I will leave the issue of reliability aside.[32] Woodman's claim about truth needs to be qualified. Indeed, truth is opposed to bias more often than to falsity in the remarks of ancient Greek and Roman historians. However, the issue with partiality is that it can lead the historian to "make up a hard core."[33] Factuality, therefore, remains a central concern of ancient Greek and Roman historians. Another element of Woodman's interpretation is problematic. There is no support in the passage of the *De oratore* for the transfer of the prescriptions for rhetorical *narratio*, which accepts both things that happened and things as if they had happened, to historical *narratio*.[34] Finally, it remains difficult to establish the limits of the "hard core" of facts required by ancient historiography,[35] and this is where misunderstandings between historians of Rome and specialists of Roman historiography occur in this debate.[36]

We might agree with J. L. Moles, who writes: "No serious ancient historian was so tied to specific factual truth that he would not sometimes help general truths along by manipulating, even inventing, 'facts.'"[37] Nevertheless, writers who inscribed themselves in the tradition of classical historiography did commit to submit their written product to a standard of truth.[38] Moreover, readers of historiography would have accepted what they read as fact.[39] We need, therefore, to look beyond classical historiography if we hope to understand generic expectations that allow the use of fiction for conveying truth.[40]

Indeed, not all narratives are historiographical. Thus, the exposition of facts in the form of a narrative is an important part of rhetoric, in Greek διήγησις and in Latin *narratio*.[41] Cicero's definition in *On Invention* is typical: "The narrative is an exposition of events that have occurred or are supposed to have occurred."[42] The type of *narratio* that interests us is the exposition of events: "That which consists of an exposition of events has three forms: *fabula, historia, argumentum. Fabula* is the term applied to a narrative in which the events are not true and have no verisimilitude, for example: 'Huge winged dragons yoked to a car' (Pacuv. trag. 397). *Historia* is an account of actual occurrences remote from the recollection of our own age, as: 'War on men of Carthage Appius decreed' (Enn. ann. 7.223). *Argumentum* is a fictitious narrative which nevertheless could have occurred. An example may be quoted from Terence: 'For after he had left the school of youth' (Ter. Andr. 51)."[43]

A similar tripartite division is used by grammarians in analyzing the subject matter of narratives.[44] Our oldest testimony for the division in a grammatical work is that of Asclepiades of Myrlea, a grammarian of the first century BCE, whose theory is discussed in the second century CE by Sextus Empiricus in his polemic against grammar.[45] "Asclepiades in his *On Grammar* ... says that under history one type is true, one is false, and one is as if true, where the actual history is true, that about myths is false, and that about fictions and such genres as comedy and mime is as if true."[46] For Asclepiades, the criterion of truth is the decisive feature, and the tripartite division in ἱστορία, μῦθος, πλάσμα is reducible to that of true (ἀληθῆ), not true or false (ψευδῆ), and as if true (ὡς ἀληθῆ).

We should be careful, however, not to identify true history as factual history. Indeed, Asclepiades describes it thus: "And of true history there are again three parts: one is about the persons of gods, heroes, and famous men, another about places and times, and the third about actions."[47] The mention of gods and heroes has many parallels in Hellenistic sources, and Roos Meijering concludes: "in Hellenistic theory ἱστορία consists of legendary matter rather than of true facts of history; it is traditional and in any case potentially (ἐν δυνατῷ) historical."[48] This is no doubt due to the nature of these sources, which for most part are scholia that comment on poetry.[49] Πλάσμα in Greek and *argumentum* in Latin are often translated as "fiction." It is important, however, to note that the criterion of verisimilitude distinguishes this invented narrative from μῦθος/ *fabula*, also invented but simply false.[50]

Through rhetorical education and its preliminary exercises, this tripartite division became more than a tool for exegetes of literary works. As attested in the *Progymnasmata*, however, the tripartite division actually results in only two types of exercises: μῦθος on one hand, and διήγησις (or διήγημα) on the other,[51] thus attenuating the distinction between ἱστορία/*historia* and πλάσμα/*argumentum*.[52] In ancient theories, therefore, there is room for narratives that satisfy the requirements of both ἱστορία/*historia* and πλάσμα/*argumentum*.

Though it is not clear that this theory of narrative would be widespread enough to inform an ancient audience's expectations, with the category of πλάσμα/*argumentum* we have something close to fiction as it is understood in modern theories. Indeed, the criterion of verisimilitude introduces a pragmatic dimension into the reception of the narrative[53] and thus, though implicitly, the notion of fictional complicity.

Modern theories often insist on two features of fiction: nonreferentiality and make-believe.[54] Hence the importance of the notion of a contract between writer and reader. In the words of Jean-Marie Schaeffer, a fiction "should be announced as fiction, the function of this announcement being to institute the pragmatic frame that limits the space of the game at the interior of which the semblance can operate without representation induced by the mimemes being treated in the same manner as would be the 'real' representations mimed by the fictional device."[55] As we may recall, Bart Ehrman argues from the absence of an explicit contract of this type that MPol is a forgery, not a fiction.[56] Several objections can be raised against such an approach.[57]

Nonreferentiality is a criterion that would limit fiction to nineteenth-century novels, and, though it is useful to trace the apparition of nonreferentiality in literature, it cannot be used to date the development of fiction itself.[58] The notion of make-believe, or "shared ludic feint,"[59] also imposes on fiction a narrowly modern point of view that eliminates from the sphere of fiction works such as seventeenth-century hagiographical and devout novels or, closer to late antiquity, didactic fictions such as the *Sacred Inscription* of Euhemerus.[60] Finally, the notion of an explicit contract is too rigid and largely anachronistic. Modern theories need to face the challenge of ancient works and come to terms with the other ways that fiction has been signaled.[61]

One that seems very promising for ancient works, and martyr narratives in particular, is the topos. Jan Herman writes: "Le *topos* implique un effet de déjà-vu ou, précisément, de reconnaissance, qui peut recanaliser la référentialité en la faisant pointer, non plus vers un référent, mais vers sa nature même de signe. Signe qui par sa récurrence et son réemploi ne peut renvoyer qu'au geste de la répétition et de la reprise et désigner par là, non pas la véridicité du texte, mais au contraire sa facticité."[62] Thus, a type of fictional complicity can be established through the use and recognition of topoi.[63] The topos works like a signal, marking the textuality of the narrative and hinting at its poeticity, in the etymological sense of "being made."

I suggest that the phrase "I am Christian," which frequently appears in martyr narratives, is a topos of this type.[64] It is vain to try to identify the first martyr who uttered this answer and then to postulate that the other martyrs imitated him or her. The narrative does not claim that the martyr actually said the phrase as much as it refers the audience to other martyr narratives. A form of fictional complicity is thus established.

There is, however, another anachronism to avoid. We should not deduce that the establishment of fictional complicity implies that the audience would assess the entire narrative as fictitious and therefore false. As we have seen, contrary to μῦθος/*fabula*, πλάσμα/*argumentum* is not false; furthermore, πλάσμα/*argumentum* is not submitted to the same dictates of verification as μῦθος/*fabula* and ἱστορία/*historia* are. Audiences of martyr narratives believed in the historicity of the martyrs and would assume a core of historical facts: their names, the day of their death, the manner of their execution. Cyprian mentions several times the importance of keeping a record of the names of the martyrs and of the day of their death.[65] Bede, several centuries later, also insists on these core facts: "on what day, but also by what manner of contest, and under whom as judge."[66]

In sum, when dealing with premodern texts, we need not assume that the establishment of fictional complicity implies a contract of shared ludic feint. A narrative that points to its textuality does not necessarily invite the audience to assume it is false. The blurring of fact and fiction and the centrality of verisimilitude make room for different types of verification. The audience acknowledges that many of the truth-claims of premodern texts are moral rather than factual.[67] The truth-claims need, therefore, to be understood at the level of the narration, as I will now show through a close study of the narration in some of the earliest martyr narratives.[68]

## Narration in Martyr Narratives

By narration, I mean the telling of the story, the narrative act. In other words, I am going to look at what the texts say about the way they are written, and a main focus will be on the narrator. I understand the narrator as a textual category; as most of our texts are anonymous, the distinction between narrator and author is all the more important.[69]

### MPion

The short preface opens with a call for the commemoration of holy men from the past and for their imitation in the present before it introduces Pionius himself. There is no indication of the person of the narrator beyond a first-person plural pronoun that identifies him with the audience: "[Pionius] being an apostolic man among us."[70] It is difficult to decide whether the reference is to shared religion in general or to shared belonging to the local Christian group.[71]

The preface ends with a statement that seems to mention a writing left by Pionius himself and that has led most scholars to assume that MPion was based on an autobiographical text. Indeed, the passage reads: τὸ σύγγραμμα τοῦτο κατέλιπεν εἰς νουθεσίαν ἡμετέραν ἐπὶ τὸ καὶ νῦν ἔχειν ἡμᾶς μνημόσυνα τῆς διδασκαλίας αὐτοῦ. It is usually translated as: "He left this writing for our admonition so that even now we have a reminder of his teaching."[72] This "autobiography" is supposed to cover sections 2 to 18 of MPion. As the narrative is in the third person, scholars assume that it has been transposed from a narrative in the first person by the editor, who was also responsible for the rest of the narrative (19–23).[73] They also point out that he did a bad job as he failed to transpose the first person in two passages.[74]

No serious attack was mounted against this scenario until 2010, when Dutch scholar Antoon Hilhorst presented the following series of arguments.[75] First, Hilhorst points out that a transposition of the narrative back to the first person would obviously produce "a most unlikely document."[76] Second, he easily dismisses attempts to locate the "divergences" between the autobiographical section and the rest of the narrative, and he further establishes the many similarities between the two sections.[77] In passing, he notes that beyond this initial statement nothing in the text indicates where the autobiographical section would start and end.[78] Finally, he objects that the whole narrative is known to Eusebius as "a document about Pionius."[79] Hilhorst builds a strong case against the traditional scenario. However, his solution to the problem posed by the statement "he left this writing for our admonition" is ultimately unsatisfying. He suggests that we gloss τὸ σύγγραμμα τοῦτο as "the teachings stored in this writing."[80] Indeed, Hilhorst argues that the whole clause "decidedly suggests a written text with a doctrinal content."[81]

The statement τὸ σύγγραμμα τοῦτο κατέλιπεν εἰς νουθεσίαν ἡμετέραν cannot be explained satisfactorily. A transposition in the third person is a most unlikely scenario, especially as nothing in the text marks clearly the beginning and end of such an autobiographical section. It would also be difficult to account for the long speeches in an "autobiography."[82] In the end, I propose that we adopt a solution that Hilhorst entertains but rejects as too banal: Pionius's martyrdom is the teaching.[83] However, rather than glossing τὸ σύγγραμμα τοῦτο, I suggest that we take the martyrdom as the subject of κατέλιπεν, and translate as follows: "His martyrdom left this writing for our admonition so that even now we have a reminder of his teaching."[84]

Despite what might seem an initial erasure of his role, the narrator does intervene in his narration. Overall, the narration is written in the third person, except for three first-person plural passages.[85] In 10.5, we read: "Someone else said: 'Look! The little fellow goes to sacrifice.' He was talking about Asclepiades who was with us."[86] We can reject the interpretation of the first person as a remnant of Pionius's voice.[87] "With us" undeniably identifies Asclepiades as a Christian. The use of the first person, however, cannot be separated from what this sentence does in the narration: it identifies the person labeled as "the little fellow," an identification that only an eyewitness would be able to make.[88]

The use of the first person in 18.13 is of a different kind. Pionius and his companions were brought back to prison after both Lepidus and Euctemon had tried in vain to convince them to sacrifice. Then, the narrator reports a story he later heard about Euctemon: "Later it was said that Euctemon had required that we be forced, that he had brought himself the lamb to the Nemeseion, and that after he had eaten from it, he wanted to bring all the roasted meat back home."[89] The "we" in this case could express the narrator's (and his audience's) special connection as a Christian to the victims of Euctemon's pressures. It is not necessary to assume that the narrator is included among these victims, though the other uses of "we" would suggest to the audience that it was the case.

Indeed, the final first-person plural is a clear case of eyewitness statement: "And his crown was signaled through his body also. For, after the fire was put out, we who were present saw that his body was similar to that of a decorated athlete in his prime."[90] The first-person plural of the verb (εἴδομεν), reinforced by the substantivized participle (οἱ παραγενόμενοι), "who were present," is used here to authenticate the somewhat miraculous preservation of Pionius's body through the fire of the pyre.

In the last paragraph of the text, in which the narrator gives the date of the martyrdom according to different calendars, the use of the first person plural establishes a strong connection with the audience: "according to us, in the kingship of our Lord Jesus Christ."[91]

The use of such an intermittent first person, which is not a common feature of historiography, appears three times in Acts,[92] a text that seems to be quite familiar to the narrator.[93] As William S. Campbell has shown for Acts, this intermittent first person is not just an authenticating device; it also establishes a connection with the audience.[94]

The narrator sometimes comments on his narration. After reporting the first speech of Pionius, the narrator suggests that Pionius said a lot more, as did the people who tried to convince him to sacrifice.[95] This points to his role as narrator since it suggests that he selected the material he included in his narration. There are also two passages where the arrangement of the narration directs attention to itself as a narration. Polemon, the *neokoros*, is done with his interrogation of Pionius and ready to move on to Sabina: "Then he went to Sabina. Pionius had previously told her: 'Say that your name is Theodota,' so that she might not, because of her name, fall back into the hands of the lawless Politta, who was her mistress. For this woman, during the reign of Gordian, as she wanted Sabina to change her faith, bound and exposed her on the mountains, where Sabina secretly got provisions from the brothers. After this they strived to free her both from Politta and from her bonds. She then spent most of her time with Pionius and was arrested in this persecution. Now Polemon said to her: 'What is your name?' She said: 'Theodota.'"[96] Just after the narrator has mentioned that Polemon was going to interrogate Sabina, he opens what is clearly demarcated in the text as parenthetical,[97] a flashback—or an external analepsis[98]—that the audience needs in order to understand why Sabina, when asked about her name, answers "Theodota." Here the narrator imparts knowledge not only of a prior exchange between Pionius and Sabina but of facts that took place before the events of the primary narration. The mention of the reign of Gordian, likely Gordian 3 (238–44), implies that the story dates back a few years as the present of the narration is the reign of Decius (249–51).[99]

Another passage is more difficult to interpret. After both Lepidus and Euctemon have tried in vain to convince them to sacrifice, Pionius and his companions are brought back to prison: "Later it was said that Euctemon had required that we be forced, that he had brought himself the lamb to the Nemeseion, and that after he had eaten from it, he wanted to bring all the roasted meat back home. Thus, he ridiculed himself by his perjury: he swore by the emperor's genius and the goddesses Nemeses, with a garland on his head, that he was not a Christian, and that, unlike the others, he would neglect nothing to further his denial."[100] The passive ἐλέγετο indicates that what follows was reported to the narrator. It is difficult to decide when it took place as the μετὰ ταῦτα is rather vague, and because the narration itself resumes with another μετὰ ταῦτα.[101] It could, therefore, be a prolepsis, or flash-forward,[102] unless we suppose that the narrator temporarily changes the focus of the narration onto Euctemon. It is clear, nevertheless, that the embedding of this secondary story in the narration, as well as that of Sabina and Politta, works as a signal for the audience that they are dealing with a carefully composed narration.

The last element to note is the insertion of an extract from the minutes of Pionius's interrogation into the narration. The passage reads as follows in our unique manuscript: Μετὰ δὲ ταῦτα ἦλθεν ὁ ἀνθύπατος εἰς τὴν Σμύρναν καὶ προσαχθεὶς ὁ Πιόνιος ἐμαρτύρησε γενομένων ὑπομνημάτων τῶν ὑποτεταγμένων πρὸ τεσσάρων εἰδῶν Μαρτίων. (After this, the proconsul came to Smyrna and when he was brought before him Pionius became a martyr. The following minutes were recorded three days before the Ides of March.)[103] Gebhardt in the *editio princeps* adds ὑπὸ before τῶν ὑποτεταγμένων, which gives the following translation: "Minutes were recorded by secretaries three days before the Ides of March."[104] The correction, likely introduced because of the position of the date in the sentence, is unnecessary.[105] Furthermore, it suppresses the indication that a document is inserted in the narration. The document starts with the date and ends with the reading of the sentence.[106] Because the format was very familiar, the narrator does not need to set more formal boundaries to the section he presents as a transcription of the official minutes. Earlier, the narrator mentions the presence of scribes during the interrogation by the *neokoros* and the fact that they were writing everything down.[107] There, however, he does not say that he transposes the official minutes. Commentators have pointed out that several features of the transposed minutes betray if not a fabrication at least an adaptation.[108] Such attempts at authentication miss the point. What matters is that the narrator himself claims that it is a document. This is a recurring feature of martyr narratives that we will examine in closer detail later.

The narrator in MPion thus points to his own work of composition in several ways. We need not focus solely on what appear to be authenticating devices as do those commentators who discuss the historical liability of MPion. If we leave aside the issue of authenticity, which did not especially matter to an audience who believed in the historicity of the martyrs, we start finding in the text cues to which the audience would have responded. These cues trigger the type of fictional complicity that I have proposed.

## MPol

Most commentators describe MPol simply as a letter, even a real letter, and deem the colophons to be a later addition.[109] I have already explained why I consider this position untenable and how important the colophons are to our understanding of the text. I will now investigate how the narration of Polycarp's martyrdom is constructed.

In MPol the narrator presents himself as a copyist and claims responsibility for the final transmission and reproduction of a document. The copyist gives his name as Pionius and explains that Polycarp told him about the existence of the document in a revelation. He then searched for it and found a document worn out by time that he reassembled (22.3). The document that Pionius edits mainly consists of a letter from the church of Smyrna to the church of Philomelion (1–20). There follow a few paragraphs: the first gives the date of Polycarp's martyrdom (21); next comes a commendatory postscript (22.1); finally, there is a paragraph written by a certain Socrates who discloses that he copied in Corinth a copy established by a certain Gaius who made his own copy from material he transcribed from Irenaeus, a disciple of Polycarp (22.2). The modern divisions of the text reflect modern prejudices about its authenticity more than its actual organization.[110]

The letter itself presents features, such as its inscription and a farewell, that the audience would expect to find in a letter and that contribute toward establishing it as a document.[111] There is no prologue or preface. The audience finds out that the letter is embedded in a slightly larger text only with the paragraph that follows the farewell formulas and gives the date of the martyrdom. It is easy to understand how the redundancy of the paragraphs that follow the letter led modern scholars to reject them as later additions, and it is difficult to escape the impression that these paragraphs try so hard to present the letter as authentic that they undermine its authenticity. Hence the temptation for the modern scholar who seeks to salvage the authenticity of the letter to reject the final paragraphs, just as Eusebius had ignored them when he excerpted the letter in the *Ecclesiastical History*. The audience, who were both familiar with such authentication devices and had no doubt about the historicity of Polycarp and his martyrdom, would have arrived at a very different conclusion.[112]

Indeed, explanations of the survival and transmission of documents are a common strategy in narratives of the period. It has been described as "pseudo-documentarism," with "pseudo" implying invention and playfulness.[113] As we have seen, however, it is not necessary to introduce the notion of make-believe when dealing with such devices. A well-known example of pseudo-documentarism is the prologue to *A Journal of the Trojan War*. The narrative is presented as written by a contemporary of the war, Diktys of Crete; it was buried with him and rediscovered much later at the time of the emperor Nero.[114] Another example is the second of two letters with which Antonius Diogenes prefaces *The Incredible Things beyond Thule*. Antonius Diogenes relates how a text, written on cypress tablets, was discovered by Alexander the Great, copied by one of his generals, Balagros, who then sent it to his wife.[115] Similarly, at the beginning of Book I of *The Life of Apollonius of Tyana*, Philostratus describes how the empress Julia Domna brought to his attention the memoirs of Damis, a disciple of Apollonius.[116] All these texts were composed in the second and third centuries CE.

William Hansen lists three formal features of pseudo-documentarism: accumulation of details that are often structured by relays, exotic and romantic pedigree, and celebrity association.[117] MPol's colophons definitively accumulate details about the transmission of the letter and structure them by describing successive relays (Irenaeus, Gaius, Socrates, Pionius). They also feature celebrity association both by insisting on the role of Polycarp himself and by mentioning Irenaeus.[118] Though there is no attempt at giving an exotic or romantic pedigree to the story, the first two features are enough for the audience to have recognized the device. This would certainly have triggered a form of fictional complicity.

We now need to consider how the letter format was exploited for the narrative. It is striking that with the exception of the inscription and the farewell formula, epistolary elements are present only at the beginning and at the end of the letter.[119]

The apostrophe "brothers" only appears twice. The first occurrence is in the first few lines of the letter: "We write to you, brothers, about those who suffered martyrdom and about the blessed Polycarp, who concluded the persecution when he, so to speak, set a seal on it with his own martyrdom."[120] The second one occurs before the beginning of the narrative of Polycarp's martyrdom:[121] "Therefore, because of this, brothers, we do not commend those who surrender of their own accord since the gospel does not so teach."[122] The presence of the addressee is thus limited to a mere minimum.

The second person, another way of engaging the addressee that characterizes epistolarity, reappears only in the last paragraph after the initial "we write to you": "Though you asked that the events be fully revealed to you, we have, for the present, made them known only summarily through our brother Marcion. Once you have learned these things, send the letter on to brothers further away, that they too may glorify the Lord who makes his selection from his own servants."[123] These second-person elements participate in the construction of the epistolary scenario: the church of Philomelion requested a letter; once they have it, they should circulate it.

The first person, also a feature that characterizes epistolarity, nearly disappears in the narrative section.[124] With the exception of the "we who were present" that guarantees that a voice came from heaven when Polycarp entered the stadium,[125] all the uses of "we" occur after Polycarp uttered his final "Amen."[126] The other instances of "we" refer to the Christians of Smyrna as actors in the narrative: they are witnesses to the miraculous preservation of Polycarp on the pyre;[127] they are prevented from taking away his body;[128] and finally, after the body was burned, they gather his remains.[129]

Thus, the epistolary framework is quite limited,[130] and the narrative itself does not take much advantage of the epistolary form.[131] One passage, an intrusion of the narrator, is interesting in this regard. When the pyre is ready,

Polycarp undresses: "He also attempted to remove his shoes, though he did not usually do this in the past, because each of the faithful was always eager to see which of them might touch his body sooner. For he had been held in all honor because of his virtuous way of life, even before his martyrdom."[132] The comment aims to explain why Polycarp has difficulty removing his sandals. This insight into Polycarp's prior life provided the brothers of Smyrna with an opportunity to boast of the honor they themselves rendered to Polycarp, but instead, οἱ πιστοί are credited for it in a very general way.

Clearly, the epistolary form was not chosen for the narrative potential it offers.[133] The choice of a letter seems to be dictated mainly by the "imagined status" of letters "as somehow inherently truthful and reliable."[134] The audience would be familiar with the role of letters as documentary evidence when quoted in historiography or biography.[135] Similar use of documents seems to have been quite common in martyrdom narratives, as we will see.

## The Martyrs of Lyon and Vienne

There also is a letter in the dossier on the martyrs of Lyon and Vienne, which was available to Eusebius. Because there is no testimony other than the excerpts in Eusebius, it is impossible to determine how the letter was embedded in the dossier. Eusebius could well have ignored any paratextual elements—as he did with the colophons from MPol—when he chose to excerpt large passages from the letter and shorter extracts from other documents.[136]

In the preserved extracts, the receivers are not addressed in the second person, but the use of the first person is much more common than in MPol. Eusebius, however, deliberately skipped over passages that were not strictly narrative. He thus omits the prefatory material and twice cut what he qualifies as side comments.[137] He had warned his readers previously that besides the narrative the σύγγραμμα contains lessons to be drawn from the events, and that he would only excerpt what he thought was relevant.[138] Thus, we know very little about the arrangement of the narration of the martyrs of Lyon and Vienne.

We should note in passing that the two texts that are traditionally presented as letters are in fact texts in which a letter is embedded. Thus, the epistle cannot be considered as one of the genres prevalent among martyr texts,[139] and Giuseppe Lazzati's theory about the forms of martyr literature needs to be revisited as the epistle can no longer be considered as the first form of it.[140]

## PMar

At the beginning of *The Passion of Marian and James*, the narrator presents his narrative as a commission of the martyrs themselves:

> When the most blessed martyrs of almighty God and of his Christ make a modest request to their dearest ones in their hurry to reach the promised kingdom of heaven, they do it with modesty, remembering that humility always makes them greater in faith. The more moderately they asked, the more readily they received. So also to us the most noble witnesses of God have left the duty of announcing their glory, I mean Marian, one of our most beloved brothers, and James. You know that they were attached to me because, in addition to our pious common allegiance, we also lived together and had familial affection for each other.[141]

The establishment of his credentials, both the request of the martyrs and his companionship with them, is repeated at the end of this short preface: "And it is not without reason that with their intimate trust they imposed on me the request I am about to fulfill. For, who would doubt our community of life in times of peace, when the same period of persecution found us living with unbroken love?"[142] Thus, the narrator describes himself as a close companion of the martyrs and a witness of the events. The commission he received from them further legitimizes his narrative. It should be noted that the rhetorical quality of the preface already reveals that the producer of the text is a *lettré*.[143]

Then, the narrative starts in the first person: "So, we were traveling to Numidia," and thus continues until Marian and James are sent to Lambaesis to be tried by the governor.[144] From this point, however, the narrator disappears from the story and the narration shifts to the third person. There is no indication of what happened to him, nor about the source of his information for what follows. Thus, the narrator does not say that he was among the brothers to whom James reported his final vision.[145] When James mentions that he saw Agapius welcoming him and other martyrs to a banquet, the narrator, before he reports the vision, interrupts his narration and explains who this Agapius is by means of a flashback,[146] a device that is characteristic of a third-person narration. The description of the execution is even introduced by an impersonal *cerneres*: "One would have observed. . . ."[147] At the time of

their execution, many martyrs saw or heard horses, the white horses of
Revelation:

> As is customary, their eyes were covered before the sword stroke, but
> no darkness blocks the sight of a free mind: there shone an abundant
> and unthinkable beam of great light. Indeed, though no sight was vis-
> ible to their terrestrial eyes, many, with their relatives and brothers
> sitting near them, said that they saw marvelous things: from above
> appeared to them horses shining bright white, on which rode youths
> clad in white. And there were many from the same number of mar-
> tyrs who attested with their ears to what their companions reported:
> they recognized the sound and the neighing of horses.[148]

The narrator reports that the martyrs shared their visions or what they heard
with those who were present without including himself among them. There is,
therefore, a marked inconsistency in the narration, a shift from a first-person to
a third-person narrator.[149]

We should not take this inconsistency for a lack of ability. As I mentioned
earlier, the text betrays a producer who is well educated and knows both classical
and Christian literature. As Joëlle Soler has shown, he skillfully weaves the
metaphor of travel into an intertextual dialogue with Apuleius.[150] I suggest that
this inconsistency points to the issue of narrative transmission, an issue that is
particularly at stake with martyr narratives. I will discuss this further in the
conclusion.

## *VCypr*

The *Life of Cyprian* is not usually included among martyr narratives; it has been
part of a different discussion, particularly as regards its genre. Harnack describes
it as the first Christian biography,[151] whereas according to Reitzenstein, it was a
panegyric.[152] Peter Lebrecht Schmidt has recently applied insights from modern
discussions about orality, suggesting that Pontius had composed a funerary ora-
tion to be delivered publicly and later revised it for publication.[153] We need, as I
mentioned earlier, to adopt a much more dialogical conception of genre, and in
any case, my focus here is on the narration and the narrator.[154]

The attribution to Pontius, a deacon of the church of Carthage, is made by
Jerome.[155] The text in the manuscripts is anonymous until the twelfth century;

there is no mention of Pontius even in the fourth-century list of Cyprian's works at the end of which it appears.[156] The narrator, who uses the first person, both singular and plural, does not name himself. The title given to the text by Jerome is *Life and Passion of Cyprian*; *Life of Cyprian* is the title attested in the fourth-century list of Cyprian's works and in the manuscript tradition.[157] That the intent of the narrator, however, is to write a martyr narrative is clearly highlighted in the preface, where he refers to the *Passion of Perpetua and Felicity* and claims that he is a better writer than the author of that text and that his subject matter is a superior hero.[158]

The repeated use of *conscribere* in the preface and the narrator's stated concern for the length of his *uolumen* clearly indicate that the text we read was intended as a written text.[159] However, the narrator does address his audience directly a few times, especially in the preface and in the conclusion.[160] Such an address occurs only once in the body of the narrative but in a crucial context. The narrator comments upon Cyprian's withdrawal outside of Carthage and asks: "Do you wish to be sure that this withdrawal was not out of fear?"[161] Cyprian, who had left Carthage even before the edict of Decius began to be enforced, had to defend himself against the accusation of flight, and the narrator answers here the accusations that were made at the time.[162]

The narrator establishes his credentials at the very beginning of the text, when he declares the sources of his information: "I will tell whether I was present or if my knowledge comes from my elders."[163] Establishing a chain of tradition through the elders is important, as the narrator is about to embark on the narrative of Cyprian's path to faith, baptism, and bishopric. The narrator first affirms his status as a primary witness when he reports the exile of Cyprian to Curubis: "For as a favor of his love he had chosen me also, among his close companions, as a voluntary exile."[164] This statement precedes a direct speech in which Cyprian reports his famous dream about his martyrdom. The second passage in which the narrator makes his presence explicit occurs after Cyprian is brought to Carthage for his trial: "He was kept there for one night under a lenient guard, such that we, his companions and dear friends, could be in his company as usual."[165] There is a long tradition of reporting the final moments of a soon-to-be-executed companion, the participation in which is presented as a privilege.[166]

These are not the only instances of the first person. Indeed, the narrator intervenes several times to comment on his own narration. When he is about to begin, he asks: "Where then should I start? Where should I set the beginning of his good qualities except at the origin of his faith and his heavenly birth?"[167] He cuts short the enumeration of Cyprian's good works: "It would take long to go through each of his deeds individually, burdensome to count them all. As a demonstration of his good works, I think this alone is enough."[168] Sometimes these interventions are more rhetorically complex. Thus, at one point he uses what the handbooks of ancient rhetoric called a *locus a fictione*.[169] Cyprian, in exile, arrives at Curubis: "I do not now want to describe the charm of the place and for the moment I pass over the provision of all delights."[170] Instead, he proposes to the reader a thought experiment: "Let us imagine this place, its foul location, its filthy appearance,"[171] and then concludes that even such a place would not be a place of exile for a man like Cyprian.[172]

The narrator also uses the first person to weigh in when he addresses those aspects of Cyprian's life that are controversial. The narrator intervenes very emphatically when he reports the opposition to Cyprian's election as bishop: "Unwillingly do I speak, but speak I must: some resisted him, so that he even won a victory."[173] His explanation of Cyprian's withdrawal is similarly introduced: "Finally, I think that I ought to say something about the usefulness of the delay, although we have already touched on it briefly. For if we consider attentively what happened afterward, we can prove that his withdrawal was not conceived by human cowardice but that it was—as is truly the case—divine."[174] The shift from the first person singular to the first person plural is meant to involve the audience in the rebuke against Cyprian's critics. Another example is when the narrator reports that Cyprian stayed in his own villa (*horti*) after he was recalled from exile: "The gardens, I mean these gardens, which he had sold at the beginning of his faith and which were restored to him by God's generosity, he certainly would have sold again to benefit the poor, were he not trying to avoid the ill will aroused by the persecution."[175]

The narration is singular in that it does not embed any document. There is, however, an explicit reference to such a document when the narrator reports the first trial: "What the bishop of God answered to the questions of the proconsul is reported in the official record."[176] The minutes are not quoted, but their content is not summarized either, a point to which I will come back. The use of the first person in the *Life of Cyprian* is also by far more insistent than in any of the other martyr narratives. The anonymity of the text in its immediate reception, however, should warn the modern reader against ascribing this use to the role of the "author," Pontius. VCypr, even if in a different way, faces the same textual challenge as the other martyr narratives, as we will see.

## PLuc

The strategy of the narrator in the first part of the *Passion of Lucius and Montanus* is similar to that of the copyist in the *Martyrdom of Polycarp*. PLuc begins as a letter: "We too have a contest to fight among you, most beloved brothers. Nothing else can be done by servants of God and by those devoted to his Christ except to have regard for the multitude of brothers. By the force of this reason, love and duty compelled us to write this letter, so that we might leave to the brothers who come after us a faithful testimony of God's greatness and a memory of the pain from our endurance through the Lord."[177] The use of *litterae* is an explicit marker for the letter. Though it lacks an inscription, it concludes with a short farewell.[178] The reference to their pain and endurance identifies the authors of the letter as the martyrs to be. They consistently use the first person plural and address their audience as their "most beloved brothers."[179]

It is only after the farewell that the narrator intervenes: "This is what they wrote together from prison. But it was necessary to collect the whole conduct of the blessed martyrs in a full narrative. Also, out of modesty, they said too little about themselves and, what is more, Flavianus privately imposed on us the task of completing what was missing in their letter. We therefore added the rest as necessary."[180] The narrator legitimizes his narrative by presenting it as commissioned by one of the martyrs. He will offer not only a continuation to the martyrs' letter—they could not write about their own execution—but a complement to their narrative.

The narrator mentions the commission again when he arrives at the time in which it occurs in the narrative: "After that Flavianus was glad because, with the sentence given, he was certain of his suffering. He even enjoyed pleasant conversation. Thus, it was then that he ordered these words to be written and to be added to his own. He also wanted his visions to be added, some of which are related to his two-day delay."[181] The repetition strengthens the authentication of the commission and, therefore, of the narrative.

The narration itself is in the third person, with a few statements in the first person singular or plural. The first person plural clarifies the narrator's status as an eyewitness. Thus, for example, after he reports how Montanus prayed that Flavianus be executed two days after him, he writes: "And before our eyes what the Lord promised in his gospel was fulfilled: whoever would seek something in complete faith would obtain what he sought (Matt. 21:22). For, two days later, just as he had asked, Flavianus too was led out and fulfilled his glory in suffering."[182] Similarly, when Flavianus is led to the praetorium: "There we were arrayed around him, joined tightly and clinging to each other, so that we held each other's hands, displaying the honor due a martyr and the love felt for a companion."[183]

The first person singular seems to be used for comments on the narration itself, in particular statements on its order:

—"However, he himself also commanded, as I mentioned earlier, that we add the two-day delay to the account and recall its reason."[184]
—"I will pass over his extraordinary fasting in prison."[185]
—"So, I come to these facts."[186]

The only exception is a comment on the spirit of Flavianus: "I will tell you what I think: he endured the third day after those two not as a day of suffering but as a day of resurrection."[187] Similar interventions of the narrator—pointing out lessons for the audience—take the form of apostrophes. One example will suffice. In one of the visions of Flavianus that the narrator reports, Cyprian gives the martyr encouragements, and the narrator comments: "O the words of a martyr encouraging a martyr!"[188]

The very presence of the narrator within the narration contrasts quite strongly with the insertion of the letter of the martyrs-to-be at its beginning without anything in the text marking it as an embedded document. This tension between the erasure of the narrator in favor of a document that is a direct testimony and the narrator's omnipresence in the narration characterizes the challenges that martyrdom narratives faced, as I will suggest in conclusion.

## PPerp

The same tension appears in the *Passion of Perpetua, Felicity, and Their Companions*. As is well known, it is composed of heterogeneous elements. The narrator is responsible for the prologue (1), a short introduction (2), the narrative of the execution (14–21.1–10), and the epilogue (21.11).[189] Before the narrative of the execution, there are two texts that the narrator presents as written by two of the martyrs, Perpetua (3–10) and Saturus (11–13).

The narrator carefully signals the inclusion of the texts written by Perpetua and Saturus. He thus introduces the text authored by Perpetua: "She herself has related in full her course toward martyrdom, and from this point it is as she left it written in her own hand and according to her own understanding."[190] Saturus's text is also clearly announced: "But the blessed Saturus too divulged this vision of his, which he himself recorded."[191] And at the end of this, the narrator clearly marks the resumption of his own voice: "These were the very remarkable visions of the most blessed martyrs Saturus and Perpetua, which they themselves recorded."[192]

There are no comments on the transmission of these documents, unless we interpret very literally the last sentence of the exordium: "For this reason we too proclaim to you, brothers and young sons, what we have heard and touched."[193] The use of *contrectare* could refer to the narrator's access to the writings of Perpetua and Saturus and mean literally that he had the texts in his hands. The sentence, moreover, is a paraphrase of 1 John 1:1: "What we have seen, what we have heard, what we have looked at with our eyes, and what our hands had touched."[194] The omission of "what we have seen" leads some commentators to suggest that the narrator was not an eyewitness: he only heard testimonies (*audiuimus*) and had in his hands (*contrectauimus*) the texts of Perpetua and Saturus.[195] Such an interpretation assumes that the narrator makes a direct quotation of 1 John rather than cites from memory.[196]

It is true that there is no explicit statement by the narrator that he is an eyewitness to the events he reports in the third person. Nevertheless, he does claim some special form of legitimacy in the only passage in which he uses the first person: "Since therefore the Holy Spirit has permitted and by that permission has willed that the course of the games be written, though unworthy to add to the recounting of such great glory, nevertheless we carry out the command of the most holy Perpetua, or rather her sacred trust. Indeed, we added one proof of her boldness and sublimity of spirit."[197] The narrator has just mentioned what happened to Secundulus and Felicity during the time covered by the narratives of Perpetua and Saturus, and now that he is ready to start the narrative of the execution, he refers to the wish Perpetua expresses at the end of her narrative: "I have taken this account up to the day before the games. As for the record of the games themselves, whoever should wish to do so, let him write."[198]

Indeed, using two legal notions, he presents himself acting as Perpetua's mandatary and trustee. We should note also that at the same time as he signals his indignity, he boasts to the audience that he is able to supplement her narrative. It seems that the audience would deduce from this statement that the narrator was an eyewitness to the events. Whatever the case, the insertion of documents is once more a major device in the narration.

*    *    *

The study of the narration in some of the earliest martyrdom narratives reveals an insistence on their textuality. It does not lead the audience to question their truthfulness—a concern that has weighed upon the interpretation of such devices for as long as scholars have been anxious to salvage their "authenticity." The emphasis on the literariness of the narration and the tension in which it engages with the use of documents create the type of fictional complicity I described in the first part of this chapter. Whether we call it "fictionalization" or prefer the more traditional term "stylization,"[199] the result is that these techniques "interrogate, destabilize or challenge, if only for a minute, the narrative's intention to be believed or its claim to be truthful."[200] It is important to realize, however, that these techniques do not make the narratives fictional nor fictitious for their audience. The prominent use of documents, which I will now address specifically, can be understood within this framework.

## The Use of Documents

The use of documents, that is, inset texts that are not by the narrator, is ubiquitous in the martyr narratives I just reviewed. MPion quotes the minutes of Pionius's interrogation by the proconsul.[201] The colophon of MPol informs the audience that what precedes in the text is a copy of a letter from the church of Smyrna to the church of Philomelion.[202] The first part of PLuc is a letter of the martyrs-to-be.[203] The inclusion of texts written by Perpetua and Saturus is a well-known feature of PPerp.[204] Other texts just look like documents. With no metadiscourse, they mimic the format of court proceedings: AScil, ACypr, and the *Acts of Justin* are among the best-known examples.[205] Scholars have discussed these documents mainly in terms of their authenticity. Do some texts reproduce the transcript of the trials? The *Acts of Justin* and AScil are still considered by some scholars to do just that.[206] Unending seems to be the discussion about the amount of editing that has to be acknowledged in the "diary" of Perpetua.[207] Many scholars still consider the colophon of MPol as an addition to the authentic letter of Smyrna.[208] The discussion focuses on the informational value of the documents, the opportunity with which they present the historians for "an inferential reconstruction of the 'reality.'"[209] Here, I will follow instead the lead of Averil Cameron, who recently invited us to drop an instrumentalist reading of Christian texts that considers them as "essentially functional—there for a purpose, that purpose being historical rather than literary, with literary issues regarded as serving the historical-theological purpose."[210] I will consider the literary issues attached to the use of documents for themselves and thus focus on the narrative work that these documents—independently of the question of their authenticity—accomplish in the texts.

One obvious function of the documents is to authenticate the narrative. A good example of this function is the role played by the letter of the church of Smyrna in MPol. As we have seen, the narrative potential of the epistolary form was clearly not what motivated its adoption.[211] Yet, the audience would be familiar with the role of letters as documentary evidence when quoted in historiography or biography. If we want to go beyond this first function of documents as authenticating device, we need to look into how other, contemporary texts use documents.

The verbatim quotation of documents is a practice known to Greek and Latin historiography. Though "documents" do not benefit from a privileged status as evidence in ancient historiography, historians do occasionally quote documents.[212] While Eusebius used to be credited as the first historian to quote documents,[213] David DeVore has shown that his quotational practices do appear in previous Greek and Jewish historians.[214] It is quite clear, nonetheless, that the practice of quoting long documents verbatim was the exception rather than the rule. Furthermore, ancient historians seem to confine the practice to official documents.[215]

Among the earliest martyr narratives, only MPion claims to use an official state document: an extract from the minutes of Pionius's interrogation.[216] DeVore suggests that for Eusebius and a Christian audience, documents emanating from churches and Christian leaders fall within a category similar to that of state documents.[217] We could then categorize as official documents the letter from the church of Smyrna in MPol, the letter from the churches of Lyon and Vienne in the original martyrdom account, and the letter at the beginning of PLuc.

When we look how the documents are used in historiography, however, important differences appear with the use of documents in martyr narratives. DeVore describes two types of quotation in historiography. The first type works as "narrative catalysts." As DeVore writes: the historian quotes a document and "then plays out the effects" of the document in his narrative.[218] For instance, Eusebius quotes the edict of Gallienus in Book 7 of the *Ecclesiastical History* and then describes the peace that ensued for the church.[219] The second type is a corroborative quotation: it confirms the historian's narrative by telling the same story.[220] For instance, Eusebius in Book 3 tells how Pliny is upset with the many Christians he finds in Bithynia and then quotes Tertullian's version of the same story.[221]

Documents in martyr narratives are not used as corroborative quotations. They do not seem either to work as catalyst. We could say that to some extent the extract of Pionius's trial minutes are played out in the following narrative of his execution. However, it does more in the narrative than to cause the execution. It accomplishes the narration of the trial itself. In martyr narratives the quotation of documents does not serve to drive the narrative action, nor does the narrative develop their effects. Instead, they are used in lieu of narrative: they do the narration.

Documents are also used in biographical literature in which they serve as "character references."[222] DeVore gives the example of Diogenes Laertius, who in the *Lives and Opinions of Famous Philosophers* quotes wills of philosophers to illustrate how they take care of their legacy, or decrees that honor them in their cities of origin, in order to reinforce their portrait. Again, martyrdom narratives do not use documents in this way, though they clearly intend to present their characters to the audience as worthy of imitation. In PPerp, to give only one example, the insertion of Perpetua's writing does not reinforce her portrayal by the narrator. Instead, it *is* the portrayal, which the narrator merely reinforces.

If we seek other contemporary narratives that are based on documents or that quote documents that do the narration, we need to turn once more to the series of texts that have been described under the label of "pseudo-documentarism."[223] As I have already noted, "pseudo-" here assumes that it matters that the documents are acknowledged to be fabrications by the audience. Hansen defines pseudo-documentarism as "an author's untrue allegation that he (or she) has come upon an authentic document of some sort that he (or she) is drawing upon or passing on to his (or her) readers."[224] Karen ní Mheallaigh insists that the device is characteristic of "an increasingly self-conscious fiction" that developed from the late first century to the early third century CE, when a growing readership "enjoyed testing the boundaries separating fact from fiction."[225] However, the ancient reception of texts such as *A Journal of the Trojan War* or *The Life of Apollonius of Tyana* should give us pause: the *Journal* was considered a more reliable source than Homer on the Trojan War, and both Hierocles and Eusebius read Philostratus's *Life* as a factual biography of Apollonius.[226] I suggest, therefore, that the device works independently of the authenticity or inauthenticity of the documents, and that it does not require the audience to adopt a specific position on the issue of truthfulness.[227]

The embedding of documents, used in lieu of narrative or portrayal, works like a topos that the audience would recognize. We need, however, to take one more step in our interpretation. I will now suggest that the device both thematizes and challenges what has been described as the impossibility of testimony.

Indeed, as Giorgio Agamben writes in *The Remnants of Auschwitz*, all testimony contains a "lacuna." About the specific case of Auschwitz survivors, he says: "The 'true' witnesses, the 'complete witnesses,' are those who did not bear witness and could not bear witness. ... The survivors speak in their stead, by proxy, as pseudo-witnesses; they bear witness to a missing testimony."[228] The "impossibility of bearing witness," which is inherent to testimony, has been commented on by many authors from Primo Levi to Hannah Arendt and Derrida.[229] Derrida's running commentary on Maurice Blanchot, *The Instant of My Death*, called *Demeure: Fiction and Testimony*, is particularly relevant to our understanding of martyrdom narratives.[230] Derrida's reading of Blanchot's fictional testimony about an encounter with death shows how the possibility of fiction is embedded in the structure of testimony itself. Derrida even refers to early Christian martyrdom: "In memory of its Christian-Roman meaning, 'passion' always implies martyrdom, that is—as its name indicates—testimony."[231] He continues:

> As a promise to *make truth*, according to Augustine's expression, where the witness must be irreplaceably alone, where the witness alone is capable of dying his own death, testimony always goes hand in hand with at least the possibility of fiction, perjury, and lie. Were this possibility to be eliminated, no testimony would be possible any longer; it could no longer have the meaning of testimony. If testimony is passion, that is because it will always *suffer* both having, undecidably, a connection to fiction, perjury, or lie and never being able or obligated—without ceasing to testify—to become a proof.[232]

Testimony and story are in necessary tension, as a testimony, a unique experience inscribed in the instant, cannot be reproduced.[233] Any story of martyrdom, therefore, makes the distinction between fiction and testimony "tremble," to use Derrida's term.[234] There is, in other words, "a disturbing complicity between fiction and testimony."[235]

I contend that the use of documents in martyrdom narratives is a textual strategy adopted to meet the specific challenge of the impossibility of testimony.

In VCypr, Pontius expresses this challenge when he arrives at the end of his narration:

> What should I do now? My mind is divided between my joy in his suffering and my sadness at remaining in life; these twofold emotions burden a heart that is too constricted. Shall I grieve that I am not his companion? But the triumph of his victory must be celebrated. Shall I celebrate the triumph of his victory? But I grieve that I am not his companion. Nevertheless, I must truly and simply confess to you that which you too have experienced. This was my sentence: I rejoice much, even very much in his glory, yet I grieve more that I remained in life.[236]

Pontius cannot both suffer martyrdom with Cyprian and write a narrative about it. Cyprian bore witness with his life; Pontius with his story. While Pontius thematizes the impossibility of testimony, other martyrdom narratives challenge it by embedding documents from the martyrs themselves and by incorporating them in the narrative as much as possible. I suggest that the inconsistency in the narration of PMar is due to the impossibility of testimony: the narrator could not share any longer "in the glory of the brothers," as he says when he reports his own arrest, and thus disappears from his own narrative.[237]

The device, as it becomes a topos, is recognized by the audience and creates a fictional complicity. Just as martyrdom narratives constantly remind their audience of their textuality they also invite their audience to explore the boundaries between testimony and fiction, not in a playful complicity in "ironic textual games,"[238] but in a complicit textual challenge to the impossibility of testimony.

*     *     *

History, fiction, document, testimony: I hope this chapter has completed the demonstration that martyrdom narratives cannot be studied with the traditional categories mobilized in favor of or against their authenticity. An understanding of fiction that better fits the conditions of textual production of the time, an attempt to bring martyrdom narratives within the ambit of both other Christian texts and non-Christian texts, and a close reading that does not consider them only as "historical documents" or "tokens for the faith" reveal textual practices that respond to the challenge that is specific to testimony: the identity and reliability of witnesses who, as survivors, can only be pseudo-witnesses.[239]

# Conclusion

Though my main goal in this book is to change the conversation about martyr narratives, I will start the conclusion with a recap of some of my claims that engage with more traditional approaches to these texts.

First, I do not renounce isolating a group of texts that can be considered as the earliest martyr narratives. However, I propose to do it on a radically different basis, without considering their authenticity and without dating them on the basis of internal elements. Thus, there are a few texts that are attested in other texts that can be dated prior to 300. This method does not and cannot collect all the texts composed before 300, but it provides a more robust basis for a study of the incipient production of martyr narratives. A complementary approach is to study the earliest attested contexts in which these texts were used, which can give some cues about the reason why they were composed. The combined methods produce a list of seven texts: the *Martyrdom of Polycarp*, the *Martyrdom of Pionius*, the *Martyrdom of the Christians from Lyon and Vienne*,[1] the *Life and Passion of Cyprian*, the *Passion of Perpetua*, the *Passion of Lucius and Montanus*, and the *Passion of Marian and James*.

Along the way, I suggest dating the composition of the *Passion of Perpetua* as a whole, that is, including the parts that are not written by Perpetua and Saturus, to the period following the persecution of Valerian. I move forward to the fourth century, after the Great Persecution, the composition of the *Acts of the Scilitan Martyrs* and that of the *Acts of Cyprian*. More generally I offer strong arguments against taking the protocol format as an index of authenticity or antiquity.

The combined methods also lead to the conclusion that the earliest martyr narratives—the same is obviously true for the latest ones—were not a product of the circumstances. They were mostly composed after the fact, in contexts of actual peace for the Christians. It was not, however, within the scope of this study to look into the memory work they did or into the ways they constructed martyrdom. A number of excellent studies have done this, even if the textual basis of those studies was traditionally constructed. My primary interest is to look at a number of literary issues the texts raise and to the consequences they have on the way historians can approach the texts.

Both the search for authentic accounts and the witch hunt for forgeries are irrelevant to the understanding of Christian martyr texts. I advocate that we abandon approaches that regard the texts as authored in favor of treatments that respond to them as living texts, texts that are anonymous, that present no or little stable textual tradition, and that appear in several languages. Each version is to be understood as a performance of a story that has been adapted to a particular context. Not only should manuscript variations not be viewed only as corruptions or interpolations, but given systematic attention they can, in many cases, provide information on the agenda of their production.

Living texts, however, are not just texts that present a lot of variants. They invite their producers to give a performance of the story that fits the context of production, and they invite their audience to expect a different, even if only slightly different, performance each time it is performed. The audience of martyr texts would not question whether the words of the martyrs are their *ipsissima verba*. The question is irrelevant, and we saw that an Augustine could adapt these words to fit the context of his homily.

Thus, among the many versions that are preserved none is more authentic than the other. There is no "original text."[2] Searching for the earliest (preserved) text makes sense only if we are looking for the earliest context in which a story was used. This is exactly what I have done with the earliest accounts of the ancient martyrs, and I have found that the narratives and the authority of the martyrs were deployed in contexts that had little to do with their martyrdom.

Because there is no authentic version, there is consequently no room for forgery. Indeed, I propose an understanding of fiction that better fits ancient texts, one that does not require an explicit contract that defines "the space for the game," but allows for other cues, such as topoi, to establish a complicity with the audience. A narration that points to its own textuality or the use of documents are not attempts to fool the audience into believing that the texts provide a true account. The distinction between true and false, authentic and forged is not meaningful; the audience generally believed in the historicity of the martyrs and did not expect more than a small core of factually true details. The moral truth of the story was what mattered. A fictional complicity was established with the audience so that the audience knew that claims to authenticity should be understood at the narrative level. Thus, I suggest that the protocol format adopted by some texts, the embedding of interrogation scenes that mimic this format, and the use of documents more generally should all be understood as textual devices that address the impossibility of testimony.

Where does this approach lead us? I noted that we must decouple the history of the persecutions from the history of martyr narrative writing. As a matter of fact, the historian does not need martyr narratives to write the history of the persecutions. To take only one example (though the same is true in other areas of the empire), Tertullian provides significantly more information about the execution of Christians in second-century North Africa than the few texts that deal with Christians executed before the edict of Decius.[3]

I have attempted to establish a list of the earliest narratives, adopting an entirely new set of criteria that disposes of assumptions about authenticity and dating based on elements within the accounts. I do not want, however, the weight of a new "canon" to bear on these texts. Far from it, the rest of the book shows that the earliest texts share the characteristics of later narratives; they are and claim to be literature. In other words, all martyr narratives are like the "passions épiques" or "passions artificielles" of Delehaye,[4] the infamous, and amorphous, category of texts that scholars have sought to weed out of their collections. As Delehaye noted, many of these texts were produced before the end of the fourth century,[5] and they ought to be read on their own terms.

In conclusion, we need to retire the early martyr texts from being used by historians of the repression and persecution of Christians and promote their study as textual productions in the larger context of Christian writings. I have shown that the way documents are used in martyrdom narratives starts to make sense only when one looks into the role they play in the text, serving no other purpose than the literary purpose of challenging the impossibility of testimony. Many other aspects of these texts await to be studied with a similar approach.

APPENDICES

---

APPENDIX A

## Text and Translation of Aug. ep. 29*

APPENDIX B

## Materials for a Synoptic Edition of the
## *Acts of the Scilitan Martyrs*

Domino merito dilectissimo et sincerissimo filio et condiacono Paulino Augustinus in domino salutem.

1. Quemadmodum obtemperem uoluntati tuae de rebus gestis martyrum nostro sermone digerendis, cum maxime cupiam, nondum colligo. Legi enim quod dignatus es mittere et inueni quaedam aliorum sermone narrata, quaedam uero solis forensibus gestis quae me maxime delectauerunt expressa. Proinde si illa in quibus nos alii praecesserunt post ipse narrare uoluero, quasi doctor importunus uidebor, uel superfluus operator; si autem illa quae solis gestis forensibus loquendo commemorare uoluero, uereor ne non solum non adiuuem germaniorem affectum quem mihi ipsi fecerunt, cum a me sola ipsa gesta legerentur < . . . >.

2. Vt enim mouerer tale aliquid facere, quando de hac re tuae caritati locutus sum, delectauerant me quaedam de martyribus conscripta a uenerabilis memoriae sene Ambrosio quae comparata ceteris quorum scripta de his rebus legeram non postposui: sed ea maxime narrauit senex Ambrosius quae in publicis gestis cognosci non possent. Et ideo non tantum minime superfluum, uerum etiam maxime necessarium opus eius apparet < . . . > sicut legitur a nescio quo conscriptum etiam de beatissimo martyre Cypriano, quod in hortis suis cum accitus est ad passionem < . . . >, quod Vico Saturni cum tenebatur et multitudo fratrum pro foribus excubabat, iussit puellas custodiri, et si quid huiusmodi est quod forensibus gestis non potest inueniri.

3. Ego autem quid faciam, qui non habeo unde cognoscam quod praeter gesta publica de martyribus cognoscendum est, nisi quod eorum legeram qui me in hoc opere praeuenerunt? Quod autem in gestis publicis lego, si hoc solum meo sermone narrare uoluero, decolorare id potius quam illustrare conabor. Hanc suggestionem meam peto consideres et quid tibi uideatur fiducia fraterna rescribe.

# Text and Translation of Aug. ep. 29*

To his rightly most beloved lord and most sincere son and fellow deacon, Paulinus, Augustine sends greetings in the Lord.

1. I do not yet see, though I desire to do so very much, how I may carry out your wishes concerning the writing of martyr accounts in my own language. For I have read what you were so gracious as to send, and I found some narrated in the language of others, but also some reported by the sole judicial protocols—these gave me the greatest pleasure. Hence, if I want to narrate myself afterward those for which others have preceded me, I will seem like an untimely teacher or a useless worker. But if I want to recall in my language those from the judicial protocols, I fear that I will not only not add to the feeling of greater authenticity that they produced for me when I read only <. . .>.[1]

2. Indeed, some accounts that our old Ambrose of venerable memory had composed about the martyrs had delighted me so that I could be moved to do something of the sort, when I spoke with Your Charity about the topic.[2] I did not disregard them compared to the other accounts I had read on this topic.[3] But our old Ambrose narrated especially what could not be known from the public records. And for that reason, his work seems not only not superfluous but also highly necessary <. . .> like the account composed by someone or other, in which one can read about the most blessed martyr Cyprian that in his garden when he was marched off to his martyrdom <. . .> that, when he was being held at Vicus Saturni and a large number of the brethren kept watch at the gates, he ordered that the young girls be protected, and anything else of this sort that cannot be found in the judicial protocols.

3. But what would I do, since I do not have any way of knowing what one should know about the martyrs apart from the public records, except for the works I had read of those who have preceded me in this undertaking? If, however, I want to narrate in my own language what I only read in the public records, I would be trying to make the account less vivid rather than more vivid. I ask that you consider my opinion and write back with brotherly confidence what you think.

# Materials for a Synoptic Edition of the
## *Acts of the Scilitan Martyrs*

It is the first time that the original texts, accompanied by an English translation, of six versions of AScil are printed together. Unfortunately, they cannot be printed as a synoptic edition, but it is my hope that the material presented will help readers realize the potential of such an approach.

The rationale for their selection and the information about the six texts are given in Chapter 3. The texts are based on the following editions (translations are mine):

1. BHL 7527: Robinson 1891, 112-16.
2. BHL 7529: Anonymous 1889.
3. BHL 7531: Aubé 1881a, 30-31.
4. BHL 7532: Aubé 1881a, 33-36.
5. BHL 7533: Aubé 1881a, 36-39.
6. BHG 1645: Robinson 1891, 113-17.

Aubé in his Étude of the Greek text gives texts 3, 4, 5, and 6. He prints in italics all the elements that seem to him to be an addition, an amplification, or a gloss to the Greek text that he deemed to be the original version.[1] After his discovery of a new Latin version, which he considers as the original Latin form, Robinson publishes text 1 and text 6 facing each other, and then gives texts 3 and 5 with "their interpolations and modifications" in italics.[2] Delehaye compares extracts of eleven versions that he groups in three families. His selection of extracts, however, is entirely dictated by what he wants to demonstrate, that is, that the work of copyists and retouchers alter the original text.[3]

The materials I propose here serve a very different purpose. In terms of the FRBR taxonomy, which was presented in Chapter 3, text 1, deemed the original text, would be considered traditionally as the Work, whereas I consider it as one

Item of a Manifestation of one Expression of the story about the martyrs from Scili, the Work, which has other Expressions. On the other hand, whereas New Philology would consider each text published here as both an Item and a Manifestation of one Expression of the Work, I adopt a more complex approach that both accepts the results of critical philology and rejects the fallacy of the original text. Text 1 is one of three Items of the Manifestation of a first Expression of the story, Expression 1. Text 2 is one Item of another Manifestation of this first Expression 1. Text 3 is the only Item of a Manifestation of a different Expression, Expression 2. Texts 4 and 5 are two Items of two different Manifestations of yet another Expression, Expression 3. Text 6 is a different Expression, a translation in Greek, Expression 4 of the story. To sum up, the texts edited below are six Items that represent four Expressions of the story of the Scilitan martyrs; two of these Expressions have two Manifestations, of which I publish one Item (Figure 1).

In the texts printed below, I mark in bold the differences between Expressions (comparing texts 3 to 1, 4 to 1, and 6 to 1)[4] and in italics the differences between Manifestations (comparing text 2 and 1 for Expression 1; text 5 and 4 for Expression 3).

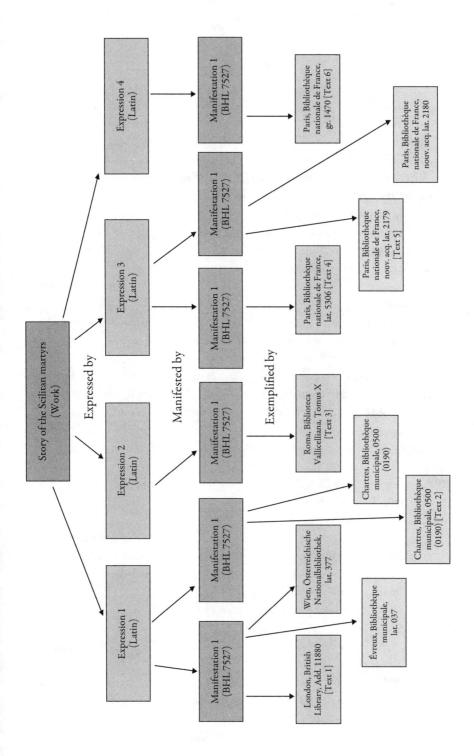

## Text 1: Latin

1. In diebus illis presidente bis Claudiano consule, XVI Kalendas Augustas, Kartagine in secretario inpositis Sperato, Nartzalo et Cittino, Donata, Secunda, Vestia, Saturninus proconsul dixit: Potestis indulgentiam domni nostri imperatoris promereri, si ad bonam mentem redeatis.

2. Speratus dixit: Numquam malefecimus, iniquitati nullam operam praebuimus; numquam malediximus, sed male accepti gratias egimus; propter quod imperatorem nostrum obseruamus.

3. Saturninus proconsul dixit: Et nos religiosi sumus, et simplex est religio nostra, et iuramus per genium domni nostri imperatoris, et pro salute eius supplicamus, quod et uos quoque facere debetis.

4. Speratus dixit: Si tranquillas praebueris aures tuas, dico mysterium simplicitatis.

5. Saturninus dixit: Initianti tibi mala de sacris nostris aures non praebebo; sed potius iura per genium domni nostri imperatoris.

6. Speratus dixit: Ego imperium huius seculi non cognosco; sed magis illi Deo seruio, quem nemo hominum uidit nec uidere his oculis potest. Furtum non feci; sed siquid emero teloneum reddo: quia cognosco domnum meum, regem regum et imperatorem omnium gentium.

7. Saturninus proconsul dixit ceteris: Desinite huius esse persuasionis. Speratus dixit: Mala est persuasio homicidium facere, falsum testimonium dicere.

8. Saturninus proconsul dixit: Nolite huius dementiae esse participes. Cittinus dixit: Nos non habemus alium quem timeamus nisi Domnum Deum nostrum qui est in caelis.

9. Donata dixit: Honorem Caesari quasi Caesari; timorem autem Deo. Vestia dixit: Christiana sum. Secunda dixit: Quod sum, ipsud uolo esse.

10. Saturninus proconsul Sperato dixit: Perseueras Christianus? Speratus dixit: Christianus sum. Et cum eo omnes consenserunt.

11. Saturninus proconsul dixit: Numquid ad deliberandum spatium uultis? Speratus dixit: In re tam iusta nulla est deliberatio.

12. Saturninus proconsul dixit: Quae sunt res in capsa uestra? Speratus dixit: Libri et epistulae Pauli uiri iusti.

13. Saturninus proconsul dixit: Moram XXX dierum habete et recordemini. Speratus iterum dixit: Christianus sum. Et cum eo omnes consenserunt.

14. Saturninus proconsul decretum ex tabella recitauit: Speratum, Nartzalum, Cittinum, Donatam, Vestiam, Secundam et ceteros ritu christiano se

# Text 1: English

1. In those days, as Claudianus, consul for the second time, presided, on the sixteenth of the Kalends of August, Speratus, Nartzalus, Cittinus, Donata, Secunda, and Vestia were brought to the governor's chambers in Carthage. The proconsul Saturninus said: "You can obtain the forgiveness of our lord the emperor, if you return to your senses."

2. Speratus said: "We have never done wrong, we have never given ourselves over to wickedness. Never have we uttered a curse, but when abused, we have given thanks, for we hold our Emperor in honor."

3. Saturninus the proconsul said: "We too are a religious people, and our religion is a simple one: we swear by the genius of our lord the emperor and we offer prayers for his health, as you also ought to do."

4. Speratus said: "If you will give me a calm hearing, I will tell you the mystery of simplicity."

5. Saturninus said: "Since you begin to malign our sacred rites, I will not listen to you. But swear rather by the genius of our lord the emperor."

6. Speratus said: "I do not recognize the imperial authority of this world. Rather, I serve that God whom no man has seen, nor can see with these eyes. I have not committed theft and if I make any purchase I pay the tax, for I recognize my Lord, the King of the kings and the Emperor of all nations."

7. Saturninus the proconsul said to the others: "Cease to be of this persuasion." Speratus said: "It is an evil persuasion to commit murder, to give false testimony."

8. The proconsul Saturninus said: "Do not participate in this folly of his." Cittinus said: "We have no one else to fear but our Lord God who is in heaven."

9. Donata said: "Honor to Caesar as Caesar, but fear to God." Vestia said: "I am Christian." Secunda said: "I want to be what I am."

10. The proconsul Saturninus said to Speratus: "Do you persist in remaining a Christian?" Speratus said: "I am Christian." And all agreed with him.

11. The proconsul Saturninus said: "Do you want time for reflection?" Speratus said: "In so just a matter there is no need for reflection."

12. The proconsul Saturninus said: "What is in your case?" Speratus said: "Books and letters of Paul, a just man."

13. The proconsul Saturninus said: "Take a reprieve of thirty days and think it over." Once again Speratus said: "I am Christian." And all agreed with him.

14. The proconsul Saturninus read the sentence from the tablet: "Speratus, Nartzalus, Cittinus, Donata, Vestia, Secunda, and the others, who have confessed

uiuere confessos, quoniam oblata sibi facultate ad Romanorum morem redeundi obstinanter perseuerauerunt, gladio animaduerti placet.

15. Speratus dixit: Deo gratias agimus. Nartzalus dixit: Hodie martyres in caelis sumus: Deo gratias.

16. Saturninus proconsul per praeconem dici iussit: Speratum, Nartzalum, Cittinum, Veturium, Felicem, Aquilinum, Laetantium, Ianuariam, Generosam, Vestiam, Donatam, Secundam duci iussi.

17. Vniuersi dixerunt: Deo gratias. Et ita omnes simul martyrio coronati sunt, et regnant cum Patre et Filio et Spiritu Sancto per omnia secula seculorurn. Amen.

that they live according to the Christian rite, because they persevered in their obstinacy though given the opportunity to return to Roman custom, are hereby sentenced to be executed by the sword."

15. Speratus said: "We thank God." Nartzalus said: "Today we are martyrs in heaven. Thanks be to God."

16. The proconsul Saturninus made the following announcement through the herald: "Speratus, Nartzalus, Cittinus, Veturius, Felix, Aquilinus, Laetantius, Januaria, Generosa, Vestia, Donata, and Secunda—I have ordered that they be led forth to execution."

17. They all said: "Thanks be to God." And thus they were all crowned together with martyrdom, and they reign with the Father, the Son, and the Holy Spirit, for all the ages of the ages. Amen.

## Text 2: Latin

1. Praesente Claudiano consule, sexto decimo kalendas Augusti apud Carthaginem in seonitario[5] impositis Sperato, Nartallo, Cithino, Donata, Secunda et Bestia, Saturninus proconsul dixit: Potestis indulgentiam domini imperatoris promereri, si ad bonam mentem redeatis *et sacrificetis diis omnipotentibus.*

2. Speratus dixit: Numquam male fecimus, nullam operam *malo* praebuimus. Numquam malediximus, sed male accepti gratias egimus. Propter quod imperatorem nostrum obseruamus *et timemus et adoramus, et ipsi cotidie sacrificium nostrae laudis offerimus.*

3. Saturninus proconsul dixit: Et nos religiosi sumus, et simplex est religio nostra, et iuramus per genium domini nostri imperatoris, et pro salute eius supplicamus, quod et uos quoque facere debetis.

4. Speratus dixit: Si tranquillas praebueris aures tuas, dico mysterium simplicitatis.

5. Saturninus dixit: Initiasti male de sacris nostris; aures non praebebo. Potius iurate per genium imperatoris.

6. Speratus dixit: Ego imperium huius saeculi non cognosco, sed magis illi seruio quem nemo hominum uidit nec uidere his oculis *carnalibus* potest*, nisi oculis cordis; si fidem habuerimus, uidebimus lumen uerum.* Furtum nunquam feci; sed si quid emero, theloneum reddo, quia cognosco dominum imperatorem regum et omnium gentium.

7. *Saturninus proconsul dixit: Desine* huius persuasionis esse. Speratus dixit: Siquidem mala est persuasio, homicidium perpetrare, falsum testimonium dicere.

8. Saturninus proconsul dixit: Nolite *furoris huius et* dementiae participes esse. Cithinus dixit: Nos non habemus alium quem timeamus nisi Dominum nostrum qui est in caelis. *Ipsum solum timere studemus ex toto corde nostro et ex tota anima nostra.*

9. *Saturninus dixit: Tu quid dicis, Bestia?* Bestia respondit: Christiana sum, *nec aliam me esse profiteor. Saturninus dixit: Quid tu dicis, Secunda?* Respondit Secunda: Quod sum ipsa esse uolo.

10. Saturninus proconsul Sperato dixit: Perseueras Christianus esse? Speratus dixit: Christianus sum. Et cum eo omnes *unanimiter* consenserunt.

11. Saturninus proconsul dixit: Nisi ad deliberandum spatium uultis? Speratus dixit: In re tam *bona* non est deliberatio.

12. Saturninus proconsul dixit: Quae sunt res in *causa* uestra? Speratus dixit: *Venerandi libri legis diuinae et epistolae Petri apostoli uiri iusti.*

# Text 2: English

1. In the presence of Claudianus, consul, on the sixteenth of the Kalends of August, Speratus, Nartallus, Cithinus, Donata, Secunda, and Bestia were brought to the governor's chambers in Carthage. The proconsul Saturninus said: "You can obtain the forgiveness of our lord the emperor, if you return to your senses *and sacrifice to the all-powerful gods.*"

2. Speratus said: "We have never done wrong, we have never given ourselves over to *evil.* Never have we uttered a curse, but when abused, we have given thanks, for we hold our Emperor in honor, *we fear him, we adore him, and we offer him the sacrifice of our praise every day.*"

3. Saturninus the proconsul said: "We too are a religious people, and our religion is a simple one: we swear by the genius of our lord the emperor and we offer prayers for his health, as you also ought to do."

4. Speratus said: "If you will give me a calm hearing, I will tell you the mystery of simplicity."

5. Saturninus said: "You began to malign our sacred rites, I will not listen to you. Swear rather by the genius of our emperor."

6. Speratus said: "I do not recognize the imperial authority of this world. Rather, I serve Him whom no man has seen, nor can see with these *carnal* eyes, *but only with the eyes of the heart; if we have faith, we will see the true light.* I have never committed theft and if I make any purchase I pay the tax, for I recognize the Lord, the Emperor of the kings and of all nations."

7. *Saturninus the proconsul said: "Cease* to be of this persuasion." Speratus said: "It indeed is an evil persuasion, to perpetrate murder, to give false testimony."

8. The proconsul Saturninus said: "Do not participate *in his madness* and folly." Cithinus said: "We have no one else to fear but our Lord who is in heaven. *We strive to fear only Him with all our heart and all our soul.*"

9. *Saturninus said: "What do you say, Bestia?"* Bestia answered: "I am Christian, and I will not confess that I am anything else." *Saturninus said: "What do say, Secunda?"* Secunda answered: "I want to be what I am."

10. The proconsul Saturninus said to Speratus: "Do you persist in being a Christian?" Speratus said: "I am Christian." And all agreed with him *unanimously.*

11. The proconsul Saturninus said: "Do you want time for reflection?" Speratus said: "In so *good* a matter there is no need for reflection."

12. The proconsul Saturninus said: "What is in your *cause*?" Speratus said: *"Venerable books of the divine law and letters of the apostle Peter, a just man."*

13. Saturninus proconsul dixit: Moram XXX dierum habete et recordemini. Speratus dixit: Christianus sum, *et indesinenter Dominum Deum meum colo et adoro, qui fecit caelum et terram, mare et omnia quae in eis sunt.* Et cum eo omnes consenserunt.

14. *Saturninus proconsul dixit: Decretum ex tabella recitaui.* Speratum, Nartalum, Cithinum, Donatam, Bestiam, Secundam, christiano ritu se uiuere confessos, et quod post oblatam sibi facultatem ad Romanorum morem redeundi obstinanter perseuerauerunt, gladio animaduerti placet.

15. Speratus dixit: Deo *omnipotenti insufficienter* gratias agimus. Nartalus dixit: Hodie martyres in caelis *esse meruimus.* Deo gratias agimus.

16. Saturninus proconsul per praeconem iussit duci *sanctos ut decollarentur,* Speratum, Nartallum, Cithinum, Bethurium, Felicem, Aquilinum, Letacium, Ianuariam, Generosam, Bestiam, Donatam, Secundam.

17. Vniuersi *uno ore* dixerunt: Deo gratias *et laudes, qui nos pro suo nomine ad gloriosam passionem perducere dignatus est. Et statim decollati sunt pro nomine Christi.* Amen.

13. The proconsul Saturninus said: "Take a reprieve of thirty days and think it over." Speratus said: "I am Christian, *and I ceaselessly worship and adore the Lord, my God, who made heaven and earth, the sea, and all that is in them.*" And all agreed with him.

14. *The proconsul Saturnus said: "I have read the sentence from the tablet.* Speratus, Nartallus, Cithinus, Donata, Bestia, Secunda, have confessed that they live according to the Christian rite. Because they persevered in their obstinacy after they had been given the opportunity to return to Roman custom, they are hereby sentenced to be executed by the sword."

15. Speratus said: "We cannot thank *almighty God sufficiently.*" Nartallus said: "Today we *are granted to become* martyrs in heaven. We thank God."

16. The proconsul Saturninus ordered through the herald that *the holy martys be led away to be decapitated,* Speratus, Nartallus, Cithinus, Bethurius, Felix, Aquilinus, Letacius, Januaria, Generosa, Bestia, Donata, Secunda.

17. They all said *in one voice*: "Thanks *and praise* to God, *who deigned to lead us in his name to our glorious death." And they were at once beheaded in the name of Christ.* Amen.

# Text 3: Latin

1. Existente Claudio consule XIV kalendas Augustas Carthagine **metropoli, statuto forensi conuentu, praeceperunt magistratus adstare sibi** Speratum, Narzalem, Cittinum, Donatam, Secundam et Vestinam. **Et adstantibus eis** Saturninus proconsul dixit: Potestis **ueniam** a dominis nostris imperatoribus **Seuero et Antono**[6] promereri, **si bono animo conuersi fueritis ad deos nostros.**

2. Speratus dixit: Nos minime aliquando malum fecimus, neque iniquitatem sequentes **in peccatis egimus operationem**, nec aliquando cuiquam malediximus, sed male suscepti a uobis, gratias egimus semper. Quamobrem dominum uerum et regem adoramus.

3. Saturninus proconsul dixit: **Et nos electi sumus, et mitissima est elegantia nostra**; et iuramus per genium domini nostri imperatoris, et pro salute illius intercedimus, quod et uos facere debuistis.

4. Speratus dixit: Si tranquillas adhibeas mihi aures tuas, dicam mysterium **mansuetudinis.**

5. Saturninus proconsul dixit: **Dicente te de mysterio non inferam mala**: tantum iura per genium regis nostri.

6. Speratus dixit: Ego **imperatoris mundi genium nescio**, sed **caelesti** Deo meo seruio quem nullus hominum uidit, nec uidere potest. Ego enim nec furatus sum aliquando; sed quodcumque emam **tributum** do quoniam cognosco eum dominum meum; **sed adoro** Dominum meum Regem regum et omnium gentium Dominum.

7. Saturninus proconsul dixit: **De caetero a tumultu garrulitatum quiescite, et accedentes sacrificate diis.** Speratus respondit: Illa est mala **concitatio**, quae facit homicidium et falsam accusationem aduersus aliquem.

8. Saturninus proconsul **ad alios conuersus** dixit: Nolite **furoris huius insipientiae** participes fieri, **sed timete potius regem nostrum, obedientes praeceptis eius.** Cittinus dixit: Nos non habemus alium quem timeamus nisi Dominum Deum nostrum qui est in coelis. **Saturninus proconsul dixit: detrudantur in carcerem, ponantur in ligno, in diem crastinum. Sequenti die Saturninus proconsul, sedens pro tribunali eos praesentari iubet. Qui cum adstitissent dicit ad foeminas: honorate regem nostrum et sacrificate diis.**

9. **Tunc** Donata dixit: Honorem quidem Caesari tanquam Caesari, **Deo autem nostro honorem et orationem offerimus. Stans** Vestina dixit: Et ego

## Text 3: English

1. With Claudianus the consul in attendance, on the fourteenth of the Kalends of August, **in the great city of Carthage, the assize court in session**, the magistrates ordered that Speratus, Narzalis, Cittinus, Donata, Secunda, and Vestina be present. **When they were present,** the proconsul Saturninus said: "You can obtain **pardon** from our lords, **the emperors Severus and Anton(in) us, if you will be restored to our gods in good spirits.**"

2. Speratus said: "We have never done wrong at all, **nor in pursuit of wickedness have we committed sins**; we have never cursed anyone, but when abused by you, we have always given thanks. Wherefore we adore our true lord and king."

3. Saturninus the proconsul said: **"We too are chosen, and our graceful discernment is very mild:** we swear by the genius of our lord the emperor, we pray for his health, as you also ought to do."

4. Speratus said: "If you will provide me with a calm hearing, I will tell you the mystery **of grace.**"

5. Saturninus the proconsul said: **"Since you talk about a mystery, I will not bring evil upon you.** Just swear by the genius of our king."

6. Speratus said: **"I do not know the genius of the emperor of the world,** but I serve my **celestial** God whom no man has seen nor can see. For I have never committed theft but whatever I buy I give **the tribute** because I recognize him as my lord, **but I adore** my Lord, King of kings and Lord of all nations."

7. Saturninus the proconsul said: **"Then put an end to the mayhem of your babbling, and come here and sacrifice to the gods."** Speratus said: "It is an evil **tumult** that commits murder and makes a false accusation against someone."

8. The proconsul Saturninus **turned to the others** and said: "Do not participate **in the folly of his madness, but fear rather our king and obey his commands.**" Cittinus said: "We have no one else to fear except the Lord our God who is in heaven." **The proconsul Saturninus said: "Have them thrust into prison; put them in the pillory until tomorrow." The following day the proconsul Saturninus, sitting in the tribunal, orders that they be brought forth. When they had stood there, he says to the women: "Honor our king and sacrifice to the gods."**

9. **Then** Donata said: "Honor to Caesar as Caesar, **but to our God we offer honor and prayer." Standing up,** Vestina said: "I too am Christian."

christiana sum. Secunda similiter dixit: **Et ego credo in Deo meo et uolo in ipso esse; diis autem tuis non seruimus, neque adoramus.**

10. **Saturninus proconsul auditis his praecepit eas seruari. Aduocatis uiris** dixit Sperato: Perseueras ut christianus sis? Speratus dixit: **Etiam perseuero et omnes audite quia** christianus sum. **Audientes omnes qui cum illo retenti fuerant, consenserunt confessioni illius dicentes: sumus et nos pariter christiani.**

11. Saturninus proconsul dixit: **Nec liberationem, nec remissionem** uultis? Speratus respondit: **In certamine iusto nulla est remissio. Fac quod uis. Nos enim pro Christo gaudentes morimur.**

12. Saturninus proconsul dixit: **Qui sunt libri quos adoratis legentes?** Speratus respondit: **Quatuor Euangeulia Domini nostri Iesu Christi et** Epistolas sancti Pauli apostoli **et omnem diuinitus inspiratam Scripturam.**

13. Saturninus proconsul dixit: **Spatium trium dierum tribuo uobis ut resipiscatis.** Speratus dixit: Christianus sum **et omnes qui mecum sunt et a fide Domini nostri Iesu Christi non discedimus. Fac quod uis.**

14. **Proconsul uidens etiam ipsorum mentis stabilitatem et fidei firmitatem dedit in eos sententiam per exceptorem, dicens sic**: Speratum, Narzalem, Cittinum, Veturium, Felicem, Acyllinum, Loetantium, Januariam, Generosam, Vestinam, Donatam et Secundam **christianos se esse confitentes et imperatori honorem et dignitatem dare recusantes, capite truncari praecipio.**

15. **Haec cum essent ex tabella recitata, Speratus et qui cum eo erant omnes dixerunt**: Deo gratias conferimus **qui dignatur nos hodie martyres accipere in coelis pro confessione sua.**

16. **His dictis ducti sunt, et flexis genibus unanimiter, cum iterum gratias Christo agerent truncata sunt singulorum capita.**

17. **Consummati sunt Christi martyres mense Iulio, die septimo decimo, et intercedunt pro nobis ad Dominum nostrum Iesum Christum cui honor et gloria cum Patre et Spiritu Sancto in saecula saeculorum.** Amen.

Similarly, Secunda said: **"And I believe in my God and I want to be in Him; but we do not serve your gods nor do we adore them."**

10. **Upon hearing this, the proconsul Saturninus, ordered that they be set aside. The men were summoned and** he said to Speratus: "Do you persist that you are Christian?" Speratus said: **"I do persist. Listen all:** I am Christian." **Hearing this, all who had been detained with him agreed with his confession, saying: "We too are likewise Christians."**

11. The proconsul Saturninus said: "Do you want **neither liberation nor remission?"** Speratus replied: **"In a just fight there is no remission. Do what you want. For we will die for Christ with joy."**

12. The proconsul Saturninus said: **"What are the books that you adore when you read them?"** Speratus said: **"The four Gospels of our Lord Jesus Christ,** the letters of **the holy apostle** Paul, **and all the divinely inspired Scripture."**

13. The proconsul Saturninus said: **"I grant you three days so that you may return to your senses."** Speratus said: "I am Christian **and so are all who are with me, and we will not forsake faith in our Lord Jesus Christ. Do what you want."**

14. **When he saw the steadfastness of their spirit and the strength of their faith, the proconsul gave his sentence against them through a scribe, speaking thus:** "I order that Speratus, Narzalis, Cittinus, Veturius, Felix, Acyllinus, Laetantius, Januaria, Generosa, Vestina, Donata, and Secunda, **who confess that they are Christians and refuse to give honor and dignity to the emperor, be decapitated."**

15. **When this had been read from the tablet, Speratus and all those who were with him said:** "We give thanks to God **who for our confession deigned to receive us today as martyrs in heaven."**

16. **With these words they were led to their execution. They all bent their knees, and, as they again gave thanks to God, one by one they were beheaded.**

17. **The martyrs of Christ achieved their martyrdom on the seventeenth of July, and they intercede for us with our Lord Jesus Christ to whom is honor and glory with the Father and Holy Spirit for the ages of ages.** Amen.

# Text 4: Latin

1. **Adductis ergo** in secretario Carthaginis **apparitorum officio** Sperato, Nazario, Cicio, Donata, Secunda et Vesta, sociis eorum Saturninus proconsul **his omnibus generaliter** dixit: Potestis indulgentiam omnes a domnis nostris imperatoribus promereri, si ad bonam mentem redeatis, **et deorum nostrorum caeremonias obseruetis.**

2. **Sanctus** Speratus dixit: Nunquam **gessisse conscii sumus** iniquitatem, **opem atque adsensum** non praebuimus; nulli unquam nos maledixisse **recolimus,** sed male tractati ac **lacessiti semper** Deo gratias egimus: **si quidem et pro iis orauimus quos iniuste patiebamur infestos, pro qua re et imperatorem nostrum adtendimus a quo nobis haec uiuendi norma concessa est.**

3. Saturninus dixit: Et nobis **religiosissima** et simplex est nostra religio et iuramus per **regnum dominorum nostrorum imperatorum** et pro salute eius supplicamus, quod uos facere debeatis.

4. Speratus **sanctus** dixit: Si tranquillas praebueris aures tuas, dicam mysterium **christianae** simplicitatis.

5. Saturninus proconsul dixit: **Incipienti** tibi dicere male de sacrificiis nostris aures praebebo? Sed potius iurate per **regnum dominorum nostrorum imperatorum ut uitae istius laetitia perfruatis.**

6. Speratus **sanctus** dixit: Ego imperium huius seculi non cognosco, sed magis illi **fide, spe et caritate** deseruio Deo quem nemo hominum uidit, nec uidere potest. **Facinus quod legibus publicis et diuinis comperitur esse damnabile** non feci. Si quid autem **in publicum egero, de id exactoribus publicis uectigalia** reddo. Imperatorem omnium gentium Deum et Dominum meum agnosco: **Querelas nulli intuli, sustinere non debeo.**

7. Saturninus proconsul **ad caeteros ora conuertit et socios sancti Sperati sic adorsus est dicens**: Desinite huius etiam persuasionis, **qua Speratus inlectus est; quos eius habuerit professio socios nihilominus habebit et paena.** Speratus **sanctus** dixit: Mala est persuasio falsum testimonium dicere, **mala utique probatur esse consensio,** si contra diuinis legibus agatur et publicis legibus quibus humanae uitae ordo disponitur. **Persuasio uero diuinae culturae sectanda est potius quam deserenda.**

8. Saturninus proconsul dixit: **In praeteritis iam ego admonui ut furoris** huius dementiae **non annuatis** esse participes. **Sanctus** Cythius respondit: **Non aliud oportet a nobis audire, proconsul, nisi quae socius noster Speratus**

## Text 4: English

1. **By the attendants were brought** to the governor's chambers, in Carthage, Speratus, Nazarius, Cicius, Donata, Secunda, and Vesta, their companions. **To all in general** the proconsul Saturninus said: "You can all obtain the forgiveness of our lords the emperors, if you return to your senses and observe the ceremonies of our gods."

2. **Holy** Speratus said: "We have never **knowingly committed** wickedness, we have not given ourselves **over to it, nor have we acquiesced to it; we do not recall** having ever cursed anyone, but when badly treated **and provoked**, we have always given thanks to God, **since indeed we have prayed also for those whose hostility we unjustly suffered. For this reason, we attend to our Emperor from whom this rule of life has been granted to us.**"

3. Saturninus said: "For us too our religion is **very pious** and simple; we swear by **the reign of our lords the emperors** and make supplications for his health, as you also ought to do."

4. **Holy** Speratus said: "If you will give me a calm hearing, I will tell you the mystery of **Christian** simplicity."

5. Saturninus said: "Will I listen to you **when you start** to malign our sacrifices? But swear rather by **the reign of our lords the emperors so that you may enjoy the delight of this life.**"

6. **Holy** Speratus said: "I do not recognize the imperial authority of this world. Rather, I serve **with faith, hope, and love** God whom no man has seen, nor can see. I have not committed **the crime that is found damnable by the public and divine laws.** If I make any purchase **in public**, I pay **the tax for it to the public tax collectors.** I recognize the Emperor of all nations, my God and Lord. **I have not caused anyone complaint, and I ought not endure complaint.**"

7. Saturninus the proconsul **turned his face toward the others and assaulted the companions of holy Speratus speaking thus:** "Cease to be of this persuasion **that seduces Speratus. The companions in his doctrine will be no less his companions in punishment.**" **Holy** Speratus said: "It is an evil persuasion to give false testimony. **It certainly is proven an evil conspiracy** if you act against the divine laws and against the public laws that organize the order of human life. **But the persuasion of divine worship ought to be followed rather than abandoned.**"

8. The proconsul Saturninus said: "**I have already previously warned you that** you not consent to participate in the madness **of his lunacy.**" **Holy**

**confessus est. Scito enim quod** non habemus aliumquem timeamus nisi unum Deum et Dominum nostrum qui est in coelo.

9. **Sancta** Donata **similiter** dixit: Honorem Caesari reddimus, timorem autem **aut cultum Christo Deo uero praestamus.** Vestia **uero uenerabilis secuta est dicens: Hoc semper meditabitur cor meum et labia mea pronuntiabunt quia** Christiana sum. **Sancta uero** Secunda **similiter ait: Quod sum Christiana,** ipsa id esse uolo **et a meorum sociorum professione non ullo obstante recedo.**

10. Saturninus proconsul **sancto** Sperato dixit: Perseueras **ut uideo** esse christianus. **Sanctus** Speratus dixit: **Hanc perseuerantiam Christianam non meis uiribus sed diuini muneris me habere confido. Proinde si uis fixam cordis mei scire sententiam,** Christianus sum. **In hac ergo confessione** et caeteri **Dei martyres** consenserunt.

11. Saturninus proconsul dixit: Forsitan ad liberandum spatium uultis accipere. **Sanctus** Speratus dixit: In rem tam **bonam** non quaeritur **secunda** deliberatio? **Tunc enim deliberauimus nos a cultura Christi non deserere, quando baptismi gratia renouati et diabolo abrenuntiauimus et Christi uestigia secuti sumus.**

12. Saturninus proconsul dixit: **Quae est, dicite mihi, res doctrinarum in causa et religione uestra?** Speratus **sanctus** respondit: Libri **Euangeliorum** et epistolae Pauli uiri **sanctissimi apostoli.**

13. Saturninus proconsul dixit: Accipite moram triginta dierum **ut retractetis huius sectae confessionem. Forsitan ad deorum sacras caerimonias reuertemini.** Speratus **sanctus** respondit: **Non triginta dierum mora mutare poterit professionem nostram, sed potius optatae uitae hoc spatium deliberandi accipere ut de tam turpi cultura idolorum christianae religionis amator existeres. Caeterum si hoc non es dignus accipere, suspende moram, sententiam recita. Nam quales nos hodie cernis, tales post hanc induciam futuros esse non dubites.**

14. **Cernens** proconsul Saturninus **sanctorum perseuerantiam** decretum recitauit ex tabella: Speratum, Nazarium, Cythium, Donatam, Secundam et omnes christiano ritu uiuere se confessos, et quod oblatam sibi facultatem redeundi ad deorum culturam obstinate non receperunt gladio namque animaduerti placet.

15. **Sanctus** Speratus dixit: Gratias Christo agimus. Nazarius **sanctus** dixit: Hodie martyres in coelo sumus. Deo gratias.

Cythius answered: "It is not proper, proconsul, to hear from us anything other than what our companion Speratus has confessed. Know indeed that we have no one else to fear except the only God and our Lord who is in heaven."

9. Holy Donata similarly said: "We bestow honor to Caesar, but we offer fear and worship to Christ, the true God." The venerable Vestia followed, saying: "This is what my heart will always meditate, what my lips will proclaim because I am Christian." Holy Secunda similarly said: "I am Christian. This is what I want to be, and I do not withdraw from the confession of my companions despite all pressure."

10. The proconsul Saturninus said to holy Speratus: "You persist, I see, in being Christian." Holy Speratus said: "I trust I owe this persistence in being Christian not to my strengths, but to those of a divine gift. Now if you want to know the firm position of my heart: I am Christian." Therefore, all the martyrs of God agreed in this confession.

11. The proconsul Saturninus said: "Maybe you want time for reflection?" Holy Speratus said: "In so good a matter is a second reflection required? For we then decided not to abandon the worship of Christ, when we were renewed in the grace of baptism, when we renounced the devil and followed in the steps of Christ."

12. The proconsul Saturninus said: "What are, tell me, the doctrinal matters in your cause and religion?" Holy Speratus answered: "The Gospels and the letters of Paul, the most holy apostle."

13. The proconsul Saturninus said: "Receive a reprieve of thirty days so that you may withdraw the confession of this sect. Maybe you will return to the sacred ceremonies of the gods." Holy Speratus said: "A reprieve of thirty days will not be able to change our profession of faith. But rather you take this time to reflect on the life you want so that you abandon such shameful cult of idols for the love of Christian religion. But if you are not worthy of receiving this, drop the reprieve, read the sentence. For you should have no doubt that after this delay we will be such as you see us today."

14. When he grasped the perseverance of the holy martyrs, the proconsul Saturninus read the decision from the tablet: "Speratus, Nazarius, Cythius, Secunda, and all those who have confessed that they live according to the Christian rite, because they did not accept in their obstinacy the opportunity given to them to return to the cult of the gods, are hereby sentenced to be executed by the sword."

15. Holy Speratus said: "We thank God." Holy Nazarius said: "Today we are martyrs in heaven. Thanks be to God."

16. Saturninus proconsul per praeconem **sanctos** duci iussit, id est Speratum, Nazarium, Cythium, Verum, Felicem, Aquilinum, Laetantium, Januariam, Generosam, Vestam, Donatam atque Secundam.

17. **Et sic uenientes ad locum martyrii, gladio sunt percussi et beatas Deo animas tradiderunt. Dominus autem suscepit martyres suos in pace, cui est honor et gloria in secula seculorum.** Amen.

16. The proconsul Saturninus ordered through the herald that the **holy martyrs** be led to the execution, Speratus, Nazarius, Cithius, Verus, Felix, Aquilinus, Laetantius, Januaria, Generosa, Vesta, Donata, and Secunda.

17. **Thus, arriving at the place of their martyrdom, they were struck with a sword and they delivered up their blessed souls to God. The Lord received his martyrs in peace. To him is honor and glory for the ages of the ages.** Amen.

# Text 5: Latin

1. *In diebus illis* adductos in secretario Carthaginis ab apparitorum officio Speratum, Narzalum, Donatam, Secundam et Vestigiam, Saturninus proconsul his omnibus generaliter dixit: Potestis indulgentiam a dominis nostris imperatoribus promereri si ad bonam mentem redeatis et deorum caerimonias obseruetis.

2. Sanctus Speratus dixit: Nunquam *male* egisse conscii sumus, iniquitati opem atque adsensum non praebuimus. Nulli unquam maledixisse recolimus; sed male tractati ac lacessiti semper Deo gratias egimus, si quidem et pro eis orauimus quos iniuste patiebamur infestos. Pro qua re et imperatorem nostrum adtendimus a quo nobis haec uiuendi norma concessa est.

3. Saturninus *proconsul* dixit: Et nos *religiosi sumus* et simplex est nostra religio et iuramus per *genium* dominorum nostrorum, pro salute eorum supplicamus quod et uos facere debeatis.

4. Sanctus Speratus dixit: Si tranquillas praebueris aures tuas dicam mysterium christianae simplicitatis.

5. Saturninus proconsul dixit: Incipienti tibi dicere malum de sacrificiis nostris aures non praebebo. Sed potius iurate per *genium* dominorum nostrorum imperatorum *ut istius mundi* laetitia perfruamini *nobiscum.*

6. Sanctus Speratus dixit: Ego imperium huius seculi non cognosco, sed magis illi fide spe deseruio Deo quem nemo hominum uidit, nec uidere potest. Facinus quod legibus publicis et diuinis comperitur esse damnauile non feci. Si quid autem in publicum emero *et de exactoribus publicis euenit,* uectigalia reddo. Imperatorem omnium gentium Deum et Dominum meum agnosco. Querelas nulli intuli, sustinere non debeo.

7. Saturninus proconsul ad caeteros ora conuertit et socios Sperati sic adorsus est dicens: Desinite huius esse persuasionis *cultores* qua Speratus inlectus est, *quoniam si uos* eius habuerit professio socios, nihilominus habebit et paena. Sanctus Speratus dixit: Mala est persuasio falsum testimonium dicere, *si mala utique prouatur concessio* si contra diuinis legibus agitis et publicis quibus uitae humanae ordo disponitur. Persuasio uero diuinae culturae sectanda est potius quam deserenda.

8. Saturninus proconsul dixit: In praeteritis iam ego admonui ut *huius* dementiae non annuatis esse participes. Sanctus Cittinus dixit: Non a nobis aliud oportet audire, o proconsul, nisi et quae socius noster Speratus confessus est. Scito enim quod non habemus alium quem timeamus nisi unum Deum et Dominum nostrum qui est in coelo.

## Text 5: English

1. *In these days* were brought to the governor's chambers, in Carthage, by the attendants: Speratus, Narzarlus, Donata, Secunda, and Vestigia. To all in general the proconsul Saturninus said: "You can obtain the forgiveness of our lords the emperors, if you return to your senses and observe the ceremonies of the gods."

2. Holy Speratus said: "We have never knowingly committed *evil*, we have not given ourselves over to it, nor have we acquiesced to it; we do not recall having ever cursed anyone, but when badly treated and provoked, we have always given thanks to God, since indeed we have prayed also for those whose hostility we unjustly suffered. For this reason, we attend to our Emperor from whom this rule of life has been granted to us."

3. Saturninus *the proconsul* said: "*We too are a religious people,* and our religion is a simple one: we swear by *the genius* of our lords the emperors, make supplications for their health, as you also ought to do."

4. Holy Speratus said: "If you will give me a calm hearing, I will tell you the mystery of the Christian simplicity."

5. Saturninus the proconsul said: "Since you start to malign our sacrifices I will not listen to you. But swear rather by *the genius* of our lords the emperors so that you may enjoy the delight *of this world* with us."

6. Holy Speratus said: "I do not recognize the imperial authority of this world. Rather, I faithfully serve with hope Him whom no man has seen, nor can see. I have not committed the crime that is found damnable by the public and divine laws. If I make any purchase in public *and if it involves the public tax collectors*, I pay the tax. I recognize the Emperor of all nations, my God and Lord. I have not caused anyone complaint, and I ought not endure complaint."

7. Saturninus the proconsul turned his face toward the others and assaulted the companions of holy Speratus speaking thus: "Cease to be *supporters* of this persuasion that seduces Speratus, *because if you are* companions in his doctrine you will be no less his companions in punishment." Holy Speratus said: "It is an evil persuasion to give false testimony, certainly, *if an admission is proven evil,* if you act against the divine laws and against the public laws that organize the order of human life. But the persuasion of the divine worship ought to be followed rather than abandoned."

8. The proconsul Saturninus said: "I have already previously warned you that you not consent to participate in his lunacy." Holy Cittinus said: "It is not proper, o proconsul, to hear from us anything other than what our companion

9. Sancta similiter Donata *adjecit*: Honorem Caesari *quasi Caesari* reddimus, timorem autem et cultum Christo Domino praestamus. Vestigia uero uenerabilis secuta est dicens: Hoc semper meditabitur cor meum et labia mea pronuntiabunt quia Christiana sum. Sancta uero Secunda similiter ait: Quod sum Christiana, ipsa esse uolo et a meorum sociorum professione nullo obstante recedo.

10. Saturninus proconsul Sperato sancto dixit: Perseueras ut uideo esse christianus. Sanctus Speratus dixit: Hanc perseuerantiam non meis uiribus sed diuini muneris me habere confido. Proinde si uis fixam cordis mei *habere* sententiam quia christianus sum, *quidquid mihi et suppliciis inferre uolueris libenter pro nomine Domini Dei mei Iesu Christi suscipiens sustineam*. In hac ergo confessione *exerceri* Dei martyres consenserunt.

11. Saturninus proconsul dixit: Forsitan ad deliberandum spatium uultis accipere? Sanctus Speratus dixit: In rem tam bonam *qua erit* secunda deliberatio? Tunc enim deliberauimus nos culturam Christi non deserere, quando baptismi gratia renouati et diabolo abrenuntiauimus et Christi uestigia secuti sumus.

12. Saturninus proconsul dixit: Quae sunt, dicite mihi, res doctrinarum in causa et religione uestra? Sanctus Speratus dixit: Libri Euangeliorum et epistolae Pauli uiri sanctissimi apostoli.

13. Saturninus proconsul dixit: Accipite moram triginta dierum ut retractetis huius sectae confessionem. Forsitan ad deorum sacras caerimonias reuertimini. Sanctus Speratus dixit: *Nos triginta dierum spatium non petimus. Nam ipsi erimus post triginta dies qui et hodie sumus*. Nec in triginta dierum moras poterit professionem nostram in aliquo permutari; sed potius *obtarem* et hoc te spatium deliberandi accipere ut de tam turpi cultura idolorum christianae religionis amator existeres. Caeterum si non es dignus accipere, suspende moram, sententiam recita tuam. Nam quales nos hodie cernis tales post hanc induciam futuros esse non dubites.

14. Cernens Saturninus proconsul sanctorum perseuerantiam decretum ex tabella recitauit: Speratum, Narzalum, Cittinum, Donatam, Vestigiam et omnes qui christiano ritu uiuere se confessi sunt et quotquot oblatam sibi facultatem redeundi ad deorum culturam obstinanter non receperunt gladio animaduertere placet.

15. Sanctus Speratus dixit: Gratias Deo agimus. Narzalus sanctus dixit: Hodie martyres in coelo sumus. Deo gratias.

Speratus has confessed. Know indeed that we have no one else to fear except the only God and our Lord who is in heaven."

9. Holy Donata similarly *added*: "We bestow honor to Caesar *as Caesar*, but we offer fear and worship to Christ, the Lord." The venerable Vestigia followed, saying: "This is what my heart will always meditate, what my lips will proclaim because I am Christian." Holy Secunda similarly said: "I am Christian. This is what I want to be, and I do not withdraw from the confession of my companions despite all pressure."

10. The proconsul Saturninus said to holy Speratus: "You persist, I see, in being Christian." Holy Speratus said: "I trust I owe this persistence not to my strengths, but to those of a divine gift. Now if you want to *get* the firm position of my heart: Because I am Christian, *whatever tortures you want to inflict upon me, I will sustain them gladly, as I incur them in the name of the Lord, my God, Jesus Christ*." Therefore, all the martyrs of God agreed to be *tormented* in this confession.

11. The proconsul Saturninus said: "Maybe you want time for reflection?" Holy Speratus said: "In so good a matter *what will be* a second reflection? For we then decided not to abandon the worship of Christ, when we were renewed in the grace of baptism, when we renounced to the devil and followed in the steps of Christ."

12. The proconsul Saturninus said: "What are, tell me, the doctrinal matters in your cause and religion?" Holy Speratus answered: "The Gospels and the letters of Paul, the most holy apostle."

13. The proconsul Saturninus said: "Receive a reprieve of thirty days so that you may withdraw the confession of this sect. Maybe you will return to the sacred ceremonies of the gods." Holy Speratus said: "*We do not seek a period of thirty days. For in thirty days we will be the very same as we are today.* And our profession of faith will in no wise be able to be changed during a delay of thirty days. But rather *I would wish that* you take this period for reflecting so that you abandon such a shameful cult of the idols for the love of Christian religion. But if you are not worthy of receiving this, drop the reprieve, read your sentence. For you should have no doubt that after this delay we will be such as you see us today."

14. When he grasped the perseverance of the holy martyrs, the proconsul Saturninus read the decision from the tablet: "Speratus, Narzalus, Cittinus, Donata, Vestigia, and all the others, who have confessed that they live according to the Christian rite and did not accept in their obstinacy the opportunity given to them many times to return to the cult of the gods, are hereby sentenced to be executed by the sword."

16. Saturninus proconsul per praeconem sanctos iubet adduci id est Speratum, Narzalum, Citinum, Venerium, Felicem, Aquilinum, Laetantium, Januariam Generosam, Donatam, Vestigiam atque Secondam.

17. Et illi uenientes ad locum martyrii beatas Deo animas tradiderunt. Dominus vero *Iesus Christus* suscepit martyres suos in pace cui est honor et gloria *cum Patre et Spiritu Sancto una et coaequalis essentia* in secula seculorum. Amen.

15. Holy Speratus said: "We thank God." Holy Narzalus said: "Today we are martyrs in heaven. Thanks be to God."

16. The proconsul Saturninus ordered through the herald that the holy martyrs be led to the execution, Speratus, Narzalus, Citinus, Venerius, Felix, Aquilinus, Laetantius, Januaria, Generosa, Donata, Vestigia, and Secunda.

17. And they, arriving at the place of their martyrdom, *delivered up their blessed souls to God.* The Lord *Jesus Christ* received his martyrs in peace. To him is honor and glory, *with the Father and the Holy Spirit, in their unique and coequal essence,* for the ages of the ages. Amen.

# Text 6: Greek

1. Ἐπὶ Πέρσαντος τὸ δεύτερον καὶ Κλαυδιανοῦ τῶν ὑπάτων, πρὸ ις καλανδῶν αὐγούστων ὅπερ ἐστιν Ἰουλίῳ ιζ, ἐν τῷ κατὰ Καρθαγένναν βουλευτηρίῳ ἤχθησαν παραστάσιμοι Σπερᾶτος Νάρτζαλος καὶ Κιττῖνος Δονᾶτα Σεκούνδα καὶ Ἑστία, πρὸς οὓς Σατουρνῖνος ὁ ἀνθύπατός φησιν· Ἐδύνασθε παρὰ τοῦ ἡμῶν αὐτοκράτορος συγχωρήσεως ἀξιωθῆναι, ἐὰν ἄρα σόφρονα λογισμὸν ἀνακαλέσησθε.

2. Ὁ δὲ **ἅγιος** Σπερᾶτος ἀπεκρίνατο λέγων· Οὐδέποτε ἐκακουργήσαμεν, οὐδέποτε κατηρασάμεθα, ἀλλὰ μὴν καὶ κακῶς δεχθέντες εὐχαριστοῦμεν, ἐπειδὴ τῷ θεῷ ἡμῶν καὶ βασιλεῖ δουλεύομεν.

3. Σατουρνῖνος ὁ ἀνθύπατος ἔφη· Ἀλλὰ καὶ ἡμεῖς θρησκεύομεν, καὶ ἁπλῆ ἡ καθ᾽ ἡμᾶς θρησκεία καθέστηκεν· καὶ δὴ ὀμνύομεν κατὰ τῆς συμπεφυκυίας εὐδαιμονίας τοῦ δεσπότου ἡμῶν βασιλέως καὶ ὑπὲρ τῆς αὐτοῦ σωτηρίας ἱκετεύομεν· ὃ καὶ ὑμᾶς ὡσαύτως χρῆ ποιεῖν.

4. Ὁ δὲ **ἅγιος** Σπερᾶτος εἶπεν· Ἐὰν γαληνιώσας μοι τὰς σὰς ἀκοὰς παράσχοις, ἐρῶ τὸ τῆς ἀληθοῦς ἁπλότητος μυστήριον.

5. Σατουρνῖνος ὁ ἀνθύπατος ἔφη· Ἐναρξαμένου σου πονηρὰ λέγειν κατὰ τῶν ἡμετέρων ἱερέων τὰς ἀκοάς μου οὐ προσθήσω· ἀλλ᾽ ὀμόσατε μᾶλλον κατὰ τῆς εὐδαιμονίας τοῦ δεσπότου ἡμῶν αὐτοκράτορος.

6. Ὁ **ἅγιος** Σπερᾶτος λέγει· Ἐγὼ τὴν βασιλείαν τοῦ νῦν αἰῶνος οὐ γινώσκω· αἰνῶ δὲ καὶ λατρεύω τῷ ἐμῷ θεῷ, ὃν οὐδεὶς τῶν ἀνθρώπων τεθέαται· οὐδὲ γὰρ οἶόν τε τούτοις τοῖς **αἰσθητοῖς** ὄμμασι. Κλοπὴν οὐ πεποίηκα· ἀλλ᾽ εἴ τι καὶ πράσσω, τὸ τέλος ἀποτίνυμι, ὅτι ἐπιγινώσκω τὸν κύριον ἡμῶν καὶ βασιλέα τῶν βασιλέων καὶ δεσπότην πάντων τῶν ἐθνῶν.

7. Σατουρνῖνος ὁ ἀνθύπατος ἔφη πρὸς τοὺς λοιπούς· Ἀπόστητε ἀπὸ τῆς **ἀποδειχθείσης** ταύτης πιθανότητος. Ὁ **ἅγιος** Σπερᾶτος ἔφη· Ἐκείνη ἐστὶν ἐπισφαλὴς πιθανότης, τὸ ἀνδροφονίαν κατεργάζεσθαι ἢ ψευδομαρτυρίαν κατασκευάζειν.

8. Σατουρνῖνος ὁ ἀνθύπατος εἶπεν· Μὴ βουληθῆτε τῆς τοσαύτης μανίας **καὶ παραφροσύνης γενέσθαι ἢ δαιχθῆναι** συμμέτοχοι. Ὁ δὲ **ἅγιος** Κιττῖνος ὑπολαβὼν ἀπεκρίνατο· Ἡμεῖς οὐκ ἔχομεν ἕτερον ὃν φοβηθῶμεν, εἰ μὴ κύριον τὸν θεὸν ἡμῶν τὸν ἐν τοῖς οὐρανοῖς κατοικοῦντα.

9. Ἡ δὲ **ἁγία** Δονᾶτα ἔφη· Τὴν μὲν τιμὴν τῷ Καίσαρι ὡς Καίσαρι, τὸν φόβον δὲ τῷ θεῷ ἡμῶν ἀποδίδομεν. Ἡ δὲ **ἁγία** Ἑστία λέγει· Ἐγὼ χριστιανὴ καθίσταμαι. Ἔτι δὲ ἡ **ἁγία** Σεκοῦνδα ἔφη· **Ὅπερ εἰμί, καὶ διαμεῖναι πορεύομαι.**

10. Τότε Σατουρνῖνος ὁ ἀνθύπατος τῷ **ἁγίῳ** Σπερᾶτῳ εἶπεν· Ἐπιμένεις ὡσαύτως χριστιανός; Ὁ **ἅγιος** Σπερᾶτος εἶπεν· Χριστιανὸς ὑπάρχω. Τὸ αὐτὸ δὲ καὶ οἱ λοιποὶ πάντες **ἅγιοι** εἶπαν.

# Text 6: English

1. In the consulship of Praesens, for the second time, and Claudianus, on the sixteenth day before the Kalends of August, that is the seventeenth of July, Speratus, Nartzalus, and Cittinus, Donata, Secunda and Vestia were led and produced in the governor's chambers in Carthage. The proconsul Saturninus says to them: "You can earn the pardon of our emperor, if you return to your senses."

2. The **holy** Speratus answered, saying: "We have never done wrong, we have never called down curses. But when wronged, we have given thanks, because we honor our God and King."

3. The proconsul Saturninus said: "But we too are religious and our religion is simple. We swear by the innate genius of our ruler and king and we pray for his well-being. You too should do this."

4. **Holy** Speratus said: "If you lend me your ears in peace, I will tell the mystery of true simplicity."

5. The proconsul Saturninus said: "If you are beginning to speak evil words about our sacred rites, I will not bend my ears. Instead, swear by the genius of our ruler and emperor."

6. **Holy** Speratus speaks: "I acknowledge no empire in the present world. I praise and serve my God, whom no man has seen. For neither can He be seen with these here **carnal** eyes. I have committed no theft, but if I buy anything I pay the tax, since I acknowledge our Lord, the King of kings and Ruler of all nations."

7. The proconsul Saturninus said to the rest of them: "Turn away from this **flaunted** persuasion." **Holy** Speratus said: "It is a dangerous conviction to commit murder or to give false testimony."

8. The proconsul Saturninus said: "Do not choose **to be or to show yourself** a partaker of such folly **and derangement.**" But **holy** Cittinus answered in response: "We have no one else to fear but the Lord our God, who lives in heaven."

9. And **holy** Donata said: "We offer honor to Caesar as Caesar, but fear to our God." **Holy** Vestia says: "I am Christian." And still **holy** Secunda said: **"As I am, so I will continue."**

10. Then the proconsul Saturninus said to the holy Speratus: "Do you likewise remain Christian?" **Holy** Speratus said: "I am Christian." All the other **holy ones** said the same.

11. Σατουρνῖνος ὁ ἀνθύπατος ἔφη· Μὴ ἄρα πρὸς διάσκεψιν ἀναμονῆς χρῄζετε; Ὁ **ἅγιος** Σπερᾶτος ἔφη· Ἐν πράγματι οὕτως ἐγκρίτῳ οὐδεμία καθίσταται βουλὴ **ἢ διάσκεψις.**

12. Σατουρνῖνος ὁ ἀνθύπατος ἔφη· Ὁποῖαι πραγματεῖαι τοῖς ὑμετέροις ἀπόκεινται σκεύεσιν; Ὁ **ἅγιος** Σπερᾶτος εἶπεν· **Αἱ καθ'ἡμᾶς βίβλοι** καὶ αἱ προσεπιτούτοις ἐπιστολαὶ Παύλου τοῦ ὁσίου ἀνδρός.

13. Σατουρνῖνος ὁ ἀνθύπατος ἔφη· Προθεσμία τριάκοντα ἡμερῶν ὑμῖν ἔστω **εἴ πως σωφρονήσητε.** Ὁ **ἅγιος** Σπερᾶτος παρ' αὐτὰ ἀπεκρίνατο· Χριστιανὸς **ἀμετάθετος** τυγχάνω. Τοῦτο δὲ καὶ οἱ λοιποὶ ὁμοθυμαδὸν συναπεφθέγξατο.

14. Τότε Σατουρνῖνος ὁ ἀνθύπατος τὴν περὶ αὐτῶν ψῆφον ἐξεφώνησεν **οὕτω περιέχουσαν·** τὸν Σπερᾶτον, Νάρτζαλλον καὶ Κηττῖνον, Δονᾶτόν τε Ἑστίαν καὶ Σεκοῦνδαν, **καὶ τοὺς ἀφάντους,** ὅσοι τῷ χριστιανικῷ θεσμῷ ἑαυτοὺς κατεπηγγείλαντο πολιτεύεσθαι, ἐπεὶ καὶ χαριστικῆς αὐτοῖς προθεσμίας τοῦ πρὸς τὴν τῶν Ῥωμαίων[7] ἐπανελθεῖν παράδοσιν, ἀκλινεῖς τὴν γνώμην διέμειναν, ξίφει τούτους ἀναιρεθῆναι δέδοκται παρ'ἡμῖν.

15. Τότε τοίνυν **ὁ ἀθλοφόρος τοῦ Χριστοῦ** Σπερᾶτος **ἐπαλλόμενος εὐχαριστίαν τῷ θεῷ ἡμῶν τῷ προσκεκληκότι αὐτοὺς εἰς τὸν ὑπὲρ αὐτοῦ θάνατον ἀνέπεμψεν.** Ὁ δὲ **ἅγιος** Νάρτζαλλος χαίρων εἶπεν· Σήμερον **ἀληθῶς** μάρτυρες ἐν οὐρανοῖς τυγχάνομεν **εὐάρεστοι τῷ θεῷ.**

16. Τότε τοίνυν Σατουρνῖνος ὁ ἀνθύπατος διὰ τοῦ κήρυκος **τὰ τῶν ἁγίων μαρτύρων ὀνόματα** κηρυχθῆναι προσέταξεν, τουτέστι τὸν Σπερᾶτον, Νάρτζαλλον, Κηττῖνον, Οὐετούριον, Φίληκα, Ἀκουϊνον, Κελεστῖνον, Ἰανουρίαν, Γενερῶσαν, Ἑστίαν, Δονάταν καὶ Σεκούνδαν.

17. Τηνικαῦτα οὖν πάντες **οἱ ἅγιοι** τὸν θεὸν **δοξολογοῦντες ὁμοφώνως** ἔφασκον· Σοὶ εὐχαριστοῦμεν, **τρισάγιε κύριε, καὶ σὲ μεγαλύνομεν,** ὅτι τὸν ἀγῶνα τῆς ὁμολογίας ἵλεως ἐτελείωσας, καὶ διαμένει σου ἡ βασιλεία εἰς τοὺς αἰῶνας τῶν αἰώνων, ἀμήν. Καὶ ἀναπεμψάντων αὐτῶν τὸ ἀμὴν ἐτελειώθησαν τῷ ξίφει, μηνὶ Ἰουλίῳ ιζʹ. Ἦσαν οὖν ὁρμώμενοι οἱ ἅγιοι ἀπὸ Ἰσχλὴ τῆς Νουμηδίας, κατάκεινται δὲ πλησίον Καρθαγέννης μητροπόλεως· ἐμαρτύρησαν δὲ ἐπὶ Πέρσαντος καὶ Κλαυδιανοῦ τῶν ὑπάτων καὶ Σατουρνίνου ἀνθυπάτου, καθ'ἡμᾶς δὲ βασιλεύοντος τοῦ κυρίου ἡμῶν Ἰησοῦ Χριστοῦ· ᾧ πρέπει πᾶσα δόξα, τιμὴ καὶ προσκύνησις σὺν τῷ παναγίῳ καὶ ζωοποιῷ πνεύματι νῦν καὶ ἀεὶ καὶ εἰς τοὺς αἰῶνας τῶν αἰώνων. Ἀμήν. Ἐπλήσθη σὺν θεῷ τὸ μαρτύριον τῶν ἁγίων Σπεράτου, Ναρτζάλου, Κηττίνου, Οὐετουρίου καὶ τῶν σὺν αὐτοῖς.

11. The proconsul Saturninus said: "Do you need a delay to deliberate?" **Holy** Speratus said: "In a matter so agreed upon, no counsel **or deliberation** is needed."

12. The proconsul Saturninus said: "What affairs are stored in your boxes?" **Holy** Speratus said: "**These are books of ours** and also the letters of Paul, a saintly man."

13. The proconsul Saturninus said: "Take a period of thirty days, **perhaps to come to your senses**." **Holy** Speratus answered this: "I am **unchangeably** Christian." The rest of them together pronounced this in agreement.

14. Then the proconsul Saturninus pronounced their verdict, **thus formulated**: "Speratus, Nartzalus and Cittinus, Donata, Vestia and Secunda **and those in hiding**, who have confessed that they live according to the Christian rite, since they were granted a period of time for returning to the tradition of the Romans, but have stubbornly persisted in their practice, I resolve that they be executed by the sword."

15. Then Speratus **the victorious in Christ leapt up and gave thanks to our God who summoned them to death on his behalf**. And **holy** Nartzalus rejoicing said: "Today we are **truly** martyrs in heaven and well-pleasing to God."

16. Then the proconsul Saturninus ordered that **the names of the holy martyrs** be announced by the herald, that is: Speratus, Nartzallus, Cittinus, Verturius, Felix, Aquilinus, Celestinus, Januaria, Generosa, Vestia, Donata and Secunda.

17. Then all **the holy martyrs in one voice gave praise to God and** said: "We thank you, **thrice-holy Lord, and we magnify you, because you graciously brought about the contest of confession. Your kingdom will live for ever and ever. Amen.**" And as they offered up the amen, they achieved death by the sword.

**This was the seventeenth of July. The holy martyrs were natives of Iscli in Numidia, which lay near the city of Carthage. They were martyred when Praesens and Claudianus were consuls and Saturninus proconsul, but as far as we are concerned under the kingship of the Lord Jesus Christ. For him shine all glory, honor and adoration, with the all-holy and life-giving Spirit now and always and for ever and ever. Amen. With God's help, the martyrdom of the holy Speratus, Nartzalus, Cittinus, Verturius and those with them was accomplished.**

# NOTES

## INTRODUCTION

1. Eusebius's *Collection of Ancient Martyrdom* is lost, but Eusebius mentions it in the *Ecclesiastical History*; see below.

2. At the turn of the century, several new volumes appeared within just a few years: the collection of Knopf (1901) and that of Gebhardt (1902), and the first version of Delehaye's classification of hagiographical texts (1903).

3. See Rebillard (2017, 2–14) for a more detailed history of collecting martyr narratives.

4. On Humanist hagiography, see Frazier 2005, Collins 2008.

5. Kolb 1987, 11–40; Cavallotto 2001, 248–51; see Cavallotto 2009, 283–325.

6. See Cavallotto 2009, 283–307 on Bonnus, 317–20 on Spalatin; Savvidis 1990, 205–69, in particular 247–48 on Bonnus's sources on early Christian martyrs.

7. See Ludwig Rabus's harsh judgement of the *legenda* in Kolb 1987, 11–12.

8. Boesch Gajano 2009, 13–20.

9. See Joassart 2011, 1–44. The reference is to Praef. 3.1, in *AASS*, Jan. I, xxxiii, and Praef. 3.2, ibid., xxxv.

10. On the importance of Mabillon for Ruinart's project, see Dolbeau 2002, 83–84.

11. Ruinart 1689, x–xj (= Ruinart 1859, 8): Qui vero ea vetera monumenta, prout in antiquis codicibus habentur, exhibere aggressi sunt, cum omnium omnino sive Martyrum sive Confessorum gesta, tam dubia, aut falsa, quam sincera simul in unum colligere proposuerint, rem eo promovere coguntur, ut pluribus, & quidem ingentibus voluminibus opus fit, ne pauca Acta habeantur, & quidem ita dubiis & falsis intermixta, ut sine magno labore, a viris etiam perspicacioribus discerni non valeant.

12. Dolbeau 2002, 91–92: "Les uns sont d'ordre historique: inexactitude des données relatives aux empereurs, incohérence chronologique, anachronisme de certaines réalités administratives, mensonges démasqués par de meilleures sources, détails fautifs sur le plan judiciaire, liturgique ou géographique. D'autres motifs de rejet sont de type plutôt littéraire, narratif ou linguistique: incohérence des textes, surabondance de citations scripturaires, présence indiscrète de merveilleux, vocabulaire tardif."

13. First version in Delehaye 1903; then Delehaye 1905 (4th ed. 1955; English translation 1998).

14. Delehaye 1955, 118 (1998, 98).

15. In Delehaye 1966, 15–109.

16. Barnes 1968.

17. Barnes 1968, 528. See Barnes 2016 for a "canon" of nineteen texts, ten of which are narratives about ancient martyrs.

18. Forgeries: Ehrman 2013, 492–507; frauds: Moss 2013a, chapter 3.

19. Derrida 1994 (1993); see Buell 2009 on the imagery and its use in early Christian studies.

20. Buell 2009, 166–67.

21. See Pezzella 1965, 31: "Si tratta della incondizionata adesione ad un'idea che è sempre stata ed è tuttora accolta come base fondamentale di ogni ricerca, che esiste cioè un documento originale ed autentico, la riproduzione degli interrogatori giudiziari cui venivano sottoposti le vittime: un 'modello' perfetto e non superabile che è garanzia del valore storico dei testi ed è all'origine del genere letterario."

22. See above for references; for the prefatory letters to the *Martyrologium Hieronymianum*, see AASS, Nov., II, 1–2; translation in Lifshitz 2006, 139–40.

23. Moss 2013a, 123; Ehrman (2013, 493–508) argues that all martyrologies are non-pseudepigraphic forgeries; see more below on Ehrman's understanding of forgery.

24. Moss 2013a, 91–92. This is the same reasoning that leads Ehrman to call them forgeries, intended to deceive; see below.

25. Castelli 2004; Grig 2004.

26. I generally use "audience" with both readers and hearers in mind; see Cobb (2017, 3–6) for important considerations on how reception differs according to whether the text is heard or read, and for a plea to emphasize a listening audience.

CHAPTER 1

1. See below for the rationale.

2. The distinction between external attestation and context of reception is elaborated below.

3. See Eus. HE 5.21.4 for the phrase; on the edict of Gallienus, see Barnes 2016, 97–105.

4. Barnes 2016, 106.

5. This is the contention of Grig 2004; for a very balanced evaluation of the "Constantinian revolution," see Lenski 2016.

6. In what follows I systematically refer to martyr narratives by their number in BHG or BHL. The system is somewhat tedious, but modern titles can refer to several versions, and this is the only way of identifying the exact text under discussion.

7. I used Eusebius as a *terminus ante quem* in Rebillard 2017; I summarize my findings below.

8. Eus. HE 4.15.46–48; 5.1.1–2; 5.4.3; 5.21.5; see Rebillard 2017, 22–25.

9. Rebillard 2017, 31.

10. Aubé (1882, 15) writes: "Il n'est pas impossible qu'elle soit celle même qui existait au temps d'Eusèbe et que celui-ci a connue."

11. Harnack (1888, 463) writes: "Eine christliche Urkunde ist uns also in dem Cod. Gr. Par. Nr. 1468 wieder geschenkt, die Eusebius gelesen hat und die wir bisher für verloren halten mussten."

12. Franchi de' Cavalieri 1920, 27–40; text: 43–45.

13. Lietzmann 1922 (= 1958, 239–50); Delehaye 1940, 145–48.

14. I adopt here a more conservative approach than in Rebillard 2017, 34.

15. Eus. HE 4.15.47; Rebillard 2017, 49.

16. Eus. HE 4.14.10 (Pionius and Polycarp are presented as contemporary); MPion 2.1 mentions an imperial decree; see also MPion 23; MPion 9.4 also mentions the emperor Gordian 3 (238–44).

17. Rebillard 2017, 24–25.

18. Dehandschutter 1979; see Hartog 2013, 167–69; Rebillard 2017, 81–83.

19. See below for further discussion.

20. BHG 1556 is the Inscription of the Letter of the Smyrneans; BHG 1557 covers chapters 1–21 (the martyrdom); BHG 1558 is the first epilogue (22.1); BHG 1559 the second (22.2–3).

21. Eus. HE 5.1–4 (BHG 1573).

22. Eus. HE 5.1.1–2 and 5.4.3; see Rebillard (2017, 145) for information about the sections omitted.

23. I use Augustine as a *terminus ante quem* in Rebillard 2017.

24. Rebillard 2017, 25–26.

25. Birley 1992; Rebillard 2015, 284–88.

26. Tert. Scap. 3.4; on Saturninus, see Birley 1992, 37–38.

27. See below for a discussion of the dating of AScil.

28. Tert. an. 55.4.

29. The distinction is important; see Rebillard 2017, 296–97.

30. Rebillard 2017, 199–200.

31. Rebillard 2017, 297–98.

32. VCypr 1.1: placuit summatim pauca conscribere, non quo aliquem vel gentilium lateat tanti uiri uita, sed ut ad posteros quoque nostros incomparabile et grande documentum in inmortalem memoriam porrigatur et ad exemplum sui litteris digeratur.

33. PPerp 1.1–2: Si uetera fidei exempla, et Dei gratiam testificantia et aedificationem hominis operantia, propterea in litteris sunt digesta, ut lectione eorum quasi repraesentatione rerum et Deus honoretur et homo confortetur, cur non et noua documenta aeque utrique causae conuenientia et digerantur? Vel quia proinde et haec uetera futura quandoque sunt et necessaria posteris, si in praesenti suo tempore minori deputantur auctoritati, propter praesumptam uenerationem antiquitatis.

34. I summarize my findings from Rebillard 2017, 200–201.

35. See above VCypr 1.1.

36. I review the passages cited by Saxer (1995, 244–48) in Rebillard 2017, 200–201.

37. In his letters, Cyprian refers to several visions (Anselmetto 1990), but there is no direct allusion to this precise vision; see Amat (1985, 131–32) for a possible indirect allusion to it in ep. 16.4.1.

38. See below and Rebillard (2017, 198–99) on Augustine's use of ACypr.

39. Moss 2010.

40. Moss 2010, 558.

41. Moss 2010, 565–68.

42. Moss 2010, 566; for a reading that does not involve relics, see, for instance, Wiśniewski 2019, 10–12.

43. Moss (2010, 567) quotes PPerp 21.1, Cypr. ep. 76.2, and ACypr 5.

44. Moss 2010, 567.

45. Moss 2010, 568; as I will suggest below, such concerns are already present in the mid-third century.

46. Moss 2010, 574; see 568 n67.

47. I borrow "prehistory" from Wiśniewski 2019, see 10–21 for a review of pre-Constantinian evidence.

48. Also Moss 2013b, 408–11.

49. Moss 2010, 573.

50. Moss 2010, 573.

51. See Sardella 1990, 265–67, to be preferred to Moriarty 1997, 312–13 (see Boeft 2012, 178).

52. Cypr. ep. 12.2; Rebillard 2017, 4.

53. See below for an interesting example in which the direction of the intertextual relationship is argued from assumptions about the authenticity of the texts.

54. Eus. HE 4.15.46–47: ἐν τῇ αὐτῇ δὲ περὶ αὐτοῦ γραφῇ καὶ ἄλλα μαρτύρια συνῆπτο κατὰ τὴν αὐτὴν Σμύρναν πεπραγμένα ὑπὸ τὴν αὐτὴν περίοδον τοῦ χρόνου τῆς τοῦ Πολυκάρπου μαρτυρίας, μεθ᾽ ὧν καὶ Μητρόδωρος τῆς κατὰ Μαρκίωνα πλάνης πρεσβύτερος δὴ εἶναι δοκῶν πυρὶ παραδοθεὶς ἀνήρηται. Τῶν γε μὴν τότε περιβόητος μάρτυς εἷς τις ἐγνωρίζετο Πιόνιος.

55. MPion 21.5.

56. The existence of an independent martyr narrative about Metrodorus is usually ruled out without further discussion; see Ehrhard 1937–52, 1.3, and Barnes 2016, 45.

57. Ameling 2008, 159.

58. Ameling 2008, 159: "shortly after Valerian (at the latest)."

59. MPol 22.3.

60. See Hartog 2013, 170–71, 331–33; well known: see Eus. HE 4.15.47.

61. See MPion 2.1, 3.6, and 8.1; on the many, complex, and polemical relationships between MPol and MPion, see Rizzi 2011.

62. See Hartog 2013, 204–5 on MPol 4 and the figure of Quintus; Moss 2010, 566–67, on MPol 17.

63. The position defended by Pionius faced opposition (Ameling 2008, 158).

64. Eus. HE 5.3.4.

65. Eus. HE 5.4.1–2.

66. Eus. HE 5.4.3.

67. Nautin 1961, 33–61.

68. Löhr 1989.

69. See Tabbernee 2007, 28–34, 173–81, 219–24.

70. There is very little new about the texts discussed in this chapter in Fialon (2018), which became available to me too late for being discussed in any detail, especially as she does not refer to Rebillard 2017.

71. See above; although Tertullian might have known of Perpetua's account, there is no evidence that he knew of the whole *Passion* (BHL 6633).

72. Before the composition of PPerp, a text attributed to Perpetua was used in a polemical context too, as it is attested by Tertullian; see González 2014.

73. VCypr 1.2: Certe durum erat, ut cum maiores nostri plebeis et catecuminis martyrium consecutis tantum honoris pro martyrii ipsius ueneratione debuerint, ut de passionibus eorum multa aut ut prope dixerim paene cuncta conscripserint, utique ut ad nostram quoque notitiam qui nondum nati fuimus peruenirent, Cypriani tanti sacerdotis et tanti martyris passio praeteriretur, qui et sine martyrio habuit quae doceret.

74. The allusion is prepared in the preceding section by several verbal parallels with PPerp 1.1–2; see above.

75. Bobertz 1988, 130–223; Burns 2002, 1–24; Dunn 2005.

76. Burns 2002, 21; Brent 2010, 251.

77. Burns 2002, 100–131.

78. Sage 1975, 393–94; Bobertz 1988, 130–31.

79. PPerp 1.6: Et nos itaque quod audiuimus et contrectauimus, annuntiamus et uobis, fratres et filioli, uti et uos qui interfuistis rememoremini gloriae Domini, et qui nunc cognoscitis

per auditum communionem habeatis cum sanctis martyribus, et per illos cum Domino nostro Iesu Christo, cui est claritas et honor in saecula saeculorum.

80. 1 John 1:7: "If we say that we have fellowship with him while we are walking in darkness, we lie and do not do what is true; but if we walk in the light as he himself is in the light, we have fellowship with one another, and the blood of Jesus his Son cleanses us from all sin."

81. I should note, however, that there is no evidence that 1 John was used in the dispute. I thank Jason R. Combs for having pointed out these allusions and their meaning to me in a response he gave to an early presentation of my arguments at Duke University in 2015.

82. PPerp 7–8.

83. PPerp 13.

84. These elements appear in the accounts written by Perpetua and by Saturus that the redactor embedded in his narrative.

85. PPerp 15.4–5.

86. PPerp 19–21.

87. PPerp(gr) subscription; APerp I 1.1; APerp II 1.1.

88. Noted by Bremmer 2012, 39–40.

89. Duval 1995, 40–45; Barnes 2016, 94–95.

90. Aug. serm. 284.2; Rebillard 2017, 175–76.

91. Barnes 2016, 86–91; see Rebillard (2015, 301–5) for a different interpretation of the circumstances of their execution.

92. See Dolbeau 1992 on PDon; Rebillard 2017, 265–66.

93. Harris and Gifford 1890, 26–27 on PLuc as a "deliberate forgery."

94. Franchi de' Cavalieri 1898, 1900 (schema on p. 13).

95. Lomanto 1975.

96. Franchi de' Cavalieri 1898 and 1900; the *index verborum* in both editions contain many references to Cyprian.

97. Dolbeau 1983, 65.

98. Lucca 2007.

99. Lucca 2007, 163–68, 172.

100. Lucca 2007, 171; see also Mazzucco 2017, 813–14.

101. See Trigg 1984, 244–46.

102. PPerp 13.

103. PMar 6.10.

104. PLuc 11.2 and 21.8.

105. PMar 8.9–10. Such a distinction is not attested in the tradition and should be considered both an innovation and a strong statement by the producer of PMar; see Lucca 2007, 161–62.

106. PLuc 5.1–2, for which I follow Franchi de' Cavalieri's interpretation (1909, 24); see Rebillard 2017, 271 n34.

107. PLuc 8.3–7 for the vision, 9.1–2 for its interpretation; see Lomanto 1975, 577–78.

108. I accept that the account of Perpetua and that of Saturus were produced at the time of their martyrdom; see below on this issue.

109. Moss 2013a, 124–62; see Robinson 1990–92, who convincingly argues that about the few executions of Christians before 250 we should refer to "repression" rather than "persecution."

110. Rebillard 2012, 35–43.

111. Tert. apol. 50.13.

112. Harnack 1924, 506–7 (1962, 492–93).

113. Praet 1993; see Bremmer 2016, 17.

114. Texts such as Tertullian, *To the Martyrs*, or Origen, *Exhortation to Martyrdom*; see Nicholson 2009 on the topic of preparation for martyrdom.

115. Delehaye 1966, 109–10; see Bastiaensen 1987a, xx.

CHAPTER 2

Epigraphs: Nicholson 2009, 62; Huebner 2019, 2.

1. Bowersock 1995, 37–38.

2. The closest attempt at a typology is Hoffmann 1966, 44–45. Cobb (2017, 34–35) considers that martyr texts in the protocol form belong to the genre of the *commentarius*; she follows Riggsby (2006, 134–45), who includes in this genre both official records and tools of scholarly inquiry. This lack of discrimination renders the category useless.

3. Barnes 2016, 357 (XIV).

4. Maraval 1990, 10–12.

5. Maraval 1990, 12. The *terminus ante quem* for both texts is the seventh century when Pedachthoe is made a bishopric; see Maraval 1990, 23 for the date.

6. Maraval 1990, 7–9. Maraval notes: "Bref, ces interrogatoires sentent le vrai" (9). Jones (1992, 245–46) accepts these conclusions. Maraval (1990, 82 n89) also wants to keep open the possibility that Hilarius, who signs as ὁ τηνικαῦτα πρῶτος τοῦ βουλευτηρίου, could be the "greffier du tribunal" who recorded the court protocol; see, however, Laniado (1995) on this misinterpretation of the subscription of Hilarius.

7. Barnes 2016, 81–82.

8. On the structure of official protocols, see Coles 1966, 29–54; Bisbee 1988, 36–61.

9. AAgap 2.4: Τὰ δὲ πραχθέντα περὶ αὐτῶν ὑπομνήματά ἐστιν τὰ ὑποτεταγμένα.

10. MPion 19.1: Μετὰ δὲ ταῦτα ἦλθεν ὁ ἀνθύπατος εἰς τὴν Σμύρναν, καὶ προσαχθεὶς ὁ Πιόνιος ἐμαρτύρησε, γενομένων ὑπομνημάτων τῶν ὑποτεταγμένων, πρὸ τεσσάρων εἰδῶν Μαρτίων.

11. See Chapter 3 for a discussion of the use of documents in martyr narratives.

12. Barnes 2016, 356–58.

13. His number XIV; see above.

14. Musurillo (1972, 42–61) gives the text (after Lazzati 1953) and an English translation of the first three texts.

15. Paris, Bibliothèque nationale de France, grec 1470; text in Lazzati 1953, 490–95.

16. Lazzati (1953, 490–95) gives a text based on three manuscripts; a search in the *Pinakes* database lists 8 manuscripts (https://pinakes.irht.cnrs.fr/).

17. Jerusalem, Patriarchikè Bibliothêkê, Panaghiou Taphou 17; text in Latyšev 1911, 2.1–4; see Franchi de' Cavalieri (1902, 71–75) for another version of this text based on Vatican, Biblioteca Apostolica Vaticana, Vat. gr. 1991.

18. Cambridge, University Library, Add. 4489; text in Burkitt 1909, 64.

19. Eus. HE 4.16–18.

20. Tatian (ad Graec. 19.3) is Eusebius's source for the circumstances of Justin's execution.

21. Chronicon Paschale 1.482 Dindorf. Eusebius's *Chronicon* places the execution in 154 (203, 13–18 Helm). As noted by Minns and Parvis (2009, 32–33), neither chronicle presents the dating as a hard fact.

22. PIR$^2$ J 814.

23. Lampe 2003, 277–78.

24. BHG 974, on the other hand, mentions the reign of Marcus Aurelius (Latyšev 1911, 2.1, l.5).

25. See discussion in Bisbee 1983, 134–37, 157; Bisbee 1988, 95–118.

26. See above; see below for the different versions of AScil.

27. AScil 1.

28. Seeck (1921) for the post-Diocletian practice; Hanslik (1963) objected that there is a first-century *secretarium* in Noricum. (Scholars citing Hanslick 1963, such as Lanata [1973, 140], do not seem to be bothered by the location of the so-called *secretarium*!) Also see Ruggiero 1991, 87–88. Ronchey (2000, 732) seems to ignore prior discussions and reverts to Seeck's position. Färber (2014, 235–81) now offers a full treatment of the evidence: he concludes that the practice started before Diocletian, but that AScil or even ACypr are delicate evidence for an early practice because of the difficulty of dating them. Also see Haensch 2003, 121.

29. See discussion in Ruggiero 1988.

30. Moss 2012, 125–27. The reference is structurally highlighted by a chiasmus; see Eastman 2011, 157–58.

31. Rebillard 2017, 353.

32. This is also how Augustine characterizes ACypr; see below.

33. See above.

34. On this group of martyrs, see Barnes 2016, 106–10.

35. Barnes 2016, 108–10, 357 (XI).

36. BHL 5253–55; see Lanata 1972.

37. Text: Bastiaensen 1987c, 238–45; see Barnes 2016, 379–86 for a review of recent attempts at dating the composition of the text, to which one ought to add Rossi 2005.

38. Text: Delehaye 1891.

39. Barnes (2016, 110 n26) notes that the governor Maximus is not a historical character.

40. Barnes 2016, 128–29, 357 (XII).

41. Delehaye 1921, 268–70.

42. Delehaye 1921, 242–59.

43. Chiesa 1996; see Lancel 2006.

44. Barnes 2016, 129–31, 357 (XIII).

45. The *Acts of Peregrinus of Bol* (Chiesa 1998) could also be included in the same category of larger narratives that include one or more interrogation scenes.

46. BHL 1989a (text in Mabillon 1723, 177–78) and BHL 1989b (text in Franchi de' Cavalieri 1902, 32–35); see Chapter 3 for a detailed discussion.

47. Aug. in Ps. 120 and 137; see Mandouze 1982, 252–53: Crispina was a *clarissima*, married with children, tortured on the catasta.

48. Barnes 2016, 126–28, 357 (XV).

49. See the hagiographical dossier in Stelladoro 2006, 100–102.

50. Corsaro (1957) establishes the anteriority of BHG 629 (text in Franchi de' Cavalieri 1928, 46–47); the other two versions in the protocol form are BHG 630b and 630c.

51. Barnes 2016, 141–42, 358 (XVIII).

52. P.Duke 438; text: Minnen 1995, 30; for the dating of the handwriting, ibid., 15.

53. Barnes 2016, 142–46, 358 (XIX).

54. Eus. HE 8.9.7.

55. The text of version Be (P.Beatty 15) is dated to 310–50: Pietersma 1984, 34–83; see Kortekaas 1987, 281–315. The text of version Bo (P.Bodmer 20) is dated to 320–50: Martin 1964, 24–52; see Kortekaas 1987, 316–36. See Bausi 2015 for an overview of the tradition on Phileas,

including the Coptic and Ethiopic versions of his *Acts*. The Latin version (BHL 6799) depends on Rufinus's translation of Eusebius; see Halkin 1963b and Kortekaas 1987, 280–314.

56. Syriac: BHO 1073; see http://syriaca.org/work/1231; text in Quentin and Tisserand 1921. Latin: BHL 2203e–f; text in Quentin 1905.

57. P.Oxy 50 3529: Parsons 1983; see Blumell and Wayment 2015, 352–54 (#98).

58. The difficulty here is that most texts cannot be dated. Brown (2003, 57) notes a shift in the fifth century "from the curt, judicial records of the martyrs of the time of the Great Persecution . . . to a world awash with blood," in which martyrdom is characterized by graphic descriptions of the tortures endured.

59. Rebillard 2017, 300–301.

60. APerp I/II. 4–5 to compare to PPerp 6.3–4. Some scholars have been seduced by the "quality" of the scene; see Amat 1996, 271.

61. Bisbee 1988, 8–11 offers a quick review of previous scholarship; also Ronchey 2000. See Coles 1966 for a list of preserved court protocols; updated in Kelly 2011, 368–80; there are few criminal trials in these proceedings.

62. See Burton 1975, 103–4; Cockle 1984; Burkhalter 1990; Haensch 1992.

63. Haensch 1992, 229–37.

64. Coles 1966, 19–24 discusses whether or not the records were abridged.

65. Anagnostou-Canas 2000, 764–67; Palme 2014a, 485–86; Palme 2014b, 402–6.

66. Haensch 1992, 224–26; Anagnostou-Canas 2000, 768–72.

67. On a shift from journals to singular transcripts, see Bickermann 1933; Palme 2014a, 496–97; Palme 2014b, 418–21, with the reservations of Haensch (2016, 309–10) that Palme (2018, 257–58) seems to accept. I thank Anna Dolganov for helping me sorting out these issues.

68. In general, there are very few criminal trials among the preserved court protocols; see above.

69. On the effects of Gallienus's edict ending the persecution of Valerian, see Barnes 2016, 97–105.

70. Humfress 2000, 2007; Hermanowicz 2008; see below.

71. P.Mil.Vogl. 6.287: Huebner 2019; Vandoni (1959, 189–90) gave the *editio princeps* of the papyrus; see Gallazzi (in Gallazzi and Vandoni 1977, 72–74) for the edition among the papyri from the Università degli Studi di Milano.

72. Huebner 2019, 8; I am not competent to discuss the readings of the papyrus nor the reconstruction proposed. Anna Dolganov (personal communication) is currently preparing a new edition of the text.

73. Vandoni 1959, 189.

74. Gallazzi 1977, 72.

75. Huebner 2019, 6.

76. Huebner 2019, 10.

77. On this crime, see Harries 2007, 72–85.

78. Mommsen 1890 (= 1907, 389–422), Mommsen 1893 (= 1910, 540–45), Mommsen 1899, 575–76.

79. Last 1937, 80–82; Sherwin-White 1952, 203–4; Robinson 1990–92, 284–85; Streeter 2006, 12–15.

80. Plin. ep. 10.96.7: Adfirmabant autem hanc fuisse summam vel culpae suae vel erroris, quod essent soliti stato die ante lucem convenire carmenque Christo quasi deo dicere se cum invicem seque sacramento non in scelus aliquod obstringere, sed ne furta, ne latrocinia, ne adulteria

committerent, ne fidem fallerent, ne depositum appellati abnegarent. The use of *sacramentum* in this passage has generated a lot of speculations; see Micunco (2006) for a recent appraisal and previous scholarship.

81. Hellegouarc'h 1972, 95; Hoben 1978, 6–7.

82. Corke-Webster 2017b, 397–404.

83. Min. Fel. 8. 3–4, Quid homines—sustinebitis enim me impetum susceptae actionis liberius exserentem—homines, inquam, deploratae inlicitae ac desperatae factionis grassari in deos non ingemescendum est? Qui de ultima faece collectis inperitioribus et mulieribus credulis sexus sui facilitate labentibus plebem profanae coniurationis instituunt, quae nocturnis congregationibus et ieiuniis solemnibus et inhumanis cibis non sacro quodam, sed piaculo foederantur, latebrosa et lucifugax natio, in publicum muta, in angulis garrula; templa ut busta despiciunt, deos despuunt, rident sacra, miserentur miseri—si fas est—sacerdotum, honores et purpuras despiciunt, ipsi seminudi. Translation Clarke 1974, 63 (slightly modified).

84. Tert. ad nat. 1.17.4: Vos tamen de nostris aduersus nostros conspiratis! Agnoscimus sane Romanam in Caesares fidem: nulla umquam coniuratio erupit.

85. Tert. apol. 28–36. The *Ad Nationes* is often described as a first draft of the *Apology*; see Schneider (1968, 26–33) for a nuanced presentation.

86. Tert. apol. 39.20–21: Haec coitio christianorum merito sane illicita, si illicitis par, merito sane damnanda, si non dissimilis damnandis, si quis de ea queritur eo titulo, quo de factionibus querela est. In cuius perniciem aliquando conuenimus? Hoc sumus congregati quod et dispersi, hoc uniuersi quod et singuli, neminem laedentes, neminem contristantes. Cum probi, cum boni coeunt, cum pii, cum casti congregantur, non est factio dicenda, sed curia. Translation Glover 1934, 181–83 (slightly modified).

87. Huebner 2019, 12.

88. The reading συνοικίον is adopted by Gallazzi 1977, 73 n5; it is a variant of συνοικία, settlement, community. For its Christian connotation, Huebner (2019, 12 n46) refers to "Kloppenburg 2019, 161," i.e., Kloppenborg (2018, 161), who only lists the feminine cognate as one of the many words that can designate an association.

89. See Schneider 1968, 285.

90. The dating of Minucius Felix after Tertullian has been broadly agreed upon since Becker 1967; see Schubert 2014, 19–26. Thomas's new arguments for a dating prior to Tertullian are not convincing (2011, 35–38).

91. Martini 1975; Harries 2009, 393–97.

92. Waltzing 1931, 81, 111 (*sacrilegium* is the theft of property consecrated to the gods; see further Bauman 1967), 207 (on *maiestas*); see Georges 2011, 198–99.

93. Corke-Webster 2017a.

94. ACypr 3.4: nefariae tibi conspirationis homines adgregasti.

95. On the edicts of Valerian, see Selinger 2002, 83–94.

96. Huebner 2019, 5.

97. Huebner 2019, 7.

98. Huebner 2019, 17–19; on the edicts of Decius and Valerian, see Selinger 2002.

99. Huebner 2019, 15–16, referring to SB 16 12497.

100. I wish to thank Anna Dolganov (personal communication) for confirming that both names were not rare.

101. See dossier in Le Blant 1879 and 1881, 62–72.

102. Geffcken 1906.

103. See Haensch 1992, 226 n45.

104. Aug. ep. 29*; the best study of the letter is Lanéry 2008, 13–21; see Duval 1987, Caltabiano 1998, Lepelley 2009. For a discussion of some of the details of the letter, see the Latin text and the English translation I give in appendix A.

105. Aug. ep 29*.1–2.

106. Aug. ep29*.1.

107. Aug. ep29*.2.

108. On the different versions, see Rebillard 2017, 197–99.

109. Contra Lepelley 2009, 152–53, who thinks that for Augustine the *Acts of Cyprian* belong to the category of texts based on the sole court protocols.

110. See Dolbeau 2003, 274–75 and Dearn 2004.

111. PSaturnDat. 1 (Franchi de' Cavalieri 1935, 49): adgredior itaque caelestes pugnas nouaque certamina gesta per fortissimos milites Christi, bellatores inuictos, martyres gloriosos; adgredior, inquam, ex actis publicis scribere.

112. Conc. Arel. a 314 c. 14 (13): De his qui scripturas sanctas tradidisse dicuntur uel uasa dominica uel nomina fratrum suorum, placuit nobis ut quicumque eorum ex actis publicis fuerit detectus, non uerbis nudis, ab ordine cleri amouetur. Nam si idem aliquos ordinasse fuerint depraehensi, et de his quos ordinauerunt ratio subsistit, non illis obsit ordinatio. Et quoniam multi sunt qui contra ecclesiam repugnare uidentur et per testes redemptos putant se ad accusationem admitti debere, omnino non permittantur, nisi ut supra diximus, actis publicis docuerint.

113. Latin texts in Ziwsa 1893, 185–97 and 197–204; English translation in Edwards 1997, 170–80 and 150–69. Duval 2000, 231–44 for a new transcription of the *Acta purgationis Felicis* and 495–98 for some notes on the text of the *Gesta apud Zenophilum*.

114. See Duval 2000 for a detailed analysis of both texts.

115. During the third session, the Donatists contest that a council of Numidian bishops met at Cirta in 303, as stated in a document handled by the Catholics. Their main argument is that no council was permitted to convene during the persecution. The Catholics then ask whether the Donatists do not have in their possession the *gesta* of martyrs who acknowledge that they took part in meetings during the persecution; Gest. col. Carth., cap. 3.421. The Donatists seem to evade the question until the Catholics send someone to fetch a copy of the *gesta*. This action is blocked, but the Donatists themselves then produce *gesta martyrum* to be read; Gest. col. Carth., cap. 3.432–34. The Catholics later produce other *gesta martyrum* to prove that Christians assembled during the persecution; Gest. col. Carth., cap. 3.448.

116. See Bastiaensen 1987a, xxviii; Bisbee 1988; Lanata 1993, 281. Barnes (2016, 63–66) is an isolated exception, who considers the *Acts of Justin* and the *Acts of the Scilitan Martyrs* as "reproducing a transcript of the trials of Christian with little or no alteration."

117. Prud. perist. 1.75–78: O uetustatis silentis obsoleta obliuio! / inuidentur ista nobis fama et ipsa extinguitur, / chartulas blasphemus olim nam satelles abstulit, / ne tenacibus libellis erudita saecula / ordinem, tempus modumque passionis proditum / dulcibus linguis per aures posterorum spargerent. Translation in Thomson 1949–53. See Fux 2013, 50–51 for a commentary.

118. Pass. Vict. Maur. 6 (AASS Maii. 2, 290): Tunc Anolinus consiliarius iussit comprehendi omnes exceptores qui erant in palatio, et fecit eos iurare per deos suos, ut si quis haberet aliquam chartam uel scedam nemo illam celaret. Tunc iurauerunt omnes per deos et per salutem imperatoris quod nemo illam celaret, et allatis omnibus chartis, fecit eas Anolinus incendi ante se ab scurrone: quod factum ualde placuit imperatori. For the date, see Lanéry 2010, 261–64.

119. Pass. Vict. Maur. (Mombrizio 1910, 2. 632): Tunc ego Maximianus notarius imperatoris christianus ab infantia iuraui per paganissimum eorum: et tamen per noctem cum luminaribus in

hippodromo circi scripsi prout memoria potui retinere. The epilogue is omitted in AASS though it belongs to the manuscript tradition (see Lanéry 2010, 262 n558).

120. Pass. Vincent. 1 (Saxer 2002, 186): Vnde reddimus fide plena relata gestorum, quae litterarum apicibus adnotari non inmerito noluit, qui uictum se erubescebat audiri. For a date before 550, see Saxer 2002, 160–63, 176.

121. See Dehandschutter 2003, 162–63, 173–74.

122. Ast. Am. Hom. 11.3 (Halkin 1965, 6): Δορυφόροι δὲ τῆς ἀρχῆς καὶ στρατιῶται πολλοί, οἱ μὲν τῶν ὑπομνημάτων ὑπογραφεῖς δέλτους φέροντες καὶ γραφίδας, ὧν θάτερος ἀναρτήσας ἀπὸ τοῦ κηροῦ τὴν χεῖρα βλέπει πρὸς τὴν κρινομένην σφοδρῶς ὅλον ἐκκλίνας τὸ πρόσωπον, ὥσπερ παρακελευόμενος γεγωνότερον λαλεῖν ἵνα μὴ κάμνων περὶ τὴν ἀκοὴν ἐσφαλμένα γράφῃ καὶ ἐπιλήψιμα. Translation in Dehandschutter 2003, 175.

123. The letter (BHG 1574a) is published in Halkin 1963a, 20–22. In the Latin version (BHL 7981), the letter constitutes the prologue to the passion.

124. See Halkin 1963a, 211–12.

125. Pass. Pont. Cim. 17 (AASS Maii. 3, 279): Iuuenis quidem Valerius, qui cum eo fuerat enutritus, timens corpus eius metu gentilium aufferre, per noctem in quo iacebat sepeliuit loco. Gesta uero martyris ab exceptoribus pecunia redimens, secum tollens, reperta nauicula, Libyæ partibus, causa persecutionis, declinauit. The passion was once thought to be a work of Valerian, bishop of Cimiez in the fifth century; Dufourcq (1905, 416–18) with the review of Delehaye 1906, 201–3. Weiss (1990) dates it to the last quarter of the eighth century; Heinzelmann (2010, 44 n74) is doubtful and points to the tenth century when the passion is attested in the manuscript tradition; see already Passet 1977, 223.

126. See Teitler 1985, 81–85 for what he calls "apocryphal *excerptores*."

127. Euseb. Gallic. hom. 56.4 (Glorie 1970–71, 652). The homily (BHL 3306; CPL 503; CPPM 4673) is sometimes attributed to Hilarius of Arles (401–49); see Cavallin (1945, 172–73). Cavallin (1952, 14–15) changed his position: clausulae are too different from those familiar to Hilarius. Bailey (2010, 33 and n26), who does not know of Cavallin 1952, thinks a good case can be made. In any case, the homily is part of the Eusebius Gallicanus collection, which was compiled in southeastern Gaul in the mid to late fifth century; see Bailey (2010, 29–38) for the *status quaestionis*.

128. There are extant a Greek version (BHG 1646) and a Latin one (BHL 7828); their relationship and dependence on a common Greek original is poorly established; see the review of Grégoire 1905 by Delehaye 1905c, 505–7. Nevertheless, the Latin version BHL 7828 was written before the sixth century when the Cappadocian martyrs were naturalized in Langres (Gaul) and the text rewritten as BHL 7829; see van der Straeten 1961, 132–33.

129. Greek text in Grégoire 1905, 22 l.15–21; Latin in Grégoire 1905, 24.

130. See Delehaye 1923, 277–78; Latin text in Knopf, Krüger, and Ruhbach 1965, 89–90.

131. Pass. Cassian. 1.4 (Knopf, Krüger, and Ruhbach 1965, 90): Quas cum sententias exciperet Cassianus, ubi deuictum deuotione tanti martyris Aurelium Agricolanum, capitalem uidit ferire sententiam, exsecrationem sui clara uoce contestans, graphium et codicem proiecit in terra.

132. *Passion of Theodore the General* 12 and 17; Greek text in Van Hoof 1883, 359–67.

133. BHG 1750 is the oldest version of the *Passion of Theodore the General*; this martyr, however, is a doublet of Theodore the Soldier and seems to appear after the sixth century, probably as late as the ninth century; see Delehaye 1909, 15.

134. Teitler 1985, 84 (his emphasis).

135. See below on authenticating devices.

136. Ando 2000, 128–29.

137. APerp I and II are not in the protocol format, but the addition of an interrogation scene is their main rewrite.

138. Augustine provides many examples; see Lapointe 1972.

139. The practice is well attested in North Africa: it was approved by the Council of Hippo in 393 (Conc. Hippon. 393 c. 5; Munier 1974, 21), but we do not know when it started; on the reading of the *passiones martyrum* in Africa and other Western churches, see Gaiffier 1954; Martimort 1992, 17.

140. See Chapter 4 on the use of documents.

141. Bowersock 1995, 5 for the quote; 7–13 for a review of figures commonly held as precedents.

142. Bowersock 1995, 27–28, quotation on p. 27.

143. Bowersock 1995, 37.

144. Boyarin 1999, 118.

145. Lieberman 1944, 19–26; on the omission of the "standard questions," see 22 about Rabbi Eliezer (Tosefta Hullin 2.24) and 24–25 for several other examples.

146. Henten and Avemarie 2002, 132–76.

147. Henten and Avemarie 2002, 133.

148. See Ando 2000, 128–29 (129 for the quote). Furthermore, the chronology I support strengthens Boyarin's arguments about what he calls the "discourse of martyrdom" and in particular his "hypothesis of shared innovation and circulation back and forth" between rabbinic and Christian texts. See Boyarin 1999, 119 and 206–8 (n116) for his "doubly conservative" chronology.

## CHAPTER 3

1. I borrow this language from Kurke 2011, 8.

2. See below for a discussion of the concept.

3. Ehrman 2013, 129, on the Neutestamentlers.

4. Ehrman 2013, 29–31.

5. Ehrman 2013, 33–35.

6. Ehrman 2013, 34.

7. Ehrman 2013, 35.

8. Ehrman 2013, 128–32; on problems with the notion of intention, see 30 n3.

9. Ehrman 2013, 31–32, 81–92.

10. Ehrman 2013, 494–97; references are to Lipsius 1874, Keim 1878, Ronchey 1990, and Moss 2010.

11. Ehrman 2013, 497.

12. When I use "author" in the following paragraphs, I merely follow Ehrman's usage, by which he means the author of the letter.

13. MPol 2.2: ἐπιδεικνυμένους ἅπασιν ἡμῖν, ὅτι ἐκείνῃ τῇ ὥρᾳ βασανιζόμενοι τῆς σαρκὸς ἀπεδήμουν οἱ γενναιότατοι μάρτυρες τοῦ Χριστοῦ, μᾶλλον δὲ, ὅτι παρεστὼς ὁ κύριος ὡμίλει αὐτοῖς.

14. Ehrman 2013, 497.

15. MPol 9.1: Καὶ τὸν μὲν εἰπόντα οὐδεὶς εἶδεν, τὴν δὲ φωνὴν τῶν ἡμετέρων οἱ παρόντες ἤκουσαν.

16. MPol 15.1–2: Μεγάλης δὲ ἐκλαμψάσης φλογός, θαῦμα εἴδομεν, οἷς ἰδεῖν ἐδόθη· οἳ καὶ ἐτηρήθημεν εἰς τὸ ἀναγγεῖλαι τοῖς λοιποῖς τὰ γενόμενα. Τὸ γὰρ πῦρ καμάρας εἶδος ποιῆσαν ὥσπερ

ὀθόνη πλοίου ὑπὸ πνεύματος πληρουμένη, κύκλῳ περιετείχισεν τὸ σῶμα τοῦ μάρτυρος· καὶ ἦν μέσον οὐχ ὡς σὰρξ καιομένη, ἀλλ' ὡς ἄρτος ὀπτώμενος ἢ ὡς χρυσὸς καὶ ἄργυρος ἐν καμίνῳ πυρούμενος. Καὶ γὰρ εὐωδίας τοσαύτης ἀντελαβόμεθα ὡς λιβανωτοῦ πνέοντος ἢ ἄλλου τινὸς τῶν τιμίων ἀρωμάτων.

17. MPol 1.1: Ἐγράψαμεν ὑμῖν, ἀδελφοί, τὰ κατὰ τοὺς μαρτυρήσαντας καὶ τὸν μακάριον Πολύκαρπον.

18. MPol 20.2: Προσαγορεύετε πάντας τοὺς ἁγίους, ὑμᾶς οἱ σὺν ἡμῖν προσαγορεύουσιν καὶ Εὐάρεστος, ὁ γράψας, πανοικεί.

19. MPol 21: Μαρτυρεῖ δὲ ὁ μακάριος Πολύκαρπος μηνὸς Ξανθικοῦ δευτέρᾳ ἱσταμένου, πρὸ ἑπτὰ καλανδῶν Μαρτίων, σαββάτῳ μεγάλῳ, ὥρᾳ ὀγδόῃ. Συνελήφθη δὲ ὑπὸ Ἡρώδου ἐπὶ ἀρχιερέως Φιλίππου Τραλλιανοῦ, ἀνθυπατεύοντος Στατίου Κοδράτου, βασιλεύοντος δὲ εἰς τοὺς αἰῶνας Ἰησοῦ Χριστοῦ ᾧ ἡ δόξα, τιμή, κράτος, μεγαλωσύνη, θρόνος αἰώνιος ἀπὸ γενεᾶς εἰς γενεάν. Ἀμήν.

20. Ehrman 2013, 499.

21. Ehrman depends on Barnes 1967; see, however, Barnes 2016, 368–73, for a new appraisal.

22. As we will see below, three different versions of section 22 are attested in the manuscript tradition; see Rebillard 2017, 83–84.

23. MPol 22.1–3: Ἐρρῶσθαι ὑμᾶς εὐχόμεθα, ἀδελφοί, στοιχοῦντας τῷ κατὰ τὸ εὐαγγέλιον λόγῳ Ἰησοῦ Χριστοῦ, μεθ' οὗ δόξα τῷ θεῷ καὶ πατρὶ καὶ ἁγίῳ πνεύματι ἐπὶ σωτηρίᾳ τῇ τῶν ἁγίων ἐκλεκτῶν, καθὼς ἐμαρτύρησεν ὁ μακάριος Πολύκαρπος, οὗ γένοιτο ἐν τῇ βασιλείᾳ Ἰησοῦ Χριστοῦ πρὸς τὰ ἴχνη εὑρεθῆναι ἡμᾶς. Ταῦτα μετεγράψατο μὲν Γάϊος ἐκ τῶν Εἰρηναίου, μαθητοῦ τοῦ Πολυκάρπου, ὃς καὶ συνεπολιτεύσατο τῷ Εἰρηναίῳ. Ἐγὼ δὲ Σωκράτης ἐν Κορίνθῳ ἐκ τῶν Γαΐου ἀντιγράφων ἔγραψα. Ἡ χάρις μετὰ πάντων. Ἐγὼ δὲ πάλιν Πιόνιος ἐκ τοῦ προγεγραμμένου ἔγραψα ἀναζητήσας αὐτά, κατὰ ἀποκάλυψιν φανερώσαντός μοι τοῦ μακαρίου Πολυκάρπου, καθὼς δηλώσω ἐν τῷ καθεξῆς, συναγαγὼν αὐτὰ ἤδη σχεδὸν ἐκ τοῦ χρόνου κεκμηκότα, ἵνα κἀμὲ συναγάγῃ ὁ κύριος Ἰησοῦς Χριστὸς μετὰ τῶν ἐκλεκτῶν αὐτοῦ εἰς τὴν οὐράνιον βασιλείαν αὐτοῦ, ᾧ ἡ δόξα σὺν τῷ πατρὶ καὶ ἁγίῳ πνεύματι εἰς τοὺς αἰῶνας τῶν αἰώνων. Ἀμήν.

24. Irenaeus grew up in Smyrna, where he heard Polycarp, who is mentioned as having had a strong influence on him; Iren. Lugd. ep. Flor. apud Eus. HE 5.20.

25. MPion 2.1 mentions that Pionius was executed on the anniversary of the death of Polycarp.

26. See Hartog 2013, 331–33 on the identification of Pionius in previous scholarship.

27. Ehrman 2013, 501; he falsely claims, however, that "we have no manuscripts that lack it"; see Rebillard 2017, 83. It would be impractical to review here the arguments against the "authenticity" of MPol 21–22; see Hartog 2013, 328–37.

28. I elaborate on this point in Chapter 4.

29. Ehrman 2013, 501.

30. Ehrman 2013, 123–26 (citation from p. 121).

31. Ehrman 2013, 123.

32. Ehrman 2013, 501.

33. See Dilley 2010. In addition to the *Apocalypse of Paul*, Dilley considers the *Acts of Pilate*, the *Revelatio Sancti Stephani*, and the *Story of Judas Kyriakos*. On the date of the *Apocalypse of Paul*, see Piovanelli 2007. Whether or not we reject the existence of a second- or third-century original, the prologue belongs to the fifth-century Latin version.

34. Ehrman 2013, 123–24; he depends here on Speyer 1970.

35. Ehrman never properly deals with the notion of fiction. Under "related phenomena," he considers what he calls "literary fictions," but because his focus is on "falsely named writings," he can affirm twice (43 and 45) that "there are no certain instances of pseudepigraphic fiction among the early Christian writings."

36. Ehrman argues against Wolter's hypothesis that anonymity is a way to claim Jesus's authority; Wolter 1988.

37. Ehrman 2013, 50.

38. I borrow this language from Kurke 2011, 8.

39. Ehrman 2003, 363. See the comment of Dehandschutter 2006, 203 n14: "Malheureusement, Ehrman ne se montre pas du tout critique à ce propos et continue de croire à un texte 'produced by Pionius.'"

40. For a typology of scribal errors, see Tarrant 2016, 9–17.

41. M or *Mosquensis* 390: Moskow, Gosudarstvennyj Istoričeskij Musej (GIM), Sinod. gr. 390.

42. K or Kosinitza 28: olim Drama, Monê Kosinitsês, 28; now Sofia, Naučen Centǎr za Slavjano-Vizantijski Proučvanija "Ivan Dujčev," D. gr. 60.

43. MPol 22.2 (M; Hartog 2013, 270): Ταῦτα μετεγράψατο μὲν Γάϊος ἐκ τῶν Εἰρηναίου συγγραμμάτων, ὃς καὶ συνεπολιτεύσατο τῷ Εἰρηναίῳ, μαθητῇ γεγονότι τοῦ ἁγίου Πολυκάρπου. Οὗτος γὰρ ὁ Εἰρηναῖος, κατὰ τὸν καιρὸν τοῦ μαρτυρίου τοῦ ἐπισκόπου Πολυκάρπου γενόμενος ἐν Ῥώμῃ, πολλοὺς ἐδίδαξεν· οὗ καὶ πολλὰ αὐτοῦ συγγράμματα κάλλιστα καὶ ὀρθότατα φέρεται, ἐν οἷς μέμνηται Πολυκάρπου, ὅτι παρ᾽ αὐτοῦ ἔμαθεν, ἱκανῶς τε πᾶσαν αἵρεσιν ἤλεγξεν καὶ τὸν ἐκκλησιαστικὸν κανόνα καὶ καθολικὸν ὡς παρέλαβεν παρὰ τοῦ ἁγίου καὶ παρέδωκεν. Λέγει δὲ καὶ τοῦτο· ὅτι συναντήσαντός ποτε τῷ ἁγίῳ Πολυκάρπῳ Μαρκίωνος, ἀφ᾽ οὗ οἱ λεγόμενοι Μαρκιωνισταί, καὶ εἰπόντος· Ἐπιγίνωσκε ἡμᾶς, Πολύκαρπε, εἶπεν αὐτὸς τῷ Μαρκίωνι· Ἐπιγινώσκω, ἐπιγινώσκω τὸν πρωτότοκον τοῦ σατανᾶ. Καὶ τοῦτο δὲ φέρεται ἐν τοῖς τοῦ Εἰρηναίου συγγράμμασιν, ὅτι ᾗ ἡμέρᾳ καὶ ὥρᾳ ἐν Σμύρνῃ ἐμαρτύρησεν ὁ Πολύκαρπος, ἤκουσεν φωνὴν ἐν τῇ Ῥωμαίων πόλει ὑπάρχων ὁ Εἰρηναῖος ὡς σάλπιγγος λεγούσης· Πολύκαρπος ἐμαρτύρησεν. Ἐκ τούτων οὖν, ὡς προλέλεκται, τῶν τοῦ Εἰρηναίου συγγραμμάτων Γάϊος μετεγράψατο, ἐκ δὲ τῶν Γαΐου ἀντιγράφων Ἰσοκράτης ἐν Κορίνθῳ. Ἐγὼ δὲ πάλιν Πιόνιος ἐκ τῶν Ἰσοκράτους ἀντιγράφου ἔγραψα κατὰ ἀποκάλυψιν τοῦ ἁγίου Πολυκάρπου ζητήσας αὐτά, συναγαγὼν αὐτὰ ἤδη σχεδὸν ἐκ τοῦ χρόνου κεκμηκότα, ἵνα κἀμὲ συναγάγῃ ὁ κύριος Ἰησοῦς Χριστὸς μετὰ τῶν ἐκλεκτῶν αὐτοῦ εἰς τὴν ἐπουράνιον αὐτοῦ βασιλείαν· ᾧ ἡ δόξα σὺν τῷ πατρὶ καὶ τῷ υἱῷ καὶ τῷ ἁγίῳ πνεύματι εἰς τοὺς αἰῶνας τῶν αἰώνων. Ἀμήν.

44. K (see below) also names the second intermediary Isocrates.

45. Iren. Lugd. Haer. 3.3.4; Eus. HE 4.14.7.

46. Hoover (2013, 487) infers from this that M might be independent from Eusebius and notes that this opens the possibility that M antedates Eusebius.

47. See Buschmann 1998, 375; Hoover 2013, 488.

48. Hoover 2013, 489 n67. Hoover does not note, however, that in 16.2 M reads τῆς ἐν Σμύρνῃ ἁγίας ἐκκλησίας instead of τῆς ἐν Σμύρνῃ καθολικῆς ἐκκλησίας so that if καθολικῆς is here polemical (meaning "catholic" rather than "universal") it would be lost on the reader of M.

49. There is no transcription of the colophon in K; only Dehandschutter's analysis is available (2009, 128–30).

50. Ign. Sm. 13.2, Pol. 8.3; on her identification with the Alce mentioned in MPol 17.2, see Hartog 2013, 318.

51. Iren. Lugd. Haer. 3.3.4.

52. Dehandschutter 2009, 130.

53. See Dehandschutter 2009, 130–31.

54. See above.

55. My critique of Ehrman is strictly limited to his use of the notion of forgery to describe martyr texts; on broader issues, see Brakke 2016.

56. Thomas 1998; see Thomas 2003. Zumthor (1992 [1972], 41–49) also associates anonymity and what he calls *mouvance* (mutability).

57. Thomas 1998, 278–79; see Morales (2006 and 2018) for an attempt to bring the Greek imperial romances into this same category.

58. Thomas 1998, 280.

59. Zwierlein (in Zwierlein and Kölligan 2014, 1.14) proposes a stemma that is based on so many assumptions about authenticity that it is best ignored.

60. BHG 1562; text in Latyšev 1911, 1.123–26; on the "Imperial Menologion," see Halkin 1985, 7–12; D'Aiuto 2018.

61. On the genre of the βίος ἐν συντόμῳ, see Delehaye 1897, 325–27.

62. Dehandschutter 2004, 479–83 (= 2007, 264–69).

63. See Rebillard 2017, 82, with bibliography.

64. Weidmann 1999, 50–58.

65. Dehandschutter (2004, 484 = 2007, 270) suggests three versions as he does not take into account M and K.

66. On the traditional distinction between story and narrative discourse, see, for instance, Fludernik 2009, 2–3.

67. Hartog 2013, 169–70.

68. See Dehandschutter 1979, 48–55; 1993, 489–90 (= 2007, 47–48).

69. Zahn 1876, liv; text: 133–67.

70. Lightfoot 1889, 3.358–60.

71. Gleede 2016, 224; see 215–22 for the dating, 222–28 for a close analysis of the translation technique.

72. Gleede 2016, 227.

73. See Lightfoot (1889, 3.360–61) for the Syriac (BHO 998) and Coptic (BHO 997) versions; Vetter (1881) for the Armenian version (BHO 999); Zwierlein and Kölligan (2014) for a shorter Armenian version that they believe to be translated from the original, lost Greek text.

74. BHO 997; see the detailed comparison in Amélineau 1888, 413–17. For the text and a French translation, see 394–413.

75. See Khomych 2010, 2012, and 2013.

76. I borrow the idea of "performance" from Thomas 1998, 289; see 2003, 40: "The text is behaving similarly to oral tradition, with each manuscript representing a new 'performance' of the work in another context."

77. Thomas 1998, 289; see Konstan 1998.

78. Konstan 1998, 127. He adds: "This is one of the reasons why such compositions are commonly anonymous." See above on anonymity and textual fluidity.

79. The concept is introduced in an article from 1959, gives its title to a book published in 1962 (1989) in which the article is included as chapter 1, and becomes a key concept in Eco's synthesis on his approach to semiotics in 1979.

80. See Eco 1979, 3: "An 'open' text cannot be described as a communicative strategy if the role of its addressee (the reader, in the case of verbal texts) has not been envisaged at the moment of its generation *qua* text. An open text is a paramount instance of a syntacticsemanticopragmatic device whose foreseen interpretation is a part of its generative process."

81. See West 1973, 37–42; according to Tarrant (2016, 54), the terms "open recension" and "closed recension" were coined by Pasquali (1934).

82. Quentin 1926, 34–36; on Lachmann, see Timpanaro 2005 (1963).

83. Quentin 1926, 43.

84. See, for instance, Génicot (1975, 27) about genealogies, Löfstedt (1976, 596) on lives of saints, Dolezalek (2002, 330) on glosses in the *Libri magistrorum*. The Hiberno-Latin scholar Ludwig Bieler (1958, 17–18) distinguishes a further category of "wild" texts, including the bulk of popular literature. Medievalist Paul Zumthor (1992 [1972], 41–49; 1972, 507 for the definition) further elaborates the concept of "mouvance": "le caractère de l'œuvre qui, comme telle, avant l'âge du livre, ressort d'une quasi-abstraction, les textes concrets qui la réalisent présentant, par le jeu des variantes et remaniements, comme une incessante vibration et une instabilité fondamentale." See also Cerquiglini (1999 [1989], 33–45) on variance.

85. Bryant (2002, 2007) defines what he calls "fluid text" in the context of print and is therefore less relevant for us. His approach, however, has been adapted to the context of ancient world text production in very interesting ways by Larsen 2018. The notion of "text network" proposed by Selden (2010) seems to work better from the point of view of the modern scholars than from that of the text producers. Brent Shaw (2018, 233) forged the label "sedimentary texts" for describing texts such as Luke-Acts that are "marked by varying layers of composition and by occasional deliberate intrusions into the text."

86. In the conclusion, I will describe a taxonomy that better illustrates the relation between story, texts, and manuscripts.

87. Monceaux 1901–23, 5.48.

88. Monceaux 1901–23, 5.48.

89. PSaturnDat 19–23; see Monceaux 1901–23, 5.53–59. On PSaturnDat, see Dolbeau 2003 and Dearn 2004. Text in Franchi de' Cavalieri 1935, 49–71. English translation in Tilley 1996, 27–49.

90. Monceaux 1901–23, 5.50–53.

91. Reitzenstein 1913, 35–37, for the text; for its Donatist character, see Franchi de' Cavalieri 1914, 211–12 (= 1962, 2.250–51) and Reitzenstein 1914, 88.

92. See Scorza Barcellona 2002, 136 for the distinction; it is ignored by Saxer 1994, Dalvit 2013, and Fialon 2018, 174–88.

93. For the existence of a unique version of PSaturnDat, see Dolbeau 2003, 276–77 (contra some confused statements by Tilley 1996, 26–27). PMax is known through a unique manuscript; see De Smedt 1890.

94. Würzburg, Universitätsbibliothek, M. p. th. f. 033 = Y, in Reitzenstein 1913, 35–37.

95. Cypr. ep. 67; Cypr. ep. 6; Cypr. ep. 4; Ps. Cypr. tract. 52 (2–3); Cypr. ep. 10; see Reitzenstein 1914, 86; Thurn 1984, 27.

96. Reitzenstein 1914, 92; see Bass 2013 for an unconvincing attempt to read the dossier as pre-Donatist.

97. See Bastiaensen 1987b, 202.

98. ACypr 2.3; Tilley 1996, 2; Bass 2013, 215. See Tilley 1996, 3 for this translation.

99. Reitzenstein 1913, 37 n1; Franchi de' Cavalieri 1914, 212 (= 1962, 2.250).

100. ACypr 3.6 (textus Y in Reitzenstein 1913, 36): Et Cyprianus: Deo laudes! Vna cum ipso credentes: Deo laudes. Et <Galerius Maximus uir clarissimus> pro consule decretum ex tabula legit: Thascium Cyprianum cum suis gladio animaduerti placet.

101. ACypr 3.6: Et decretum ex tabula recitauit: Thascium Cyprianum cum suis gladio animaduerti placet.

102. ACypr 3.6: Et decretum ex tabula recitauit: Thascium Cyprianum cum suis gladio animaduerti placet. Cyprianus episcopus dixit: Deo gratias.

103. Aug. c. Petil. 2.66.146: Considerate paululum quam multis, et quantum luctum dederint Deo laudes armatorum uestrorum (Consider for a short space to how many, and with what intensity, the cry of "Praises be to God," proceeding from your armed men, has caused others to mourn); see Klöckener 1996.

104. All the texts objected to Monceaux (1909) by Delehaye (1910, 467–68) date to after 411; see Dalvit 2013, 162–65.

105. ACypr 4.1: Post eius sententiam populus fratrum dicebat: Et nos cum eo decollemur. (After his condemnation, the people of the brothers kept saying: "Let us too be beheaded with him.")

106. See Tilley 1996, 2.

107. ACypr 4.1 (textus Y in Reizenstein 1913, 37): <Et> speculatorem expectans erexit oculos ad caelum rogans, et cum speculator furens uenisset, a caelo ad terram oculos deposuit et iussit speculatori aureos uiginti dari.

108. ACypr 4.1: Et coepit spiculatorem sustinere. Et cum uenisset spiculator, iussit suis ut eidem spiculatori aureos uiginti quinque darent.

109. Franchi de' Cavalieri 1914, 211 (= 1962, 250); Delehaye 1966, 69.

110. Maier 1987–89, 1.126 n3; Scorza Barcellona 2002, 135–36.

111. ACypr. 4.3 (textus Y in Reitzenstein 1913, 37): Et item post paucos dies Galerius Maximus uir clarissimus pro consule paenitentiae reus decessit languore consumptus.

112. ACypr. 4.3 (textus n in Biastiaensen 1987b, 230): praefocatus a diabolo mortuus est; n is Montpellier, Bibliothèque Universitaire Historique de Médecine, H 156.

113. See Bastiaensen 1987b, 198: "Y è decisamente autonomo e di buona tradizione, ma ha accetato lezioni fantasiose."

114. BHL 1989a was first published by Mabillon (1723, 177–78) from the manuscript Reims, Bibliothèque municipale, 0296 (E. 381); in his edition, Ruinart (1689, 477–79) also collated the manuscript Reims, Bibliothèque municipal, 1410 (K 786). BHL 1989b was published by Franchi de' Cavalieri (1902, 32–35) from the manuscript Autun, Bibliothèque municipal, S 034 (030); he later found a second manuscript with this version: Vatican City, Biblioteca apostolica Vaticana, Archivio di San Pietro A. 005, and published its variants (1905, 255 n2 = 1962, 131 n2). When Franchi de' Cavalieri published BHL 1989b, he thought that the two manuscripts from Reims were lost (1902, 31). However, in a supplement to the volume, he noted that the manuscripts had been located and he published the variants that were not included in his apparatus criticus. This supplement, which did not make its way in many libraries but was duly noted in the Bulletin des publications hagiographiques in *Analecta Bollandiana* (22, 1903, 487), escaped the attention of many scholars, such as Musurillo (1972, xliv), Maier (1987–89, 1.106), Scorza Barcellona (2002, 139), Dalvit (2013, 556), and Fialon (2018, 176 n14), who repeat that the manuscripts from Reims used by Mabillon and Ruinart are lost.

115. Monceaux 1903, 388–89; Dalvit 2013, 554–56, arrives at a similar conclusion.

116. Delehaye 1905a, 133. I leave aside the speculations of Rosen (1997), who distinguishes three layers: the traces of an authentic protocol in 1.2–7; a later Donatist creation in 2.1–3.3; and the two combined by a redactor responsible for 1.1 and 4.1–3.

117. The divisions of the text are those adopted by Knopf, Krüger, and Ruhbach (1965, 109–11) and followed in most modern editions and translations.

118. Monceaux 1903, 388–89; on this Donatist *signum*, see above.

119. Monceaux 1903, 389; Saxer (1994, 60–61) expresses strong reservations about the Donatist character of the doxology.

120. PCrispin 3.2.

121. Monceaux 1901–23, 5.52–53; on PMax, see Dalvit 2009.

122. The manuscript used by Mabillon is Reims, Bibliothèque municipale, 0296 (E. 381).

123. See Fialon 2018, 175–78.

124. PCrispin 4.2 (Franchi de' Cavalieri 1902, 35): Et signans frontem suam signaculum crucis, extendens ceruicem suam decollata est pro nomine domini nostri Iesus Christi, cui honor in saecula saeculorum. Amen. (English translation: Musurillo 1972, 309.)

125. PCrispin 2.3 (Mabillon 1723, 177): Quid uis? Vt sim sacrilega apud deum et apud imperatorem non sim? Absit. Deus magnus et omnipotens est, qui fecit mare et herbas uirides et aridam terram; homines autem facti ab ipso quid mihi possunt praestare?

126. PCrispin 3.2 (Mabillon 1723, 177): Caput meum perdo semel: sed si turificauero idolis.

127. PCrispin 2.3 (Franchi de' Cavalieri 1902, 34): Dii, qui non fecerunt caelum et terram, permeant! Ego sacrifico deo aeterno, permanenti in saecula saeculorum, qui est deus uerax et metuendus, qui fecit mare et herbas uirides et aridam terram; homines autem facti ab ipso quid mihi possunt praestare? (English translation: Musurillo 1972, 305.)

128. PCrispin 3.2 (Franchi de' Cavalieri 1902, 35): Caput meum libentissime pro deo meo perdere, desidero; nam uanissimis idolis mutis et surdis non sacrifico. (English translation: Musurillo 1972, 307.)

129. Thus, Saxer (1994), Scorza Barcellona (2002), Dalvit (2013), and Fialon (2018) do not discuss the hypothesis of Dolbeau (1983).

130. Dolbeau 1983, 52–61; five of the manuscripts are now lost.

131. Dolbeau 1983, 62; see Dolbeau 1992, 253. PDon, also known as the *Sermon on the Passion of Donatus and Advocatus*, is a panegyric commemorating the death of several Donatists, both laypeople and members of the clergy, killed between 317 and 321 in Carthage. Working edition in Dolbeau 1992; English translation in Tilley 1996, 52–60. Tilley (1996, 52) wrongly indicates that there are two versions, one Donatist and one Catholic, of the text.

132. PLuc 14.4 (β in Dolbeau 1983, 63): Deinde lapsorum. abruptam festinantiam, negationem pacis, ad plenam paenitentiam et Christi sententiam differebat.

133. PLuc 14.4 (α in Dolbeau 1983, 63): Deinde lapsorum abruptam festinantiam, negationem pacis, differebat.

134. PLuc 23.3–5 (β in Dolbeau 1983, 63–64): Hoc est mandatum meum ut diligatis inuicem quemadmodum dilexi uos. Et supremum illud adiunxit et in testamenti modum ultimo sermonis sui fide signauit, quod Lucianum presbyterum conmendatione plenissima prosecutus, quantum in illo fuit, sacerdotio destinauit. Nec inmerito. Non enim difficile fuit spiritu iam caelo et Christo proximanti habere notitiam.

135. PLuc 23.3–5 (α in Dolbeau 1983, 63–64): Hoc est mandatum meum ut diligatis inuicem quemadmodum dilexi uos. Et supremum illud adiunxit et in testamenti modum ultimo sermonis sui firmauit. Nec inmerito. Non enim difficile fuit spiritu iam caelo et Christo proximanti habere notitiam.

136. Dolbeau 1983, 64.

137. Bouhot 1983, 363–64.

138. See above.

139. Dolbeau 1983, 61: "Nous avons normalement écarté les variantes purement orthographiques et, quand la tradition était stable, les innovations propres à tel ou tel manuscrit."

140. See Schäfer (1986, 149–52) extending to Rabbinic literature some of the principles he applied to his edition of the Hekhalot literature (Schäfer 1981); discussion in Thomas 2003, 84–85.

141. Robinson 1891; in his edition, Robinson uses two other manuscripts that present texts very close to London, British Library, Add. 11880, though they offer a number of additions.

142. Anonymous 1889.

143. Baronius, *Annales*, ad annum 202 (ed. Theiner 1864, 477–79); see Aubé 1881a, 30–31. The manuscript is dated to the twelfth or thirteenth century; see Vichi and Mottironi 1961, 162.

144. Paris, Bibliothèque nationale de France, lat. 5306; Ruinart 1689, 79–80; see Aubé 1881a, 33–36. This fourteenth-century manuscript is part of the Moissac Legendary; see Philippart 1977, 102 n86.

145. Paris, Bibliothèque nationale de France, nouv. acq. lat. 2179 and 2180; Aubé 1881b, 503–9; see Aubé 1881a, 36–39. On the date of the manuscripts, respectively eleventh and tenth century, see Gamber 1968, 219.

146. Paris, Bibliothèque nationale de France, gr. 1470; see Robinson 1891, 113–17; Ruggiero 1991, 77–79. On the history of the text, see Conticello 2011, 228–29.

147. Mabillon 1723, 172.

148. See Anonymous 1889 and 1897.

149. Franchi de' Cavalieri 1903, 217–18 (= 1962, 2.45–46).

150. Robinson 1891, 108; see Corsaro 1955, 19 ("e chi non sa che brevità nei testi agiografici significa attendibilità storica?"); Ruggiero 1991, 69.

151. Robinson 1891, 107; Corsaro 1955, 17.

152. See Chapter 2 on this criterion.

153. See Delehaye 1966, 279; Ruggiero 1991, 56–57.

154. See Ruggiero 1991, 58–59, for a *status quaestionis* and the bibliography.

155. Robinson 1891, 108.

156. In addition to Rome, Biblioteca Vallicelliana, Tomus X, Baronius mentions two manuscripts from the Vatican library that have not been identified as far as I know; see Ruggiero 1891, 58.

157. See Quentin 1908, 89–90.

158. Delehaye 1966, 279; Ruggiero 1991, 57.

159. Ruggiero (1991, 57) seems to suggest that BHL 7531 is the most recent text; Aubé (1881a, 20) places it before BHL 7532 and BHL 7533. Aubé (1881b, 509 n3) suggests that *coaequalis essentia* in the final doxology of BHL 7533 evokes the fourth-century trinitarian discussions. The expression seems quite rare until the eighth or ninth century. Doxologies, however, are often modified by copyists, and the manuscript is dated to the tenth century.

160. For the English translations and the original texts, see Appendix B. The numbering refers to the sections of AScil.

161. The two other manuscripts that give, according to Robinson, a text very similar to 1, also contain the order to sacrifice.

162. Note that the two manuscripts that give, according to Robinson, a text very similar to 1 include the reply of Donata and follow a similar pattern, alternating between question and answer.

163. Aubé 1881a, 6.

164. Delehaye 1966, 278–83; he talks about the "sans-gêne" of the copyists (283).

165. See the conclusion for discussion of how the FRBR model can elucidate this.

166. Aug. serm. 37, 299D [Denis 16], 299E [Guelf. 30], 299F [Lambot 9]; see Lapointe 1972, 38–39. Margoni-Kögler 2010, 146, also lists (after Saxer 1980, 317) 335B [Guelf. 31]. Nothing in the sermon, however, supports this identification.

167. Aug. serm. 37.1 (see 37.23); 299D.1 (see 299D.6 and 7); 299F.1.

168. Aug. serm. 37.23: Honorem, inquit, Caesari quasi Caesari, timorem autem Deo; 299E.2: Honorem, inquit, Caesari quasi Caesari, timorem autem Deo.

169. AScil 9: Honorem Caesari quasi Caesari, timorem autem Deo.

170. There are several variants of Donata's answer. For the second part in the other versions, see the synoptic.

171. Aug. serm. 299F.2: Recordamini, carissimi, quemadmodum, cum iudex qui audiebat appellaret eorum confessionem "uanitatis persuasionem," respondit unus illorum: "Vanitatis persuasio est homicidium facere, falsum testimonium dicere."

172. AScil 7: Saturninus proconsul dixit ceteris: "Desinite huius esse persuasionis." Speratus dixit: "Mala est persuasion homicidum facere, falsum testimonium dicere."

173. Aug. serm. 299F.3: Hoc tenebant testes ueri, futura eius munera mente cernebant. Propterea cuncta transeuntia contemnebant: Vana salus hominis. Ideo non terrebatur quando audiebat: "Si Christum confessus fueris eris punitus," quia illud attendebat: testis falsus non erit impunitus. Beati sancti uerum dixerunt et occisi sunt. English translation: Hill 1994, 274.

174. Hill 1994, 276.

175. I use "manipulation" without any of the negative connotation usually associated with it.

176. IFLA 1998 (2nd ed. 2009); see an expansion of it as FRBRoo, current version 2.4 (Bekiari et al. 2016).

177. The following definitions are drawn from IFLA 2009, 17–25.

178. IFLA 2009, 24.

179. To this extent, my approach diverges from the one promoted by New Philology; see Lied and Lundhaug 2017 for a recent presentation.

180. I consider as fully valid the stemmata that have been produced for some martyr texts such as Van Beek (1936) for PPerp or Dolbeau (1983) for PLuc.

181. Fischer 2013, 89.

182. See Robinson 2000; Fischer 2010; Jänicke and Wrisley 2017; see Epp's proposal (2007) of a variant-conscious edition of the Greek New Testament.

CHAPTER 4

1. Bowersock 1994.

2. Though he does not offer an explicit definition, several statements make this clear.

3. Bowersock 1994, 141: "The martyr narratives were to provide the basis for an abundant production of instructive fiction in the centuries ahead, although the earliest martyr acts, based as they were on carefully maintained protocols of interrogation, had rather more historical veracity than was to be characteristic of the genre later."

4. Bowersock 1994, 22.

5. Thomas 2003; on Bowersock, see 4 and 92–104.

6. See Snyder 2013, 23–65.

7. Not in the sense of Hägg 1987 (= 2004, 73–98); see Thomas 2003, 94.

8. I borrow this label from Whitmarsh 2013, 35–36.

9. See Thomas 2003, 3–5, and, among many recent publications, the contributions in Pinheiro, Perkins, and Pervo 2013.

10. Thomas 2003, 88–89. These would be, thus, quite different from the imperial romances that focus on private figures in an historical framework.

11. Thomas 2003, 90.

12. Thomas 2003, 95, referring to the triad of history, myth, and plasma, on which see below.

13. Thomas 2003, 99; see Reitzenstein 1906, 84–99.

14. See below.

15. Thomas 2003, 99, with reference to Cicero's letter to Lucceius.

16. Thomas 2003, 102, with a reference to Francis 1998, on which see below.

17. Thomas 2003, 102; Wills (2015, 22–25) suggests that we substitute a constellation model for that of a point on a continuum and that we qualify these texts as popular or entertaining history.

18. Thomas 2003, 12.

19. Bale 2015, 83.

20. See Fowler 1982, 37: "Genre is much less of a pigeonhole than a pigeon."

21. Among many examples, see Penner 2004, 114–46.

22. Eduard Schwartz (1897) was the first and most influential proponent of "tragic history." See Walbank 1955 and 1960 for a thorough refutation of earlier scholarship; more recently Marincola 2003, 2010, 2013.

23. Polyb. 2.56–59.

24. Marincola 2013.

25. Marincola 2003.

26. I borrow the phrase from Marincola 2003, 287.

27. Cic. fam. 5.12 (letter in which Cicero asks Lucceius to write the history of his consulship); see Hall 1998. For its use as evidence about "tragic history," see Reitzenstein 1906, Ullman 1942, and Walbank 1955, 4–5.

28. Cic. or. 2.51–54, 62–64.

29. Woodman 1988, 2008 (citation at 23).

30. Woodman 1988, 91.

31. Woodman 1988, 197.

32. See Lendon 2009 and some comments in response by Woodman in Marincola 2011, 288–90.

33. See Marincola 1997, 158–62 (citation at 162).

34. Blockley (2001, 22) contra Woodman (1988, 86–87), who quotes Cic. inv. 1.27; also see Laird (2009, 202) who points that *inventio* is not mentioned in Cic. or. 2.62–64; already Potter 1999, 140.

35. Blockley (2001, 23–24) is a good example of this difficulty: while he concedes regarding Ammianus that "battle and siege descriptions, for instance, letters and speeches, characterizations, and historian's arguments were all dressed up with plausible generalities that we call 'fictions,'" he also protests that "to take the view that the writers, listeners and readers of ancient historiography understood that what was before them was, with the exception of a small and indeterminate core of fact, plausible fiction is to reduce all the discussion of the collection of evidence, and especially the importance accorded to autopsy, to the status of a sham or a topos."

36. On the antagonism between these two fields, see Lendon 2009.

37. Moles 1993, 120; see Pelling (1990) advocating for a category of true enough.

38. See discussion in Potter 1999, 12–18; Marincola 1997, 12–19 on tradition.

39. On the issue of reception, see Wheeldon 1989.

40. I do not find useful the opposition between "conscious fictional manipulation of history" and "conscious transformation of biographical reconstructions into hagiographic images" that Maggioni (2016, 75–76) proposes, nor the notion of "truthful fiction" introduced by Francis

(1998) about Philostratus's *Life of Apollonius of Tyana*. I suggest a shift of focus from speculation about authorial intentionality to an investigation of how the text operates.

41. On διήγησις/narratio, see Calboli Montefusco 1988, 33–77; Lausberg 1998 (1973²), 136–60. Rapp (1998) rightly emphasizes the role of διήγησις in hagiography and its dependence from ancient rhetoric.

42. Cic. inv. 1.27: narratio est rerum gestarum aut ut gestarum expositio; see Rhet. her. 1.3.4, Quint. inst. 4.2.31.

43. Cic. inv. 1.27: Ea quae in negotiorum expositione posita est tres habet partes: fabulam, historiam, argumentum. Fabula est in qua nec uerae nec ueri similes res continentur, cuiusmodi est: "Angues ingentes alites, iuncti iugo." Historia est gesta res, ab aetatis nostrae memoria remota; quod genus: "Appius indixit Karthaginiensibus bellum." Argumentum est ficta res, quae tamen fieri potuit. Huiusmodi apud Terentium: "Nam is postquam excessit ex ephebis." See Rhet her. 1.8.13. On the tripartite division, see Barwick 1928.

44. See Meijering 1987, 76–87.

45. The identification of this Asclepiades as the grammarian from Myrlea is rejected by Slater (1972, 331–32), who prefers an identification with the first-century BCE doctor, also from Bithynia, known as Asclepiades of Bithynia. On the treatise of Sextus, see Blank 1998. I leave aside the question of the origin of the tripartite division: see Hose (1996) for the argument that it is a Latin division imported into Greek theory against the theory of a Greek, Stoic origin, ascribed to Crates of Mallus by Mette (1936).

46. S.E.M. 1.252: Ἀσκληπιάδης δὲ ἐν τῷ Περὶ γραμματικῆς τρία φήσας εἶναι τὰ πρῶτα τῆς γραμματικῆς μέρη, τεχνικὸν ἱστορικὸν γραμματικόν, ὅπερ ἀμφοτέρων ἐφάπτεται, φημὶ δὲ τοῦ ἱστορικοῦ καὶ τοῦ τεχνικοῦ, τριχῇ ὑποδιαιρεῖται τὸ ἱστορικόν· τῆς γὰρ ἱστορίας τὴν μέν τινα ἀληθῆ εἶναί φησι τὴν δὲ ψευδῆ τὴν δὲ ὡς ἀληθῆ, καὶ ἀληθῆ μὲν τὴν πρακτικήν, ψευδῆ δὲ τὴν περὶ μύθους, ὡς ἀληθῆ δὲ τὴν περὶ πλάσματα οἷά ἐστιν ἡ κωμῳδία καὶ οἱ μῖμοι.

47. S.E.M. 1.253: τῆς δὲ ἀληθοῦς τρία πάλιν μέρη· ἡ μὲν γάρ ἐστι περὶ τὰ πρόσωπα θεῶν καὶ ἡρώων καὶ ἀνδρῶν ἐπιφανῶν, ἡ δὲ περὶ τοὺς τόπους καὶ χρόνους, ἡ δὲ περὶ τὰς πράξεις.

48. Meijering 1987, 78. Sextus Empiricus is therefore more of an exception when he defines it as "an exposition of true things which actually happened" (S.E.M. 1.263); on ἱστορία in Sextus, see Cassin 1990.

49. Meijering 1987, 73–75.

50. On πλάσμα/argumentum, see Rispoli 1988, 107–41.

51. Theo prog. 4–5; Hermog. prog. 1–2; Lib. prog. 1–2; Aphth. prog. 1–2; see Kennedy 2003 and Gibson 2008 on these texts.

52. See Nicolai 1992, 128–32.

53. See Sznajder 2013, 54–55.

54. Greek novels or romances would then be the only ancient texts to qualify as fiction, a position defended by several scholars; see Konstan 1998 for the nonreferentiality of ancient novels; Morgan 1993, ní Mheallaigh 2014 on make-believe.

55. Schaeffer 2010 (1999), 136–37.

56. See above.

57. The following paragraphs owe much to the insights of Lavocat 2016.

58. See Lavocat (2016, 21) on Paige (2011), who articulates a history of fiction around what he calls "the three 'regimes' of poetic invention—the Aristotelian regime [between Homer and 1670], the pseudofactual regime [between 1670 and the end of the eighteenth century], and the fictional regime."

59. See Schaeffer 2010 (1999), 121–39.

60. On hagiographical novels, see Oddo 2002, Selmeci Castioni 2012; on Euhemerus, see Whitmarsh 2013, 49–62.

61. Lavocat 2004a collects papers on sixteenth- and seventeenth-century works that pave the way for such a challenge (see Duprat 2004 and Lavocat 2004b); see Herman 2008, 8–9; also, Duprat 2009 and the contributions in the second part of Lavocat 2010, in particular Noille-Clauzade 2010.

62. Herman 2008, 11.

63. Most discussions of topoi in martyr narratives or hagiography more generally are centered on their historical value or lack thereof; see Pratsch 2003, 62–64, and 2005, 364–71.

64. Among the texts in Rebillard 2017: MCarp 5, 23, 24; MPion 8; ACypr 1; Pass. Fructuos. 2.2; AScil 9, 10, 13; see Lieu 2016, 223–43.

65. Cypr. ep. 12.2; see Salzman (1990, 45–47) on the *Depositio martyrum*, a list of Roman martyrs with location of their tombs, included in the *Codex-Calendar of 354*.

66. Bede, *Ecclesiastical History* 5.24.2.

67. For a redefinition of fiction that expands on Lavocat's definition and applies it to English literature from the late Middle Ages to the eighteenth century, see Fludernik 2018.

68. In the rest of this chapter, I focus on the earliest narratives that I have identified in Chapter 1; I review them in the order in which they respectively appear in BHG and BHL.

69. For a critical review of modern theories of the narrator, see Patron 2016 and 2015; for an introduction to the functions of the narrator, for instance, Fludernik 2009 (2006), 26–29; on "degrees of narratorhood," see Chatman 1978.

70. MPion 1.2: ἀποστολικὸς ἀνὴρ τῶν καθ'ἡμᾶς γενόμενος.

71. The phrase recalls MPol 16.2: ἐν τοῖς καθ'ἡμᾶς χρόνοις διδάσκαλος ἀποστολικὸς καὶ προφητικὸς γενόμενος. Hilhorst (1987, 453) suggests that the unusual τῶν καθ'ἡμᾶς is an equivalent of the ἐν τοῖς καθ'ἡμᾶς χρόνοις from MPol 16.2. The first-person plural could then be read as establishing the narrator as a contemporary of Pionius. Such an attempt, if any, would be lost on an audience who would know nothing about the narrator, and it seems to be in contradiction with the καὶ νῦν in the next sentence.

72. MPion 1.2; thus translated by Musurillo (1972, 137), Robert (1994, 33), Ronchey (1987, 155).

73. This scenario was established by Delehaye in 1921 (see 1966, 30–32) and has been accepted since without much discussion.

74. MPion 10.5 and 18.13.

75. Hilhorst 2010.

76. Hilhorst 2010, 107–8.

77. Hilhorst 2010, 108–11.

78. Hilhorst 2010, 111–12.

79. Eus. HE 4.15.47; Hilhorst 2010, 112–13.

80. Hilhorst 2010, 113–15 (quotation from p. 115).

81. Hilhorst 2010, 115.

82. A point also made by Hilhorst 2010, 108.

83. Hilhorst 2010, 114–15. Hilhorst notes that "it could be said of any martyr" (115), which should be seen as a recommendation rather than an objection.

84. See Rebillard 2017, 50; Hilhorst (2010, 114) glosses τὸ σύγγραμμα τοῦτο as "the example of his martyrdom as it is recorded in this writing."

85. Hilhorst (2010, 115–20) argues that the first two "we-passages" are of a *pluralis sociativus* type and need not be understood as traces of the original first-person narrative.

86. MPion 10.5: Ἄλλος δέ τις ἔλεγεν· Ἴδετε, ἀνθρωπάριον ὑπάγει ἐπιθῦσαι. Ἔλεγε δὲ τὸν σὺν ἡμῖν Ἀσκληπιάδην.

87. Contra Robert 1994, 73.

88. Because their goal is to refute the autobiography hypothesis, both Hilhorst (2010, 116–17) and Gibson (2001, 343 n8) miss the point.

89. MPion 18.13: Ἐλέγετο δὲ μετὰ ταῦτα ὅτι ἠξιώκει ὁ Εὔκτήμων ἀναγκασθῆναι ἡμᾶς, καὶ ὅτι αὐτὸς ἀπήνεγκε τὸ ὀίδιον εἰς τὸ Νεμεσεῖον, ὃ καὶ μετὰ φαγεῖν ἐξ αὐτοῦ ὀπτηθὲν ἠθέλησεν ὅλον εἰς τὸν οἶκον ἀποφέρειν.

90. MPion 22.2: Ἐσημάνθη δὲ αὐτοῦ ὁ στέφανος καὶ διὰ τοῦ σώματος. Μετὰ γὰρ τὸ κατασβεσθῆναι τὸ πῦρ τοιοῦτον αὐτὸν εἴδομεν οἱ παραγενόμενοι ὁποῖόν τε τὸ σῶμα ἀκμάζοντος ἀθλητοῦ κεκοσμημένου.

91. MPion 23: κατὰ δὲ ἡμᾶς βασιλεύοντος τοῦ κυρίου ἡμῶν Ἰησοῦ Χριστοῦ. It recalls the use of "we" in the preface.

92. See Campbell 2007, 46–47: such a "we" appears only in Polybius and only twice; see 67–85 on the "we" character in Acts.

93. See Saxer 1986, 111–25.

94. See Campbell 2007, 68: it "draws readers into the story by conveying a sense of familiarity and shared purpose."

95. MPion 5.1 and 3.

96. MPion 9.3–5: Εἶτα ἦλθεν ἐπὶ τὴν Σαβῖναν. Προειρήκει δὲ αὐτῇ ὁ Πιόνιος ὅτι Εἰπὸν σεαυτὴν Θεοδότην, πρὸς τὸ μὴ ἐμπεσεῖν αὐτὴν ἐκ τοῦ ὀνόματος πάλιν εἰς τὰς χεῖρας τῆς ἀνόμου Πολίττης τῆς γενομένης αὐτῆς δεσποίνης. Αὕτη γὰρ ἐπὶ καιρῶν Γορδιανοῦ βουλομένη μεταγαγεῖν τῆς πίστεως τὴν Σαβῖναν πεδήσασα ἐξώρισεν αὐτὴν ἐν ὄρεσιν, ὅπου εἶχε τὰ ἐπιτήδεια λάθρα παρὰ τῶν ἀδελφῶν. Μετὰ δὲ ταῦτα σπουδὴ ἐγένετο ὥστε αὐτὴν ἐλευθερωθῆναι καὶ Πολίττης καὶ τῶν δεσμῶν, καὶ ἦν τὰ πλεῖστα διατρίβουσα μετὰ τοῦ Πιονίου καὶ συνελήφθη ἐν τῷ διωγμῷ τούτῳ. Εἶπεν οὖν καὶ ταύτῃ ὁ Πολέμων· Τίς λέγῃ; Ἡ δὲ εἶπεν· Θεοδότη.

97. The δὲ after προειρήκει signals its beginning and the οὖν after εἶπεν marks its end and the return to the narration.

98. Fludernik 2009, 34–35; this is what Genette (1983 [1972], 35–47) calls anachrony.

99. See MPion 2.1.

100. MPion 18.13–14: Ἐλέγετο δὲ μετὰ ταῦτα ὅτι ἠξιώκει ὁ Εὔκτήμων ἀναγκασθῆναι ἡμᾶς, καὶ ὅτι αὐτὸς ἀπήνεγκε τὸ ὀίδιον εἰς τὸ Νεμεσεῖον, ὃ καὶ μετὰ φαγεῖν ἐξ αὐτοῦ ὀπτηθὲν ἠθέλησεν ὅλον εἰς τὸν οἶκον ἀποφέρειν. Ὡς ἐγκαταγέλαστον αὐτὸν διὰ τὴν ἐπιορκίαν γενέσθαι, ὅτι ὤμοσε τὴν τοῦ αὐτοκράτορος τύχην καὶ τὰς Νεμέσεις στεφανωθεὶς μὴ εἶναι Χριστιανὸς μηδὲ ὡς οἱ λοιποὶ παραλιπεῖν τι τῶν πρὸς τὴν ἐξάρνησιν.

101. MPion 19.1: Μετὰ δὲ ταῦτα ἦλθεν ὁ ἀνθύπατος εἰς τὴν Σμύρναν.

102. Fludernik 2009, 34–35.

103. MPion 19.1.

104. Gebhardt 1896, 169.

105. See already Schwartz 1905, 21.

106. MPion 20.7.

107. MPion 9.1.

108. See, in particular, Robert 1994, 106.

109. For a review, see Hartog 2013, 200–203.

110. The BHG adopts a different division: BHG 1556 is the Inscription of the Letter of the Smyrneans; BHG 1557 covers chapters 1–21 (the martyrdom); BHG 1558 is the first epilogue (22.1); BHG 1559 the second (22.2–3).

111. See White (1984) on the most salient features of ancient epistolography.

112. On authentication strategies for embedded letters, see Hodkinson and Rosenmeyer 2013, 15.

113. For the imperial period, see Hansen 2003 and ní Mheallaigh 2008; more generally Speyer 1970, Angelet et al. 1999.

114. Only four fragments of the Greek original of the *Ephemeris belli Troiani* are known (Gainsford 2012, 67); it was composed before Philostratus wrote the *Heroicus*, which can be dated to the 220s (Rusten and König 2014, 10, for the date of *Heroicus*; 30, for its knowledge of the *Ephemeris*). The prologue is preserved in one manuscript family of the Latin translation; see text in Eisenhut 1973, 2–3.

115. For the Greek papyri fragments of the *Incredible Things Beyond Thule* and an English translation, see Stephens-Winkler 1995, 130–57. Though some scholars reverse the relationship, Antonius Diogenes was likely known to Lucian; see Stephens and Winkler 1995, 118–19. The text of the letter is not preserved, but its content is summarized by Photius 111a41–111b18 (English translation in Stephens and Winkler 1995, 127–28).

116. Philostr. VA 1.3 (text and English translation in Jones 2005–6, 1.38–39).

117. Hansen 2003, 305–8.

118. Pionius, likely the martyr from Smyrna, would have been a local celebrity.

119. On the formal property of letters, the epistolarity, see Altman 1982; several contributions in Morello and Morrison 2007 apply the notion to ancient letters.

120. MPol 1.1: Ἐγράψαμεν ὑμῖν, ἀδελφοί, τὰ κατὰ τοὺς μαρτυρήσαντας καὶ τὸν μακάριον Πολύκαρπον, ὅστις ὥσπερ ἐπισφραγίσας τῇ μαρτυρίᾳ αὐτοῦ κατέπαυσεν τὸν διωγμόν.

121. The beginning of the narrative is marked in the text by a δὲ (5.1).

122. MPol 4: Διὰ τοῦτο οὖν, ἀδελφοί, οὐκ ἐπαινοῦμεν τοὺς προσιόντας ἑαυτοῖς, ἐπειδὴ οὐχ οὕτως διδάσκει τὸ εὐαγγέλιον.

123. MPol 20.1: Ὑμεῖς μὲν οὖν ἠξιώσατε διὰ πλειόνων δηλωθῆναι ὑμῖν τὰ γενόμενα, ἡμεῖς δὲ κατὰ τὸ παρὸν ἐπὶ κεφαλαίῳ μεμηνύκαμεν διὰ τοῦ ἀδελφοῦ ἡμῶν Μαρκίωνος. Μαθόντες οὖν ταῦτα καὶ τοῖς ἐπέκεινα ἀδελφοῖς τὴν ἐπιστολὴν διαπέμψασθε ἵνα καὶ ἐκεῖνοι δοξάζωσιν τὸν κύριον τὸν ἐκλογὰς ποιοῦντα ἀπὸ τῶν ἰδίων δούλων.

124. The narrative starts in 5.1 (see above about the δὲ) and ends at 18.3 as the comment in 19.1 indicates: "Such are the events concerning the blessed Polycarp."

125. MPol 9.1.

126. MPol 15.1.

127. MPol 15.1–2.

128. MPol 17.1.

129. MPol 18.2.

130. Buschmann (1994, 94) notes: "Zwischen MartPol 1.1a und 19.1a finden sich aber keine Briefelemente." He is, however, too concerned with defending the authenticity of the text to make much of this observation.

131. Jane McLarty (2013) suggests that the letter creates a community between sender and receiver, and she concludes that "martyrdom letters are family letters" (380). She fails, however, to note that the few elements she picks up are very sparse.

132. MPol 13.2: ἐπειρᾶτο καὶ ὑπολύειν ἑαυτόν, μὴ πρότερον τοῦτο ποιῶν διὰ τὸ ἀεὶ ἕκαστον τῶν πιστῶν σπουδάζειν ὅστις τάχιον τοῦ χρωτὸς αὐτοῦ ἅψηται· ἐν παντὶ γὰρ ἀγαθῆς ἕνεκεν πολιτείας καὶ πρὸ τῆς μαρτυρίας ἐκεκόσμητο.

133. Unlike in contemporary texts such as the letter attributed to Phlegon of Tralles or ps-Aeschines *Epistle 10*; see respectively Morgan 2013 and Hodkinson 2013.

134. Hodkinson and Rosenmeyer 2013, 15.

135. See Hodkinson and Rosenmeyer 2013, 14–15.

136. See presentation of the dossier in Rebillard 2017, 145, and Löhr 1989.

137. Eus. HE 5.1.4, 5.1.36, 5.1.62.

138. Eus. HE 5. pref. 2.

139. As does Cobb 2017, 40–46.

140. Lazzati 1956, 5–12.

141. PMar 1.1–2: Quotiens aliquid beatissimi martyres dei omnipotentis et Christi eius festinantes ad promissa regna caelorum carissimis suis uerecundius mandant, memores humilitatis quae semper in fide solet facere maiores, quantum modestius petiuerunt, tanto efficacius impetrauerunt. Et nobis quoque hoc praedicandae gloriae suae munus Dei testes nobilissimi reliquerunt, Marianum dico, ex dilectissimis fratribus nostris, et Iacobum, quos mihi scitis praeter communem sacramenti religionem, uitae etiam societate et domesticis affectibus inhaesisse.

142. PMar 1.4: Nec inmerito id obsecuturo mihi fiducia familiaris iniunxit; quis enim dubitet quae nobis in pace uitae communitas fuerit, quando nos indiuidua dilectione uiuentes unum tempus persecutionis inuenerit?

143. Amat 1999, 303–5; see Soler (2014) on his engagement with Apuleius and possibly Virgil, in addition to Scriptures and Cyprian.

144. PMar 9.5.

145. PMar 11.3–6.

146. PMar 11.1–2. The narrative resumes its order in PMar 11.3: Is ergo Agapius.

147. PMar 12.1.

148. PMar 12.4–6: Tunc oculis sub ictu ferri de more uelatis, nullae tamen aciem liberae mentis clausere tenebrae; sed largus atque inaestimabilis splendor inmensae lucis effulsit. Nam et plerique cum proximis et assistentibus sibi fratribus, quamuis carnaliter in uisum acies non pateret, uidere se tamen mira quaedam loquebantur, quod sibi apparerent equi desuper niueo colore candentes, quibus ueherentur iuuenes candidati. Nec defuere ex eodem martyrum numero qui collegarum relationem attestarentur auribus et ex audito equorum fremitu ac sono recognoscerent. The allusion is to Rev. 19:11–16.

149. See Fludernik 2009, 30–31, on the notion of person.

150. Soler 2014.

151. Harnack 1913.

152. Reitzenstein 1913.

153. Schmidt 2001.

154. See Deléani (1995) for a soft narratological analysis of the account of the death of Cyprian, and Lomiento (1968) for a careful analysis of how Scripture is the organizational principle of Pontius's *narratio*.

155. Hier. uir. ill. 68: Pontius, diaconus Cypriani, usque ad diem passionis eius cum ipso exilium sustinens, egregium uolumen Vitae et passionis Cypriani reliquit.

156. Pellegrino 1955, 59; the *Cheltenham List* is also known as *Canon Mommsenianus* or *Indiculum* [*Veteris et Novi Testamenti*]; VCypr is at the end of the list under no. 51.

157. See references above.

158. VCypr 1.2; see Chapter 1 for text and discussion.

159. VCypr 1.1–2, where *conscribere* is used three times within twelve lines; VCypr 10.1: Multa alia et quidem magna, quae temperandi uoluminis ratio non patitur prolixo onere sermonis iterari; see Pellegrino 1955, 86. The use of both *uolumen* and *sermo* shows that *sermo* does not imply an oral discourse; see also 1.1 and 1.3 in close proximity to *conscribere*.

160. VCypr 1.4–6: uos … desideratis audire … desiderium uestrum … uos nos auribus fatigatis; VCypr 19.4: uobis tamen et simpliciter confitendum est quod et uos scitis. For Bastiaensen (1975, 250), the references to a speech are merely stylistic.

161. VCypr 7.13: Vultis scire secessum illum non fuisse formidinem?

162. See Cypr. ep. 8 and Sage 1975, 192–96.

163. VCypr 2.3: si quibus eius interfui, si qua de antiquioribus comperi, dicam.

164. VCypr 12.3: nam et me inter domesticos comites dignatio caritatis eius elegerat exulem uoluntarium.

165. VCypr 15.5: Receptum eum tamen et in domo principis constitutum una nocte continuit custodia delicata, ita ut conuiuae eius et cari in contubernio ex more fuerimus.

166. See Deléani 1995, 468–69.

167. VCypr 2.1: Vnde igitur incipiam? Vnde exordium bonorum eius adgrediar, nisi a principio fidei et natiuitate caelesti?

168. VCypr 5.1: Longum est ire per singula; enumerare cuncta eius onerosum est. Ad probationem bonorum operum solum hoc arbitror satis esse, quod …

169. See Montgomery 1996, 209–10 and n52 with reference to rhetoric handbooks.

170. VCypr 11.7: Nolo nunc describere loci gratiam et deliciarum omnium paraturam interim transeo. The description is given in VCypr 12.1.

171. VCypr 11.7: Fingamus locum illum situ sordidum, squalidum uisu, …

172. VCypr 11.7: posset licet talis locus habere nomen exilii, quo Cyprianus, sacerdos Dei, uenerat?

173. VCypr 5.6: Inuitus dico, sed dicam necesse est: quidam illi restiterunt, ut et uinceret.

174. VCypr 8.1: Puto denique etiamnunc aliqua de dilationis utilitate dicenda, tametsi iamdudum pauca perstrinximus. Dum enim quae uidentur postmodum subsecuta satiamus, sequitur ut probemus secessum illum non hominis pusillitate conceptum, sed, sicuti est uere, fuisse diuinum.

175. VCypr 15.1: hortos, inquam, quos inter initia fidei suae uenditos et de Dei indulgentia restitutos pro certo iterum in usu pauperum uendidisset, nisi inuidiam de persecutione uitaret.

176. VCypr 11.1: et quid sacerdos Dei proconsule interrogante responderit, sunt acta quae referant.

177. PLuc 1.1: Et nobis est apud uos certamen, dilectissimi fratres; nihil aliud agendum Dei seruis et Christo eius dicatis quam multitudinem fratrum cogitare. Qua ui, qua ratione hic amor, hoc officium ad has nos inpulit litteras ut fratribus post futuris et magnificentiae Dei fidele testimonium et laboris ad tolerantiam nostri per dominum memoriam relinqueremus.

178. PLuc 11.7: Optamus uos bene ualere.

179. PLuc 7.1, 7.7, 10.1.

180. PLuc 12.1: Haec omnes de carcere simul scripserant. Sed quia necesse erat omnem actum martyrum beatorum pleno sermone conplecti, quia et ipsi de se per modestiam minus dixerant et Flauianus quoque priuatim hoc nobis munus iniunxit ut quicquid litteris eorum defuit adderemus, necessario reliqua subiunximus.

181. PLuc 21.1–2: Exinde iam gaudens quia post sententiam datam, scilicet passionis suae certior, etiam iocundo conloquio fruebatur, sic effectum est ut iuberet haec scribi et ad propria uerba coniungi. Addi quoque ostensiones suas uoluit, quarum pars ad moram bidui pertineret.

182. PLuc 15.4: Et perfectum est sub oculis nostris quod dominus in euangelio suo repromisit, ut qui tota fide peteret, quicquid peteret inpetraret. Nam post biduum, secundum quod postulatum fuerat, Flauianus quoque productus gloriam suam passione perfecit.

183. PLuc 19.1: Illic nos in latere eius constituti eramus, iuncti penitus et haerentes, ita ut manus manibus teneremus, exhibentes martyri honorem et contubernio caritatem.

184. PLuc 15.5: Quoniam tamen, ut supra dixi, etiam ipse mandauit ut bidui moram, memorati causam.

185. PLuc 21.12: Nam ut omittam carceris abstinentiam singularem.

186. PLuc 22.1: ad illa uenio quod.

187. PLuc 17.4: Dicam quod sentio: dies ille post biduum tertius non quasi passionis sed quasi resurrectionis dies sustinebatur.

188. PLuc 21.5: O uerba martyris martyrem cohortantis! See also PLuc 14.9, 16.4, 18.4, 23.7.

189. Amat (1996, 77–78) offers stylistic reasons for the possibility that the narrative of the execution is the work of a narrator distinct from the one responsible for the exordium and the peroration. Nothing supports the hypothesis from a narratological point of view. Heffernan (2012, 9) believes that the redactor (R) is responsible for all the sections that are not written by Perpetua and Saturus.

190. PPerp 2.3: Haec ordinem totum martyrii sui iam hinc ipsa narrauit sicut conscriptum manu sua et suo sensu reliquit.

191. PPerp 11.1: Sed et Saturus benedictus hanc uisionem suam edidit, quam ipse conscripsit.

192. PPerp 14.1: Hae uisiones insigniores ipsorum martyrum beatissimorum Saturi et Perpetuae, quas ipsi conscripserunt.

193. PPerp 1.6: Et nos itaque quod audiuimus et contrectauimus, annuntiamus et uobis, fratres et filioli, uti et uos qui interfuistis rememoremini gloriae Domini, et qui nunc cognoscitis per auditum communionem habeatis cum sanctis martyribus, et per illos cum Domino nostro Iesu Christo, cui est claritas et honor in saecula saeculorum.

194. I quote a translation of the text as it appears in Tertullian (anim. 17; adv. Prax. 15): quod uidimus, quod audiuimus, oculis nostris uidimus, et manus nostrae contrectauerunt.

195. Bastiaensen 1987d, 414. Some editors have added et uidimus to the text of the manuscripts on the basis of the Greek text; see Amat 1996, 192.

196. Boeft 2012, 174.

197. PPerp 16.1: Quoniam ergo permisit et permittendo uoluit Spiritus Sanctus ordinem ipsius muneris conscribi, etsi indigni ad supplementum tantae gloriae describendae, tamen quasi mandatum sanctissimae Perpetuae, immo fideicommissum eius exequimur, unum adicientes documentum de ipsius constantia et animi sublimitate.

198. PPerp 10.15: Hoc usque in pridie muneris egi; ipsius autem muneris actum, si quis uoluerit, scribat.

199. On "fictionalization," see De Temmerman 2016, 12–17; on "stylization," see Fontaine 1967, 1.97–134, and Uytfanghe 1993, 148.

200. De Temmerman 2016, 14.

201. MPion 19–20.

202. MPol 22.

203. PLuc 12.1.

204. PPerp 3–10 and 11–13.

205. See Chapter 2.

206. See Barnes 2016, 63–64.

207. For a recent example, see Gold 2018, 15–18.

208. Hartog (2013, 170–71) is inconclusive.

209. I borrow the expression from Dominick La Capra's famous critique of the blind confidence of historians in the documentary model (1985, 19).

210. Cameron 2016, 43.

211. See the description of the limited epistolary framework above.

212. See Marincola 1997, 104–5.

213. See Momigliano 1963, 89–91 (= 1977, 115–17).

214. DeVore 2013, 242–52; see Carotenuto (2001) for the practice among Jewish and Christian apologists.

215. On the use of documents in ancient historiography, see the many contributions in Biraschi 2003; Spielberg 2015 for Roman historiography; Wiater (2018, 152) for a compelling narratological analysis of the use of the Roman-Carthaginian treaties by Polybius.

216. MPion 19–20.

217. DeVore 2013, 246.

218. DeVore 2013, 243.

219. Eus. EH 7.13 for the edict of Gallienus.

220. DeVore 2013, 246–49.

221. Eus. EH 3.33; see DeVore 2013, 248–49, on this example.

222. DeVore 2013, 249–52; see DeVore 2014.

223. See above about MPol.

224. Hansen 2003, 302.

225. Ní Mheallaigh 2008, 404.

226. On Dictys, see Gainsford (2012) for the evidence for its reception and Pervo (2018) on how it blurs the boundaries between history and fiction; on Hierocles and Eusebius, see Hägg 1992.

227. Stott (2005, 112–14) offers a critique of the arbitrary distinction established by Speyer (1970) (and many scholars who follow his lead) between texts that he claims use the device of the "book-find report" referentially and those that he says use it rhetorically; see Stott 2008, 77–122. Also, Zadorojnyi (2013) on how imperial prose fiction and nonfiction narrativize inscriptions and destabilize their documentary character: epigraphy in a narrative is never just a document; the narrator always plays with readerly expectations about the reported text.

228. Agamben 1999 (1998), 32.

229. Levi 1996 (1947); Arendt 1963; Derrida 2000a and 2000b.

230. On this text, see Vessey 2010, especially 308–12; also, Vessey 2005, 173–75. I thank Mark Vessey for having pointed me toward this text of Derrida (1998).

231. Derrida 2000b, 27; the reference to passion comes from the title of the conference at which Derrida gave a first version of his essay "Passions de la littérature."

232. Derrida 2000b, 27–28. The citation of Augustine is to Conf. 10.1.1; see Vessey 2010, 309 and n60.

233. See Derrida 2000b, 42.

234. As Vessey (2010, 308) writes: "The body of the lecture is a line-by-line exegesis of Blanchot's recit, exposing the impossibility of ever calculating the respective parts of 'fiction' and 'testimony' in a text of this ('literary') kind or indeed, more tellingly, in any act of witness."

235. Derrida 2000b, 43; see Heinich 1998 and Baron 2005 for an articulation of fiction and testimony about the Shoah.

236. VCypr 19.3: Quid hoc loco faciam? Inter gaudium passionis et remanendi dolorem in partes diuisus animus, et angustum nimis pectus adfectus duplices onerant. Dolebo quod non comes fuerim? Sed illius uictoria triumphanda est. De uictoria triumphabo? Sed doleo quod comes non sim. Verum uobis tamen et simpliciter confitendum est, quod et uos scitis, in hac me fuisse sententia: multum ac nimis multum de gloria eius exsulto, plus tamen doleo quod remansi.

237. PMar 4.6; see above.
238. I borrow the phrase from ní Mheallaigh 2008, 422.
239. See Agamben 1999 (1998), 34.

## CONCLUSION

1. I use this uncommon title to make the point that the letter quoted by Eusebius is part of a larger document; see above.
2. See the important deconstruction of the notion in Breed 2014, 52–74.
3. Rebillard 2012, 35–43.
4. Delehaye 1966, 171–226.
5. Delehaye 1966, 224.

## APPENDIX A

I modify Teske's translation where my interpretation differs and where I follow a different Latin text; see Teske 2005, 334-35. I adopt the Latin text of Lanéry 2008, 545-46.

1. The absence of a *sed etiam* corresponding to *non solum* clearly indicates a lacuna at the end of the paragraph. Most translators have interpreted *germaniorem affectum* as referring to a feeling of authenticity. Yves-Marie Duval, however, pointed to an interesting parallel with Aug. c. Faust. 20.21 in which *affectus* refers to the feeling for the martyrs aroused by their tombs; see Duval 1987, 576. In that case *germanior affectus* would here refer to a stronger feeling of brotherhood with the martyrs.
2. For the meaning of *senex* as a term of affection rather than biographical detail, see Lanéry 2008, 19. I also follow her interpretation for *ut enim mouerer* being a hypothetical conditional; Augustine did not form the project of writing martyr accounts. Paulinus, after a discussion in which Augustine expressed his admiration for Ambrose's texts, follows up with a letter inviting him to write his own.
3. The *non proposui* of the manuscripts is a clear mistake. The reading *non postposui* is suggested by Lanéry 2008, 20.

## APPENDIX B

1. Aubé 1881a, 21.
2. Robinson 1891, 109.
3. Delehaye 1966, 278.
4. The entire text of the Greek version (Text 6) should be in bold. In order to facilitate the comparison, however, I only marked in bold the differences that do not pertain to the difference of language.
5. Thus, the manuscripts for *secretario* (?).
6. For Antonino, i.e., Caracalla.
7. ὀρωμένων in the manuscript.

# BIBLIOGRAPHY

Agamben, Giorgio. 1998. *Quel che resta di Auschwitz: L'archivio e il testimone.* Homo sacer 3. Turin: Bollati Boringhieri.

———. 1999. *Remnants of Auschwitz: The Witness and the Archive.* New York: Zone Books.

Altman, Janet G. 1982. *Epistolarity: Approaches to a Form.* Columbus: Ohio State University Press.

Amat, Jacqueline. 1985. *Songes et visions: L'au-delà dans la littérature latine tardive.* Collection des études augustiniennes. Série Antiquité 109. Paris: Institut des études augustiniennes.

———, ed. 1996. *Passion de Perpétue et de Félicité; suivi des Actes.* Sources chrétiennes 417. Paris: Éditions du Cerf.

———. 1999. "La langue des Passions africaines du IIIe siècle." In *Latin vulgaire-latin tardif. 5, Actes du Ve colloque international sur le latin vulgaire et tardif, Heidelberg, 5-8 septembre 1997,* edited by Hubert Petersmann and Rudolf Kettermann, 301–7. Bibliothek der klassischen Altertumswissenschaften. Neue Folge. 2. Reihe 105. Heidelberg: Winter.

Amélineau, Émile. 1888. "Les Actes Coptes du martyre de St. Polycarp." *Proceedings of the Society of Biblical Archaeology* 10: 391–417.

Ameling, Walter. 2008. "The Christian Lapsi in Smyrna, 250 A.D. (Martyrium Pionii 12–14)." *Vigiliae Christianae* 62 (2): 133–60.

Anagnostou-Canas, Barbara. 2000. "La documentation judiciaire pénale dans l'Égypte romaine." *Mélanges de l'École française de Rome. Antiquité* 112 (2): 735–79.

Ando, Clifford C. 2000. *Imperial Ideology and Provincial Loyalty in the Roman Empire.* Classics and Contemporary Thought. Berkeley: University of California Press.

Angelet, Christian, Jan Herman, Fernand Hallyn, and Kris Peeters, eds. 1999. *Le topos du manuscrit trouvé: Actes du colloque international, Louvain-Gand, 22–23-24 mai 1997.* Bibliothèque de l'information grammaticale 40. Louvain: Peeters.

Anonymous. 1889. "*Passio martyrum Scillitanorum*: Ex cod. Carnotensi 190(a), fol. 257v–258r." *Annalecta Bollandiana* 8: 5–8.

———. 1897. "De *Passione martyrum Scillitanorum* in codice Bruxellensi 98–100." *Annalecta Bollandiana* 16: 64–65.

Anselmetto, Claudio. 1990. "Rivelazione privata e tradizione nell'epistolario di Cipriano." *Augustinianum* 30 (2): 279–312.

Arendt, Hannah. 1963. *Eichmann in Jerusalem: A Report on the Banality of Evil.* New York: Viking Press.

Aubé, Benjamin. 1881a. *Étude sur un nouveau texte des Actes des martyrs Scillitains.* Paris: Didot.

———. 1881b. *Les chrétiens dans l'Empire romain, de la fin des Antonins au milieu du IIIe siècle (180–249).* Paris: Didier.

————. 1882. *Un texte inédit d'actes de martyrs du IIIe siècle*. Paris: Didier.

Bailey, Lisa Kaaren. 2010. *Christianity's Quiet Success: The Eusebius Gallicanus Sermon Collection and the Power of the Church in Late Antique Gaul*. Notre Dame, IN: University of Notre Dame Press.

Bale, Alan. 2015. *Genre and Narrative Coherence in the Acts of the Apostles*. Library of New Testament Studies 514. New York: Bloomsbury.

Barnes, Timothy D. 1967. "A Note on Polycarp." *Journal of Theological Studies* 18 (2): 433–37.

————. 1968. "Pre-Decian Acta Martyrum." *Journal of Theological Studies* 19 (2): 509–31.

————. 2016. *Early Christian Hagiography and Roman History*. 2nd ed. Tria Corda 5. Tübingen: Mohr Siebeck.

Baron, Christine. 2005. "Témoignage et dispositif fictionnel." In *Littérature, fiction, témoignage, vérité*, edited by Jean Bessière and Judit Maár, 81–93. Cahiers de la nouvelle Europe 3. Paris: Centre interuniversitaire d'études hongroises.

Barwick, Karl. 1928. "Die Gliederung der Narratio in der rhetorischen Theorie und ihre Bedeutung für die Geschichte des antiken Romans." *Hermes* 63 (2): 261–87.

Bass, Alden. 2013. "The Passion of Cyprian in the So-Called 'Donatist Dossier' of Würzburg M. p. Th. f. 33." In *The Use of Textual Criticism for the Interpretation of Patristic Texts*, edited by Kenneth Steinhauser and Scott Dermer, 209–31. Lewiston: Mellen Press.

Bastiaensen, Antoon A. R. 1975. "Commento." In *Vite dei Santi dal III al VI secolo. 3, Vita di Cipriano, Vita di Ambrogio, Vita di Agostino*, edited by Christine Mohrmann, 243–451. Milan: Mondadori.

————. 1987a. "Introduzione." In *Atti e passioni dei martiri*, edited by Antoon A. R. Bastiaensen, ix-xlix. Milan: Mondadori.

————. 1987b. "*Acta Cypriani*: Nota al testo." In *Atti e passioni dei martiri*, edited by Antoon A. R. Bastiaensen, 197–205. Milan: Mondadori.

————. 1987c. "*Acta Maximiliani*: Testo critico." In *Atti e passioni dei martiri*, edited by Antoon A. R. Bastiaensen, 238–44. Milan: Mondadori.

————. 1987d. "Commento alla *Passio Perpetuae et Felicitatis*." In *Atti e passioni dei martiri*, edited by Antoon A. R. Bastiaensen, 412–52. Milan: Mondadori.

Bauman, R. A. 1967. "Tertullian and the Crime of Sacrilegium." *Journal of Religious History* 4: 175–83.

Bausi, Alessandro. 2015. "Dalla documentazione papiracea (P.Bodm. XX e P.Chester Beatty XV) alle raccolte agiografiche: La lunga storia degli Acta Phileae in versione etiopica." *Adamantius* 21: 155–70.

Becker, Carl. 1967. *Der Octavius des Minucius Felix: Heidnische Philosophie und frühchristliche Apologetik*. Sitzungsberichte. Bayerische Akademie der Wissenschaften, 1967. 2. Munich: Beck.

Bekiari, Chryssoula, Martin Doerr, Patrick Le Bœuf, and Pat Riva. 2016. "Definition of FRBROO: A Conceptual Model for Bibliographic Information in Object-Oriented Formalism." https://www.ifla.org/files/assets/cataloguing/FRBRoo/frbroo_v_2.4.pdf.

Bickermann, E. 1933. "Testificatio Actorum: Eine Untersuchung über antike Niederschriften 'zu Protokoll.'" *Aegyptus* 13 (3/4): 333–55.

Bieler, Ludwig. 1958. "The Grammarian's Craft." *Folia* 10 (2): 3–42.

Biraschi, Anna Maria, ed. 2003. *L'uso dei documenti nella storiografia antica*. Incontri perugini di storia della storiografia antica e sul mondo antico 12. Naples: Ed. Scientifiche Italiane.

Birley, Anthony R. 1992. "Persecutors and Martyrs in Tertullian's Africa." *Bulletin of the Institute of Archaeology of the University of London* 29: 37–68.

Bisbee, Gary A. 1983. "The Acts of Justin Martyr: A Form-Critical Study." *Second Century* 3: 129–57.

———. 1988. *Pre-Decian Acts of Martyrs and "Commentarii."* Harvard Dissertations in Religion 22. Philadelphia: Fortress Press.

Blank, David L., ed. 1998. *Against the Grammarians = (Adversus Mathematicos. I) / Sextus Empiricus.* Clarendon Later Ancient Philosophers. Oxford: Clarendon Press.

Blockley, Roger C. 2001. "Ammianus and Cicero on Truth in Historiography." *Ancient History Bulletin* 15 (1–2): 14–24.

Blumell, Lincoln H., and Thomas A. Wayment, eds. 2015. *Christian Oxyrhynchus: Texts, Documents, and Sources.* Waco: Baylor University Press.

Bobertz, Charles A. 1988. "Cyprian of Carthage as Patron: A Social Historical Study of the Role of Bishop in the Ancient Christian Community of North Africa." Ph.D. diss., Yale University.

Boeft, Jan den. 2012. "The Editor's Prime Objective: 'Haec in Aedificationem Ecclesiae Legere.'" In *Perpetua's Passions: Multidisciplinary Approaches to the Passio Perpetuae et Felicitatis,* edited by Jan Bremmer and Marco Formisano, 169–79. Oxford: Oxford University Press.

Boesch Gajano, Sofia. 2009. "Dalle raccolte di vite di Santi agli Acta Sanctorum: Persistenze e trasformazioni fra umanesimo e controriforma." In *De Rosweyde aux Acta Sanctorum: La recherche hagiographique des Bollandistes à travers quatre siècles,* edited by Robert Godding, Bernard Joassart, Xavier Lequeux, and François De Vriendt, 5–34. Subsidia Hagiographica 88. Brussels: Société des Bollandistes.

Bouhot, Jean-Paul. 1983. Review of *La Passion des saints Lucius et Montanus,* by François Dolbeau. *Revue des études augustiniennes* 1984 (2): 363–64.

Bowersock, Glen W. 1994. *Fiction as History: From Nero to Julian.* Sather Classical Lectures 58. Berkeley: University of California Press.

———. 1995. *Martyrdom and Rome.* The Wiles Lectures given at the Queen's University of Belfast. Cambridge: Cambridge University Press.

Boyarin, Daniel. 1999. *Dying for God: Martyrdom and the Making of Christianity and Judaism.* Figurae. Stanford: Stanford University Press.

Brakke, David. 2016. "Early Christian Lies and the Lying Liars Who Wrote Them: Bart Ehrman's Forgery and Counterforgery." *Journal of Religion* 96 (3): 378–90.

Breed, Brennan W. 2014. *Nomadic Text: A Theory of Biblical Reception History.* Indiana Studies in Biblical Literature. Bloomington: Indiana University Press.

Bremmer, Jan. 2012. "Felicitas: The Martyrdom of a Young African Woman." In *Perpetua's Passions: Multidisciplinary Approaches to the Passio Perpetuae et Felicitatis,* edited by Jan Bremmer and Marco Formisano, 35–53. Oxford: Oxford University Press.

———. 2016. "Arthur Darby Nock's Conversion (1933): A Balance." In *Zwischen Ereignis und Erzählung: Konversion als Medium,* edited by Julia Weitbrecht, Werner Röcke, and Ruth von Bernuth, 9–30. Transformationen der Antike 39. Berlin: de Gruyter.

Brent, Allen. 2010. *Cyprian and Roman Carthage.* Cambridge: Cambridge University Press.

Brown, Peter. 2003. "Between Imitation and Admiration: Augustine and the Cult of the Saints in Late Antiquity and the Early Middle Ages." In *Munera amicitiae: Studi di storia e cultura sulla tarda antichità offerti a Salvatore Pricoco,* edited by Rossana Barcellona and Teresa Sardella, 51–74. Soveria Mannelli: Rubbettino.

Bryant, John. 2002. *The Fluid Text: A Theory of Revision and Editing for Book and Screen.* Ann Arbor: University of Michigan Press.

———. 2007. "Witness and Access: The Uses of the Fluid Text." *Textual Cultures: Texts, Contexts, Interpretation* 2 (1): 16–42.

Buell, Denise Kimber. 2009. "God's Own People: Specters of Race, Ethnicity, and Gender in Early Christian Studies." In *Prejudice and Christian Beginnings: Investigating Race, Gender, and Ethnicity in Early Christian Studies*, edited by Laura Salah Nasrallah and Elisabeth Schüssler Fiorenza, 159–90. Minneapolis: Fortress Press.

Burkhalter, Fabienne. 1990. "Archives locales et archives centrales en Égypte romaine." *Chiron* 20: 191–216.

Burkitt, F. C. 1909. "The Oldest MS of St. Justin's Martyrdom." *Journal of Theological Studies* 11 (41): 61–66.

Burns, J. Patout. 2002. *Cyprian the Bishop.* London: Routledge.

Burton, G. P. 1975. "Proconsuls, Assizes and the Administration of Justice Under the Empire." *Journal of Roman Studies* 65: 92–106.

Buschmann, Gerd. 1994. *Martyrium Polycarpi: Eine formkritische Studie: Ein Beitrag zur Frage nach der Entstehung der Gattung Märtyrerakte.* Beihefte zur Zeitschrift für die neutestamentliche Wissenschaft und die Kunde der älteren Kirche 70. Berlin: de Gruyter.

———. 1998. *Das Martyrium des Polykarp.* Kommentar zu den apostolischen Vätern 6. Göttingen: Vandenhoeck & Ruprecht.

Calboli Montefusco, Lucia. 1988. *Exordium, narratio, epilogus: Studi sulla teoria retorica greca e romana delle parti del discorso.* Bologna: CLUEB.

Caltabiano, Matilde. 1998. "Ambrogio, Agostino e gli scritti sui martiri." In *Nec timeo mori: Atti del congresso internazionale di studi ambrosiani nel XVI centenario della morte di sant'Ambrogio (Milano, 4–11 aprile 1997)*, edited by Luigi Franco Pizzolato and Marco Rizzi, 585–93. Studia patristica Mediolanensia 21. Milan: Vita e pensiero.

Cameron, Averil. 2016. *Christian Literature and Christian History.* Hans-Lietzmann-Vorlesungen 15. Berlin: de Gruyter.

Campbell, William S. 2007. *The "We" Passages in the Acts of the Apostles: The Narrator as Narrative Character.* Studies in Biblical Literature 14. Atlanta, GA: Society of Biblical Literature.

Carotenuto, Erica. 2001. *Tradizione e innovazione nella Historia Ecclesiastica di Eusebio di Cesarea.* Istituto Italiano per gli Studi Storici 46. Bologna: Il Mulino.

Cassin, Barbara. 1990. "L'histoire chez Sextus Empiricus." In *Le scepticisme antique: Perspectives historiques et systématiques: Actes du Colloque international sur le scepticisme antique, Université de Lausanne, 1–3 juin 1988*, edited by André-Jean Voelke, 123–38. Cahiers de la Revue de théologie et de philosophie 15. Lausanne: Revue de théologie et de philosophie.

Castelli, Elizabeth A. 2004. *Martyrdom and Memory: Early Christian Culture Making.* Gender, Theory, and Religion. New York: Columbia University Press.

Cavallin, Samuel. 1945. "Saint Genès le notaire." *Eranos* 43: 150–75.

———, ed. 1952. *Vitae Sanctorum Honorati et Hilarii.* Skrifter utgivna av Vetenskapssocieteten i Lund 40. Lund: Gleerup.

Cavallotto, Stefano. 2001. "Heiligentexte, devozione ai santi e riforma liturgica nelle Chiese protestanti (1522–1552)." *Hagiographica* 8: 233–56.

———. 2009. *Santi nella Riforma: Da Erasmo a Lutero.* Sacro/Santo, NS 12. Rome: Viella.

Cerquiglini, Bernard. 1989. *Éloge de la variante: Histoire critique de la philologie.* Des travaux. Paris: Éditions du Seuil.

———. 1999. *In Praise of the Variant: A Critical History of Philology.* Translated by Betsy Wing. Parallax. Baltimore: Johns Hopkins University Press.

Chatman, Seymour B. 1978. *Story and Discourse: Narrative Structure in Fiction and Film*. Ithaca, NY: Cornell University Press.

Chiesa, Paolo. 1996. "Un testo agiografico africano ad Aquileia: Gli Acta di Gallonio e dei martiri di Timida Regia." *Analecta Bollandiana* 114: 241–68.

———. 1998. "Pellegrino martire in urbe Bolitana e Pellegrino di Ancona: Un'altra agiografia africana ad Aquileia?" *Analecta Bollandiana* 116 (1–2): 25–56.

Clarke, Graeme W., ed. 1974. *The Octavius / Marcus Minucius Felix*. Ancient Christian Writers 39. New York: Newman Press.

Cobb, L. Stephanie. 2017. *Divine Deliverance: Pain and Painlessness in Christian Martyr Texts*. Berkeley: University of California Press.

Cockle, W. E. H. 1984. "State Archives in Graeco-Roman Egypt from 30 BC to the Reign of Septimius Severus." *Journal of Egyptian Archaeology* 70: 106–22.

Coles, Revel A. 1966. *Reports of Proceedings in Papyri*. Papyrologica Bruxellensia 4. Brussels: Fondation Égyptologique Reine Élisabeth.

Collins, David J. 2008. *Reforming Saints: Saint's Lives and Their Authors in Germany, 1470–1530*. Oxford: Oxford University Press.

Conticello, Carmelo Giuseppe. 2011. "Le projet d'un répertoire des traductions de textes chrétiens du latin au grec (IIIe–XVe siècle): Quelques exemples." In *Eukarpa: Études sur la Bible et ses exégètes*, edited by Mireille Loubet and Didier Pralon. Paris: Éditions du Cerf.

Corke-Webster, James. 2017a. "The Early Reception of Pliny the Younger in Tertullian of Carthage and Eusebius of Caesarea." *Classical Quarterly* 67 (1): 247–62.

———. 2017b. "Trouble in Pontus: The Pliny–Trajan Correspondence on the Christians Reconsidered." *TAPA* 147 (2): 371–411.

Corsaro, Francesco. 1955. "Note sugli Acta martyrum Scillitanorum." *Nuovo Didaskaleion* 6: 5–51.

———. 1957. "Studi sui documenti agiografici intorno al martirio di S. Euplo." *Orpheus* 4: 33–62.

D'Aiuto, Francesco. 2018. "Il Menologio Imperiale: Un secolo dopo l'editio princeps (1911–1912) di Vasilij V. Latyšev." In *Byzantine Hagiography: Texts, Themes & Projects*, edited by Antonio Rigo, Michele Trizio, and Eleftherios Despotakis, 55–114. Studies in Byzantine History and Civilization 13. Turnhout: Brepols.

Dalvit, Matteo. 2009. "Virgines speciosae et castimonialae: Analisi della Passio SS. Maximae, Donatillae et Secundae." *Annali di scienze religiose* 2: 115–62.

———. 2013. "Ecclesia martyrum: Analisi del corpus martirologico donatista." Ph.D. diss., Università degli Studi di Padova.

De Smedt, Charles. 1890. "Passiones tres martyrum Africanorum SS. Maximae, Donatillae et Secundae, S. Typasii veterani et S. Fabii vexilliferi." *Analecta Bollandiana* 9: 107–34.

De Temmerman, Koen. 2016. "Ancient Biography and Formalities of Fiction." In *Writing Biography in Greece and Rome: Narrative Technique and Fictionalization*, edited by Koen De Temmerman and Kristoffel Demoen, 3–25. Cambridge: Cambridge University Press.

Dearn, Alan. 2004. "The Abitinian Martyrs and the Outbreak of the Donatist Schism." *Journal of Ecclesiastical History* 55 (1): 1–18.

Dehandschutter, Boudewijn. 1979. *Martyrium Polycarpi: Een literair-kritische studie*. Bibliotheca Ephemeridum Theologicarum Lovaniensium 52. Leuven: Universitaire Pers Leuven.

———. 1993. "The Martyrium Polycarpi: A Century of Research." In *Aufstieg und Niedergang der römischen Welt (ANRW). Teil 2. Principat. Band 27. Religion, 1*, edited by Wolfgang Haase and Hildegard Temporini, 485–522. Berlin: de Gruyter.

———. 2003. "Asterius of Amasea." In *"Let Us Die That We May Live": Greek Homilies on Christian Martyrs from Asia Minor, Palestine, and Syria (c. AD 350–AD 450)*, edited by Johan Leemans, Wendy Mayer, Pauline Allen, and Boudewijn Dehandschutter, 162–93. London: Routledge.

———. 2004. "Polycarpiana: Notes on the Hagiographic Dossier of a Saint." *Ephemerides Theologicae Lovanienses* 80 (4): 475–84.

———. 2006. "Un texte perdu du Martyre de Polycarpe retrouvé : Le codex Kosinitza 28." *Ephemerides Theologicae Lovanienses* 82 (1): 201–6.

———. 2007. *Polycarpiana: Studies on Martyrdom and Persecution in Early Christianity: Collected Essays.* Edited by Johan Leemans. Bibliotheca Ephemeridum Theologicarum Lovaniensium 205. Leuven: Leuven University Press.

———. 2009. "Polycarp of Smyrna: Some Notes on the Hagiography and Homiletics About a Smyrnaean Martyr." In *Volksglaube im antiken Christentum*, edited by Theofried Baumeister, Heike Grieser, and Andreas Merkt, 125–37. Darmstadt: WBG, Wissenschaftliche Buchgesellschaft.

Deléani, Simone. 1995. "Le récit de la mort de Cyprien dans la Vita Cypriani: Structure et signification." In *La narrativa cristiana antica: Codici narrativi, strutture formali, schemi retorici : Atti del XXIII Incontro di studiosi dell'antichità cristiana, Roma, 5–7 maggio 1994*, 465–77. Studia Ephemeridis Augustinianum 50. Rome: Institutum Patristicum Augustinianum.

Delehaye, Hippolyte. 1891. "Acta Sancti Julii veterani martyris." *Analecta Bollandiana* 10: 50–52.

———. 1897. "Les ménologes grecs." *Analecta Bollandiana* 16: 311–29.

———. 1903. "Les légendes hagiographiques." *Revue des questions historiques* 30: 56–122.

———. 1905a. "Bulletin des publications hagiographiques." *Analecta Bollandiana* 24: 115–68.

———. 1905b. *Les légendes hagiographiques.* Brussels: Société des Bollandistes.

———. 1905c. "Bulletin des publications hagiographiques." *Analecta Bollandiana* 24: 487–532.

———. 1906. "Bulletin des publications hagiographiques." *Analecta Bollandiana* 25: 177–231.

———. 1909. *Les légendes grecques des saints militaires.* Paris: Picard.

———. 1910. "Bulletin des publications hagiographiques." *Analecta Bollandiana* 29: 441–505.

———. 1921. "La Passion de S. Félix de Thibiuca." *Analecta Bollandiana* 39: 241–76.

———. 1923. "Les Actes de S. Marcel le Centurion." *Analecta Bollandiana* 41: 257–87.

———. 1940. "Les Actes des martyrs de Pergame." *Analecta Bollandiana* 58: 142–76.

———. 1955. *Les légendes hagiographiques.* 4e éd. Subsidia Hagiographica 18. Brussels: Société des Bollandistes.

———. 1966. *Les passions des martyrs et les genres littéraires.* 2e éd., revue et corrigée. Subsidia Hagiographica 13B. Brussels: Société des Bollandistes.

———. 1998. *The Legends of the Saints.* Translated by Donald Attwater. Dublin: Four Courts Press.

Derrida, Jacques. 1993. *Spectres de Marx: L'état de la dette, le travail du deuil et la nouvelle Internationale.* La philosophie en effet. Paris: Éditions Galilée.

———. 1994. *Specters of Marx: The State of the Debt, the Work of Mourning, and the New International.* Translated by Peggy Kamuf. New York: Routledge.

———. 1998. *Demeure.* Paris: Galilée.

———. 2000a. "'A Self-Unsealing Poetic Text': Poetics and Politics of Witnessing." In *Revenge of the Aesthetic: The Place of Literature in Theory Today*, edited by Michael P. Clark, 179–207. Berkeley: University of California Press.

———. 2000b. *Demeure: Fiction and Testimony.* Translated by Elizabeth Rottenberg. Stanford: Stanford University Press.

DeVore, David J. 2013. "Greek Historiography, Roman Society, Christian Empire: The Ecclesiastical History of Eusebius of Caesarea." Ph.D. diss., University of California, Berkeley.

———. 2014. "Character and Convention in the Letters of Eusebius' Ecclesiastical History." *Journal of Late Antiquity* 7 (2): 223–52.

Dilley, Paul C. 2010. "The Invention of Christian Tradition: Apocrypha, Imperial Policy, and Anti-Jewish Propaganda." *Greek, Roman and Byzantine Studies* 50 (4): 586–615.

Dolbeau, François. 1983. "La Passion des saints Lucius et Montanus: Histoire et édition du texte." *Revue des études augustiniennes* 29: 39–82.

———. 1992. "La Passio sancti Donati (BHL 2303 b): Une tentative d'édition critique." In *Memoriam sanctorum venerantes: Miscellanea in onore di Monsignor Victor Saxer*, 251–67. Studi di antichità cristiana 48. Rome: Pontificio Istituto di Archeologia cristiana.

———. 2002. "Le Nain de Tillemont, conseiller de Dom Ruinart, durant la préparation des Acta primorum martyrum (1689)." In *Le Nain de Tillemont et l'historiographie de l'Antiquité romaine*, 79–110. Colloques, congrès et conférences sur le classicisme 3. Paris: Champion.

———. 2003. "La Passion des martyrs d'Abitina: Remarques sur l'établissement du texte." *Analecta Bollandiana* 121: 273–96.

Dolezalek, Gero R. 2002. "Libri magistrorum and the Transmission of Glosses in Legal Textbooks (12th and early 13th century)." In *Juristische Buchproduktion im Mittelalter*, edited by Vincenzo Colli, 315–49. Studien zur europäischen Rechtsgeschichte 155. Frankfurt am Main: Klostermann.

Dufourcq, Albert. 1905. "Lérins et la légende chrétienne." *Comptes rendus des séances de l'Académie des Inscriptions et Belles-Lettres* 49 (4): 415–22.

Dunn, Geoffrey D. 2005. "Cyprian's Rival Bishops and Their Communities." *Augustinianum* 45 (1): 61–93.

Duprat, Anne. 2004. "Fiction et définition du littéraire au XVIe siècle." In *Usages et théories de la fiction: Le débat contemporain à l'épreuve des textes anciens (XVIe–XVIIIe siècles)*, edited by Françoise Lavocat, 65–86. Interférences. Rennes: Presses universitaires de Rennes.

———. 2009. *Vraisemblances: Poétique et théorie de la fiction, du Cinquecento à Jean Chapelain (1500–1670)*. Bibliothèque de littérature générale et comparée 79. Paris: Champion.

Duval, Yves-Marie. 1987. "Introduction à la letter 29*." In *Œuvres de saint Augustin. 46B, Lettres 1*–*29\**, edited by Johannes Divjak, 573–80. Bibliothèque augustinienne. Paris: Desclée de Brouwer.

Duval, Yvette. 1995. *Lambèse chrétienne: La gloire et l'oubli: De la Numidie romaine à l'Ifrîqiya*. Collection des études augustiniennes. Série Antiquité 144. Paris: Institut d'études augustiniennes.

———. 2000. *Chrétiens d'Afrique à l'aube de la paix constantinienne: Les premiers échos de la grande persécution*. Collection des études augustiniennes. Série Antiquité 164. Paris: Institut d'études augustiniennes.

Eastman, David L. 2011. *Paul the Martyr: The Cult of the Apostle in the Latin West*. Writings from the Greco-Roman World. Supplement 4. Atlanta, GA: Society of Biblical Literature.

Eco, Umberto. 1959. "L'opera in movimento e la coscienza dell'epoca." *Incontri musicali* 3: 32–54.

———. 1962. *Opera aperta: Forma e indeterminazione nelle poetiche contemporanee*. Milan: Bompiani.

———. 1979. *The Role of the Reader: Explorations in the Semiotics of Texts*. Bloomington: Indiana University Press.

———. 1989. *The Open Work*. Translated by Anna Concogni. Cambridge, MA: Harvard University Press.

Edwards, Mark, ed. 1997. *Against the Donatists / Optatus*. Translated Texts for Historians 27. Liverpool: Liverpool University Press.

Ehrhard, Albert. 1937–52. *Überlieferung und Bestand der hagiographischen und homiletischen Literatur der griechischen Kirche von den Anfängen bis zum Ende des 16. Jahrhunderts*. 3 vols. Texte und Untersuchungen zur Geschichte der altchristlichen Literatur 50–52. Leipzig: Hinrichs.

Ehrman, Bart D., ed. 2003. *The Apostolic Fathers*. Loeb Classial Library 24–25. Cambridge, MA: Harvard University Press.

———. 2013. *Forgery and Counterforgery: The Use of Literary Deceit in Early Christian Polemics*. New York: Oxford University Press.

Eisenhut, Werner, ed. 1973. *Dictys Cretensis Ephemerídos Belli Troiani libri*. 2. Aufl. Bibliotheca scriptorum Graecorum et Romanorum Teubneriana. Leipzig: Teubner.

Epp, Eldon Jay. 2007. "It's All About Variants: A Variant-Conscious Approach to New Testament Textual Criticism." *Harvard Theological Review* 100 (3): 275–308.

Färber, Roland. 2014. *Römische Gerichtsorte: Räumliche Dynamiken von Jurisdiktion im Imperium Romanum*. Vestigia 68. Munich: Beck.

Fialon, Sabine. 2018. *Mens immobilis: Recherches sur le corpus latin des actes et des passions d'Afrique romaine (IIe–VIe siècles)*. Collection des études augustiniennes. Série Antiquité 203. Paris: Institut d'études augustiniennes.

Fischer, Franz. 2010. "The Pluralistic Approach: The First Scholarly Edition of William of Auxerre's Treatise on Liturgy." *Jahrbuch für Computerphilologie* 10: 151–68.

———. 2013. "All Texts Are Equal, but . . . Textual Plurality and the Critical Text in Digital Scholarly Editions." *Variants* 10: 77–91.

Fludernik, Monika. 2006. *Einführung in die Erzähltheorie*. Darmstadt: WBG, Wissenschaftliche Buchgesellschaft.

———. 2009. *An Introduction to Narratology*. Translated by Patricia Häusler-Greenfield and Monika Fludernik. London: Routledge.

———. 2018. "The Fiction of the Rise of Fictionality." *Poetics Today* 39 (1): 67–92.

Fontaine, Jacques, ed. 1967. *Vie de Saint Martin / Sulpice Sévère*. Sources chrétiennes 133–35. Paris: Éditions du Cerf.

Fowler, Alastair. 1982. *Kinds of Literature: An Introduction to the Theory of Genres and Modes*. Cambridge, MA: Harvard University Press.

Franchi de' Cavalieri, Pio. 1898. *Gli Atti dei SS. Montano, Lucio e compagni: Recensione del testo ed introduzione sulle sue relazioni con la Passio S. Perpetuae*. Römische Quartalschrift. Supplementheft 8. Rome: Herder.

———. 1900. *La Passio SS. Mariani et Jacobi*. Studi e Testi 3. Rome: Tipografica Vaticana.

———. 1902. *Note agiografiche*. Studi e Testi 8. Rome: Tipografica Vaticana.

———. 1903. "Le reliquie dei martiri Scillitani." *Römische Quartalschrift für christliche Altertumskunde und Kirchengeschichte* 17: 209–21.

———. 1905. "Della Passio SS. Marcelli tribuni, Petri militis et aliorum." *Nuovo bullettino di archeologia cristiana* 11: 237–68.

———. 1909. "Nuove osservazioni critiche ed esegetiche sul testo della Passio sanctorum Montani et Lucii." In *Note agiografiche*. 3, 3–31. Studi e Testi 22. Vatican City: Biblioteca Apostolica Vaticana.

———. 1914. "Di un nuovo studio sugli Acta proconsularia di S. Cipriano." *Studi Romani* 2: 189–215.

———. 1920. "Di una nuova recensione del Martirio dei SS. Carpo, Papylo et Agatonice." In *Note agiografiche*. 6, 1–45. Studi e Testi 33. Rome: Tipografica Vaticana.

———. 1928. *Note agiografiche. 7.* Studi e Testi 49. Rome: Tipografica Vaticana.

———. 1935. "La Passio dei martiri abitinensi." In *Note agiografiche. 8*, 129–99. Studi e Testi 65. Vatican City: Biblioteca Apostolica Vaticana.

———. 1962. *Scritti agiografici.* 2 vols. Studi e Testi 221–222. Vatican City: Biblioteca apostolica vaticana.

Francis, James A. 1998. "Truthful Fiction: New Questions to Old Answers on Philostratus' Life of Apollonius." *American Journal of Philology* 119 (3): 419–41.

Frazier, Alison Knowles. 2005. *Possible Lives: Authors and Saints in Renaissance Italy.* New York: Columbia University Press.

Fux, Pierre-Yves. 2013. *Prudence et les martyrs: Hymnes et tragédie: Peristephanon 1, 3–4, 6–8, 10: Commentaire.* Paradosis 55. Fribourg: Éditions Universitaires.

Gaiffier, Baudoin de. 1954. "La lecture des Actes de martyrs dans la prière liturgique en Occident: à propos du passionnaire hispanique." *Analecta Bollandiana* 73: 134–66.

Gainsford, Peter. 2012. "Diktys of Crete." *Cambridge Classical Journal* 58: 58–87.

Gallazzi, Claudio, and Mariangela Vandoni, eds. 1977. *Papiri della Università degli Studi di Milano. 6, (P. Mil. Vogliano 258–300).* Milan: Instituto Editoriale Cisalpino.

Gamber, Klaus. 1968. *Codices liturgici Latini antiquiores.* Secunda editio aucta. Freiburg: Universitätsverlag.

Gebhardt, Oscar von. 1896. "Das Martyrium des heiligen Pionios." *Archiv für slavische Philologie* 18: 156–71.

———, ed. 1902. *Ausgewählte Märtyreracten und andere Urkunden aus der Verfolgungszeit der christlichen Kirche.* Berlin: Duncker.

Geffcken, Johannes. 1906. "Die Stenographie in den Akten der Märtyrer." *Archiv für Stenographie* 57: 81–89.

Genette, Gérard. 1972. *Figures III.* Poétique. Paris: Éditions du Seuil.

———. 1983. *Narrative Discourse: An Essay in Method.* Translated by Jane E. Lewin. Ithaca, NY: Cornell University Press.

Génicot, Léopold. 1975. *Les généalogies.* Typologie des sources du Moyen Âge occidental 15. Turnhout: Brepols.

Georges, Tobias, ed. 2011. *Apologeticum / Tertullian.* Kommentar zu frühchristlichen Apologeten 11. Freiburg im Breisgau: Herder.

Gibson, Craig A., ed. 2008. *Libanius's Progymnasmata: Model Exercises in Greek Prose Composition and Rhetoric.* Writings from the Greco-Roman World 27. Atlanta, GA: Society of Biblical Literature.

Gibson, E. Leigh. 2001. "Jewish Antagonism or Christian Polemic: The Case of the Martyrdom of Pionius." *Journal of Early Christian Studies* 9 (3): 339–58.

Gleede, Benjamin. 2016. *Parabiblica Latina: Studien zu den griechisch-lateinischen Übersetzungen parabiblischer Literatur unter besonderer Berücksichtigung der apostolischen Väter.* Supplements to Vigiliae Christianae 137. Leiden: Brill.

Glorie, François, ed. 1970–71. *Eusebius "Gallicanus" Collectio homiliarum.* 3 vols. Corpus Christianorum. Series Latina 101-101A-101B. Turnhout: Brepols.

Glover, T. R., ed. 1934. *Apology, De Spectaculis / Tertullian.* Loeb Classical Library 250. Harvard, MA: Harvard University Press.

Gold, Barbara K. 2018. *Perpetua: Athlete of God.* Women in Antiquity. New York: Oxford University Press.

González, Eliezer. 2014. *The Fate of the Dead in Early Third Century North African Christianity: The Passion of Perpetua and Felicitas and Tertullian.* Studien und Texte zu Antike und Christentum 83. Tübingen: Mohr Siebeck.

Grégoire, Henri. 1905. *Saints jumeaux et dieux cavaliers: Étude hagiographique.* Bibliothèque hagiographique orientale 9. Paris: Picard.

Grig, Lucy. 2004. *Making Martyrs in Late Antiquity.* London: Duckworth.

Haensch, Rudolf. 1992. "Das Statthalterarchiv." *Zeitschrift der Savigny-Stiftung für Rechtsgeschichte: Romanistische Abteilung* 109 (1): 209–317.

——. 2003. "Römische Amtsinhaber als Vorbilder für die Bischöfe des 4. Jahrhunderts?" In *The Representation and Perception of Roman Imperial Power,* edited by Lukas de Blois, Paul Erdkamp, Olivier Hekster, Gerda de Kleijn, and Stephan Mols, 117–36. Impact of Empire 3. Amsterdam: Gieben.

——. 2016. "Die Protokolle der Statthaltergerichte der spätantiken Provinzen Ägyptens." In *Recht haben und Recht bekommen im Imperium Romanum: Das Gerichtswesen der römischen Kaiserzeit und seine dokumentarische Evidenz: Ausgewählte Beiträge einer Serie von drei Konferenzen an der Villa Vigoni in den Jahren 2010 bis 2012,* edited by Rudolf Haensch, 299–324. Journal of Juristic Papyrology Supplement 24. Warsaw: Taubenschlaga.

Hägg, Tomas. 1987. "Callirhoe and Parthenope. The Beginnings of the Historical Novel." *Classical Antiquity* 6: 184–204.

——. 1992. "Hierocles the Lover of Truth and Eusebius the Sophist." *Symbolae Osloenses* 67: 138–50.

——. 2004. *Parthenope: Selected Studies in Ancient Greek Fiction (1969–2004).* Copenhagen: Museum Tusculanum Press.

Halkin, François. 1963a. *Inédits byzantins d'Ochrida, Candie et Moscou.* Subsidia Hagiographica 38. Brussels: Société des Bollandistes.

——. 1963b. "L'Apologie du martyr Philéas de Thmuis (Papyrus Bodmer XX) et les Actes latins de Philéas et Philoromus." *Analecta Bollandiana* 81 (1–2): 5–27.

——. 1965. *Euphémie de Chalcédoine: Légendes byzantines.* Subsidia Hagiographica 41. Brussels: Société des Bollandistes.

——. 1985. *Le ménologe impérial de Baltimore: Textes grecs.* Subsidia Hagiographica 69. Brussels: Société des Bollandistes.

Hall, Jon. 1998. "Cicero to Lucceius (Fam. 5.12) in Its Social Context: Valde Bella?" *Classical Philology* 93 (4): 308–21.

Hansen, William F. 2003. "Strategies of Authentication in Ancient Popular Literature." In *The Ancient Novel and Beyond,* edited by Stelios Panayotakis, Maaike Zimmerman, and Wytse Hette Keulen, 301–14. Mnemosyne. Supplementum 241. Leiden: Brill.

Hanslik, Rudolf. 1963. "Secretarium und tribunal in den Acta Martyrum Scillitanorum." In *Mélanges offerts à Mademoiselle Christine Mohrmann,* edited by Lodewijk J. Engels, H. A. M. Hoppenbrouwers, and A. J. Vermeulen, 165–68. Utrecht: Spectrum.

Harnack, Adolf von. 1888. *Die Acten des Karpus, Papylus and der Agathonike.* Texte und Untersuchungen zur Geschichte der altchristlichen Literatur 3, 4. Leipzig: Hinrichs.

——. 1913. *Das Leben Cyprians, von Pontius: Die erste christliche Biographie.* Texte und Untersuchungen zur Geschichte der altchristlichen Literatur 39, 3. Leipzig: Hinrichs.

——. 1924. *Die Mission und Ausbreitung des Christentums in den ersten drei Jahrhunderten.* 4., verb. und verm. Aufl. Leipzig: Hinrichs.

——. 1962. *The Mission and Expansion of Christianity in the First Three Centuries.* Translated by James Moffatt. New York: Harper.

Harries, Jill. 2007. *Law and Crime in the Roman World.* Key Themes in Ancient History. Cambridge: Cambridge University Press.

———. 2009. "Tertullianus & Son?" In *A Wandering Galilean: Essays in Honour of Seán Freyne*, edited by Zuleika Rodgers, Margaret Daly-Denton, and Anne Fitzpatrick-McKinkey, 385–400. Supplements to the Journal for the Study of Judaism 132. Leiden: Brill.

Harris, J. Rendel, and Seth Kelley Gifford. 1890. *The Acts of the Martyrdom of Perpetua and Felicitas: The Original Greek Text Now First Edited from a Ms. in the Library of the Convent of the Holy Sepulchre at Jerusalem*. London: Clay and Sons.

Hartog, Paul. 2013. *Polycarp's Epistle to the Philippians and the Martyrdom of Polycarp: Introduction, Text, and Commentary*. Oxford Apostolic Fathers. Oxford: Oxford University Press.

Heffernan, Thomas J. 2012. *The Passion of Perpetua and Felicity*. New York: Oxford University Press.

Heinich, Nathalie. 1998. "Le témoignage, entre autobiographie et roman: La place de la fiction dans les récits de déportation." *Mots: Les langages du politique* 56 (1): 33–49.

Heinzelmann, Martin. 2010. "L'hagiographie mérovingienne: Panorama des documents potentiels." *Beihefte der Francia* 71: 27–82.

Hellegouarc'h, Joseph. 1972. *Le vocabulaire latin des relations et des partis politiques sous la République*. 2e éd. revue et corrigée. Paris: les Belles Lettres.

Henten, Jan Willem van, and Friedrich Avemarie, eds. 2002. *Martyrdom and Noble Death: Selected Texts from Graeco-Roman, Jewish, and Christian Antiquity*. London: Routledge.

Herman, Jan. 2008. "Introduction générale: 'ceci n'est pas un roman'." In *Le roman véritable: Stratégies préfacielles au XVIIIe siècle*, edited by Jan Herman, Mladen Kozul, and Nathalie Kremer, 1–18. Oxford: Voltaire Foundation.

Hermanowicz, Erika. 2008. *Possidius of Calama: A Study of the North African Episcopate at the Time of Augustine*. Oxford: Clarendon Press.

Hilhorst, Antoon. 1987. "Commento al *Martyrium Pionii*." In *Atti e passioni dei martiri*, edited by Antoon A. R. Bastiaensen, 453–77. Milan: Mondadori.

———. 2010. "'He Left Us This Writing': Did He? Revisiting the Statement in Martyrdom of Pionius 1.2." In *Martyrdom and Persecution in Late Antique Christianity: Festschrift Boudewijn Dehandschutter*, edited by Johan Leemans, 104–21. Bibliotheca Ephemeridum Theologicarum Lovaniensium 241. Leuven: Leuven University Press.

Hill, Edmund, ed. 1994. *The Works of Saint Augustine: A Translation for the Twenty-First Century. 3, Sermons. 8, (273–305A) on the Saints*. New York: New City Press.

Hoben, Wolfgang. 1978. *Terminologische Studien zu den Sklavenerhebungen der römischen Republik*. 1. Aufl. Wiesbaden: Steiner.

Hodkinson, Owen. 2013. "Epistolarity and Narrative in Ps.-Aeschines Epistle 10." In *Epistolary Narratives in Ancient Greek Literature*, edited by Owen Hodkinson, Patricia A. Rosenmeyer, and Evelien Bracke, 323–45. Mnemosyne. Supplementum 359. Leiden: Brill.

Hodkinson, Owen, and Patricia A. Rosenmeyer. 2013. "Introduction." In *Epistolary Narratives in Ancient Greek Literature*, edited by Owen Hodkinson, Patricia A. Rosenmeyer, and Evelien Bracke, 1–36. Mnemosyne. Supplementum 359. Leiden: Brill.

Hoffmann, Manfred. 1966. *Der Dialog bei den christlichen Schriftstellern der ersten vier Jahrhunderte*. Texte und Untersuchungen zur Geschichte der altchristlichen Literatur 96. Berlin: Akademie-Verlag.

Hoover, Jesse. 2013. "False Lives, False Martyrs: 'Pseudo-Pionius' and the Redating of the Martyrdom of Polycarp." *Vigiliae Christianae* 67 (5): 471–98.

Hose, Martin. 1996. "Fiktionalität und Lüge: Über einen Unterschied zwischen römischer und griechischer Terminologie." *Poetica* 28 (3/4): 257–74.

Huebner, Sabine. 2019. "Soter, Sotas, and Dioscorus Before the Governor: The First Authentic Court Record of a Roman Trial of Christians?" *Journal of Late Antiquity* 12 (1): 2–24.

Humfress, Caroline. 2000. "Roman Law, Forensic Argument and the Formation of Christian Orthodoxy." In *Orthodoxie, Christianisme, Histoire = Orthodoxy, Christianity, History*, edited by Susanna Elm, Éric Rebillard, and Antonella Romano, 125–47. Collection de l'École française de Rome 270. Paris: de Boccard.

———. 2007. *Orthodoxy and the Courts in Late Antiquity*. Oxford: Oxford University Press.

IFLA. 1998. *Functional Requirements for Bibliographic Records*. IFLA Series on Bibliographic Control 9. Munich: Saur.

———. 2009. "Functional Requirements for Bibliographic Records." https://www.ifla.org/files/assets/cataloguing/frbr/frbr_2008.pdf.

Jänicke, Stefan, and David Joseph Wrisley. 2017. "Visualizing Mouvance: Toward a Visual Analysis of Variant Medieval Text Traditions." *Digital Scholarship in the Humanities* 32 (suppl_2): 106–23.

Joassart, Bernard. 2011. *Aspects de l'érudition hagiographique au XVIIe et XVIIIe siècles*. École pratique des hautes études. Sciences historiques et philologiques. V, Hautes études médiévales et modernes 99. Geneva: Droz.

Jones, Christopher P. 1992. Review of *La Passion Inédite de S. Athénogène de Pédachthoé en Cappadoce. (BHG 197b). (Subsidia Hagiographica, 75)*, by Pierre Maraval. *Journal of Theological Studies* 43 (1): 245–48.

———, ed. 2005–6. *The Life of Apollonius of Tyana / Philostratus*. 3 vols. Loeb Classical Library 16, 17, 458. Cambridge, MA: Harvard University Press.

Keim, Theodor. 1878. *Aus dem Urchristentum: Geschichtliche Untersuchungen in zwangloser Folge*. Zurich: Füssli.

Kelly, Benjamin. 2011. *Petitions, Litigation, and Social Control in Roman Egypt*. Oxford: Oxford University Press.

Kennedy, George Alexander, ed. 2003. *Progymnasmata: Greek Textbooks of Prose Composition and Rhetoric*. Writings from the Greco-Roman World 10. Atlanta, GA: Society of Biblical Literature.

Khomych, Taras. 2010. "A Forgotten Witness: Recovering the Early Church Slavonic Version of the Martyrdom of Polycarp." In *Martyrdom and Persecution in Late Antique Christianity: Festschrift Boudewijn Dehandschutter*, edited by Johan Leemans, 123–33. Bibliotheca Ephemeridum Theologicarum Lovaniensium 241. Leuven: Leuven University Press.

———. 2012. "An Early Church Slavonic Translation of the Martyrdom of St. Polycarp: Three Decades Later." *Analecta Bollandiana* 130: 294–302.

———. 2013. "The Martyrdom of Polycarp in Church Slavonic: An Evidence of the Academic Menologion." *Vigiliae Christianae* 67 (4): 393–406.

Klöckener, Martin. 1996. "Deo Gratias, Deo Laudes." In *Augustinus-Lexikon*. 2: 294–96. Basel: Schwabe.

Kloppenborg, John S. 2018. "Associations, Guilds, Clubs." In *The Oxford Handbook of Early Christian Ritual*, edited by Risto Uro, Rikard Roitto, and Richard E. DeMaris, 154–70. Oxford: Oxford University Press.

Knopf, Rudolf, ed. 1901. *Ausgewählte Märtyrerakten*. Tübingen: Mohr.

Knopf, Rudolf, Gustav Krüger, and Gerhard Ruhbach, eds. 1965. *Ausgewählte Märtyrerakten*. 4. Aufl. Tübingen: Mohr.

Kolb, Robert. 1987. *For All the Saints: Changing Perceptions of Martyrdom and Sainthood in the Lutheran Reformation*. Macon, GA: Mercer University Press.

Konstan, David. 1998. "The Alexander Romance: The Cunning of the Open Text." *Lexis* 16: 123–38.

Kortekaas, G. A. A. 1987. "*Acta Phileae*." In *Atti e passioni dei martiri*, edited by Antoon A. R. Bastiaensen, 247–337. Milan: Mondadori.

Kurke, Leslie. 2011. *Aesopic Conversations: Popular Tradition, Cultural Dialogue, and the Invention of Greek Prose*. Princeton, NJ: Princeton University Press.

LaCapra, Dominick. 1985. *History & Criticism*. Ithaca, NY: Cornell University Press.

Laird, Andrew. 2009. "The Rhetoric of Roman Historiography." In *The Cambridge Companion to the Roman Historians*, edited by Andrew Feldherr, 197–213. Cambridge: Cambridge University Press.

Lampe, Peter. 2003. *From Paul to Valentinus: Christians at Rome in the First Two Centuries*. Minneapolis: Fortress Press.

Lanata, Giuliana. 1973. *Gli atti dei martiri come documenti processuali*. Milan: Giuffrè.

———. 1993. "Avvocati nei processi contro cristiani?" *Materiali per una storia della cultura giuridica* 23 (2): 277–90.

Lancel, Serge. 2006. "Actes de Gallonius: Texte critique, traduction et notes." *Revue d'études augustiniennes et patristiques* 52 (2): 243–59.

Lanéry, Cécile. 2008. *Ambroise de Milan hagiographe*. Collection des études augustiniennes. Série Antiquité 183. Paris: Institut d'études augustiniennes.

———. 2010. "Le dossier des saints Nazaire, Celse, Gervais et Protais: Édition de la Passion BHL 6043 (= 3516)." *Analecta Bollandiana* 128 (2): 241–80.

Laniado, Avshalom. 1995. "Hilarios Pyrrhachas et la Passion de Saint Athénogène de Pédachthoé (BHG 197b)." *Revue des études byzantines* 53 (1): 279–84.

Lapointe, Guy. 1972. *La célébration des martyrs en Afrique d'après les sermons de saint Augustin*. Montreal: Université de Montréal.

Larsen, Matthew D. C. 2018. *Gospels Before the Book*. New York: Oxford University Press.

Last, Hugh. 1937. "The Study of the Persecutions." *Journal of Roman Studies* 27: 80–92.

Latyšev, Vasilij V. 1911. *Menologii anonymi Byzantini saeculi X quae supersunt*. 2 vols. Saint Peterburg: Akademii Nauk.

Lausberg, Heinrich. 1973. *Handbuch der literarischen Rhetorik: Eine Grundlegung der Literaturwissenschaft*. 2., durch e. Nachtr. vermehrte Aufl. Munich: Hueber.

———. 1998. *Handbook of Literary Rhetoric: A Foundation for Literary Study*. Translated by Matthew T. Bliss, Annemiek Jansen, and David E. Orton. Leiden: Brill.

Lavocat, Françoise, ed. 2004a. *Usages et théories de la fiction: Le débat contemporain à l'épreuve des textes anciens (XVIe–XVIIIe siècles)*. Interférences. Rennes: Presses universitaires de Rennes.

———. 2004b. "Fictions et paradoxes: Les nouveaux mondes possibles à la Renaissance." In *Usages et théories de la fiction: Le débat contemporain à l'épreuve des textes anciens (XVIe–XVIIIe siècles)*, edited by Françoise Lavocat, 87–111. Interférences. Rennes: Presses universitaires de Rennes.

———, ed. 2010. *La théorie littéraire des mondes possibles*. Paris: CNRS Éditions.

———. 2016. *Fait et fiction: Pour une frontière*. Poétique. Paris: Éditions du Seuil.

Lazzati, Giuseppe. 1953. "Gli atti di S. Giustino martire." *Aevum* 27 (6): 473–97.

———. 1956. *Gli sviluppi della letteratura sui martiri nei primi quattro secoli: Con appendice di testi*. Studi superiori. Turin: Società editrice internazionale.

Le Blant, Edmond. 1879. "Les Acta Martyrum et leurs sources." *Comptes rendus des séances de l'Académie des Inscriptions et Belles-Lettres* 23 (3): 210–17.

————. 1881. "Les actes des martyrs: Supplément aux Acta sincera de Dom Ruinart." *Mémoires de l'Académie des Inscriptions et Belles Lettres* 30: 57–347.

Lendon, J. E. 2009. "Historians Without History: Against Roman Historiography." In *The Cambridge Companion to the Roman Historians*, edited by Andrew Feldherr, 41–62. Cambridge: Cambridge University Press.

Lenski, Noel. 2016. *Constantine and the Cities: Imperial Authority and Civic Politics*. Philadelphia: University of Pennsylvania Press.

Lepelley, Claude. 2009. "Les réticences de saint Augustin face aux légendes hagiographiques d'après la lettre Divjak 29*." In *Transformations of Late Antiquity: Essays for Peter Brown*, edited by Philip Rousseau, 147–58. Aldershot: Ashgate.

Levi, Primo. 1947. *Se questo è un uomo*. Biblioteca Leone Ginzburg 3. Turin: De Silva.

————. 1996. *Survival in Auschwitz: The Nazi Assault on Humanity*. Translated by Stuart Woolf. New York: Simon & Schuster.

Lieberman, Saul. 1944. "Roman Legal Institutions in Early Rabbinics and in the Acta Martyrum." *Jewish Quarterly Review* 35 (1): 1–57.

Lied, Liv Ingeborg, and Hugo Lundhaug. 2017. "Studying Snapshots: On Manuscript Culture, Textual Fluidity, and New Philology." In *Snapshots of Evolving Traditions: Jewish and Christian Manuscript Culture, Textual Fluidity, and New Philology*, edited by Liv Ingeborg Lied and Hugo Lundhaug, 1–19. Texte und Untersuchungen zur Geschichte der altchristlichen Literatur 175. Berlin: de Gruyter.

Lietzmann, Hans. 1922. "Die älteste Gestalt der Passio SS. Carpi Papylae et Agathonices." In *Festgabe von Fachgenossen und Freunden Karl Müller zum siebzigsten Geburtstag dargebracht*, 46–57. Tübingen: Mohr.

————. 1958. "Die älteste Gestalt der Passio SS. Carpi Papylae et Agathonices." In *Kleine Schriften*, 1: 239–50. Texte und Untersuchungen zur Geschichte der altchristlichen Literatur 67. Berlin: Akademie-Verlag.

Lieu, Judith. 2016. *Neither Jew nor Greek? Constructing Early Christianity*. 2nd ed. London: Bloomsbury.

Lifshitz, Felice. 2006. *The Name of the Saint: The Martyrology of Jerome and Access to the Sacred in Francia, 627–827*. Notre Dame, IN: University of Notre Dame Press.

Lightfoot, J. B. 1889. *The Apostolic Fathers: Revised Texts with Introductions, Notes, Dissertations, and Translations*. 3 vols. London: Macmillan.

Lipsius, Richard Adelbert. 1874. "Der Martyrertod Polykarps." *Zeitschrift für wissenschaftliche Theologie* 17: 188–214.

Löfstedt, Bengt. 1976. "Observations d'un latiniste sur des problèmes de critique textuelle des romanistes." In *Actes du XIIIe Congrès International de Linguistique et Philologie Romanes*, 2: 593–600. Quebec: Presses de l'Université Laval.

Löhr, Winrich A. 1989. "Der Brief der Gemeinden von Lyon und Vienne." In *Oecumenica et Patristica: Festschrift für Wilhelm Schneemelcher zum 75. Geburtstag*, edited by Damaskinos Papandreou, Wolfgang A. Bienert, and Knut Schafferdiek, 688–93. Stuttgart: Kohlhammer.

Lomanto, Valeria. 1975. "Rapporti fra la Passio Perpetuae e Passiones africane." In *Forma futuri: Studi in onore del cardinale Michele Pellegrino*, 566–86. Turin: Bottega d'Erasmo.

Lomiento, Gennaro. 1968. "La Bibbia nella *compositio* della Vita Cypriani di Ponzio." *Vetera Christianorum* 1968 (5): 23–60.

Lucca, Claudia. 2007. "Tratti profetici dei martiri nella Passio Mariani et Iacobi e nella Passio Montani et Lucii." In *Cristianesimi nell'antichità: Fonti, istituzioni, ideologie a confronto*, edited by Alberto D'Anna and Claudio Zamagni, 149–74. Spudasmata 117. Hildesheim: Olms.

Mabillon, Jean. 1723. *Vetera analecta*. 2nd ed. Paris: Montalant.

Maggioni, Giovanni Paolo. 2016. "Texts Between History and Fiction in Medieval Hagiography." In *Fiction and Figuration in High and Late Medieval Literature*, edited by Marianne Pade, Anders Culhed, Anders Hallengren, and Brian Møller Jensen, 75–82. Analecta Romana Instituti Danici. Supplementa 47. Rome: Det Danske Institut i Rom.

Maier, Jean-Louis. 1987–89. *Le dossier du donatisme*. 2 vols. Texte und Untersuchungen zur Geschichte der altchristlichen Literatur 134–35. Berlin: Akademie-Verlag.

Mandouze, André. 1982. *Prosopographie de l'Afrique chrétienne (303–533)*. Paris: Éditions du CNRS.

Maraval, Pierre, ed. 1990. *La passion inédite de S. Athénogène de Pédachthoé en Cappadoce (BHG 197b)*. Subsidia Hagiographica 75. Brussels: Société des Bollandistes.

Margoni-Kögler, Michael. 2010. *Die Perikopen im Gottesdienst bei Augustinus: Ein Beitrag zur Erforschung der liturgischen Schriftlesung in der frühen Kirche*. Sitzungsberichte der philosophisch-historischen Klasse 810. Veröffentlichungen der Kommission zur Herausgabe des Corpus der Lateinischen Kirchenväter 29. Vienna: Verlag der Österreichischen Akademie der Wissenschaften.

Marincola, John. 1997. *Authority and Tradition in Ancient Historiography*. Cambridge: Cambridge University Press.

———. 2003. "Beyond Pity and Fear: The Emotions of History." *Ancient Society* 33: 285–315.

———. 2010. "Aristotle's Poetics and Tragic History." In *Parachorēgēma: Meletēmata Gia to Archaio Theatro Pros Timēn Tou Kathēgētē Grēgorē M. Sēphakē*, 445–60. Heraklion: Panepistēmiakes Ekdoseis Krētēs.

———, ed. 2011. *Greek and Roman Historiography*. Oxford Readings in Classical Studies. Oxford: Oxford University Press.

———. 2013. "Polybius, Phylarchus, and Tragic History: A Reconsideration." In *Polybius and His World: Essays in Memory of F. W. Walbank*, edited by Bruce John Gibson and Thomas Harrison, 73–90. Oxford: Oxford University Press.

Martimort, Aimé-Georges. 1992. *Les lectures liturgiques et leurs livres*. Typologie des sources du Moyen Âge occidental 64. Turnhout: Brepols.

Martin, Victor, ed. 1964. *Apologie de Philéas évêque de Thmouis*. Papyrus Bodmer 20. Cologny: Bibliotheca Bodmeriana.

Martini, Remo. 1975. "Tertulliano giurista e Tertulliano Padre della Chiesa." *Studia et Documenta Historiae et Iuris* 41: 79–124.

Mazzucco, Clementina. 2017. "Le visioni e il carisma profetico di Perpetua, dalla Passio agli Acta." *Humanitas* 72 (5–6): 798–822.

McLarty, Jane. 2013. "The Function of the Letter Form in Christian Martyrdom Accounts: 'I Would Like My Community, My Church, My Family, to Remember.'" In *Epistolary Narratives in Ancient Greek Literature*, edited by Owen Hodkinson, Patricia A. Rosenmeyer, and Evelien Bracke, 371–85. Mnemosyne. Supplementum 359. Leiden: Brill.

Meijering, Roos. 1987. *Literary and Rhetorical Theories in Greek Scholia*. Groningen: Forsten.

Mette, Hans Joachim. 1936. *Sphairopoiia: Untersuchungen zur Kosmologie des Krates von Pergamon*. Munich: Beck.

Micunco, Giuseppe. 2006. "Sacramentum in Plinio, Ep. 10, 96." *Invigilata Lucernis* 28: 153–59.

Minnen, Peter van. 1995. "The Earliest Account of a Martyrdom in Coptic." *Analecta Bollandiana* 113 (1–2): 13–38.

Minns, Denis, and P. M. Parvis, eds. 2009. *Justin, Philosopher and Martyr: Apologies*. Oxford Early Christian Texts. Oxford: Oxford University Press.

Moles, John L. 1993. "Truth and Untruth in Herodotus and Thucydides." In *Lies and Fiction in the Ancient World*, edited by Christopher Gill and Timothy P. Wiseman, 88–121. Austin: University of Texas Press.

Mombrizio, Bonino. 1910. *Sanctuarium seu Vitae sanctorum*. Ed. Abbaye de Solesmes. Paris: Fontemoing.

Momigliano, Arnaldo. 1963. "Pagan and Christian Historiography in the Fourth Century A.D." In *The Conflict Between Paganism and Christianity in the Fourth Century*, edited by Arnaldo Momigliano, 79–99. Oxford: Clarendon Press.

———. 1977. *Essays in Ancient and Modern Historiography*. Oxford: Blackwell.

Mommsen, Theodor. 1890. "Der Religionsfrevel nach römischen Recht." *Historische Zeitschrift* 28: 389–429.

———. 1893. "Christianity in the Roman Empire." *Expositor* 4 (8): 1–7.

———. 1899. *Römisches Strafrecht*. Leipzig: Duncker & Humblot.

———. 1907. "Der Religionsfrevel nach römischen Recht." In *Gesammelte Schriften. 3, Juristische Schriften. 3*, 389–422. Berlin: Weidmann.

———. 1910. "Christianity in the Roman Empire." In *Gesammelte Schriften. 6, Historische Schriften. 3*, 540–45. Berlin: Weidmann.

Monceaux, Paul. 1901–23. *Histoire littéraire de l'Afrique chrétienne depuis les origines jusqu'à l'invasion arabe*. 7 vols. Paris: Leroux.

———. 1903. "Les Actes de sainte Crispine, martyre à Theveste." In *Mélanges Boissier: recueil de mémoires concernant la littérature et les antiquités romaines dédié à Gaston Boissier à l'occasion de son 80 anniversaire*, 383–89. Paris: Fontemoing.

———. 1909. "Épigraphie donatiste." *Comptes rendus des séances de l'Académie des Inscriptions et Belles-Lettres* 53 (4): 249–52.

Montgomery, Hugo. 1996. "Pontius' Vita S. Cypriani and the Making of a Saint." *Symbolae Osloenses* 71: 195–215.

Morales, Manuel Sanz. 2006. "The Copyist as Novelist: Multiple Versions in the Ancient Greek Novel." *Variants* 5: 129–46.

———. 2018. "Copyists' Versions and the Readership of the Greek Novel." In *Cultural Crossroads in the Ancient Novel*, edited by M. Futre Pinheiro, David Konstan, and Bruce D. MacQueen, 183–93. Trends in Classics. Supplementary Volumes 40. Berlin: de Gruyter.

Morello, Ruth., and A. D. Morrison, eds. 2007. *Ancient Letters: Classical and Late Antique Epistolography*. Oxford: Oxford University Press.

Morgan, John R. 1993. "Make-Believe and Make Believe: The Fictionality of the Greek Novels." In *Lies and Fiction in the Ancient World*, edited by Christopher Gill and Timothy P. Wiseman, 175–229. Austin: University of Texas Press.

———. 2013. "Love from Beyond the Grave: The Epistolary Ghost-Story in Phlegon of Tralles." In *Epistolary Narratives in Ancient Greek Literature*, edited by Owen Hodkinson, Patricia A. Rosenmeyer, and Evelien Bracke, 293–321. Mnemosyne. Supplementum 359. Leiden: Brill.

Moriarty, Rachel. 1997. "The Claims of the Past: Attitudes to Antiquity in the Introduction to Passio Perpetuae." In *Papers Presented at the Twelfth International Conference on Patristic Studies Held in Oxford, 1995*, edited by Elizabeth A. Livingston, 3: 307–13. Studia Patristica 31. Leuven: Peeters.

Moss, Candida R. 2010. "On the Dating of Polycarp: Rethinking the Place of the Martyrdom of Polycarp in the History of Christianity." *Early Christianity* 1 (4): 539–74.

———. 2012. *Ancient Christian Martyrdom: Diverse Practices, Theologies, and Traditions.* Anchor Yale Bible Reference Library. New Haven, CT: Yale University Press.

———. 2013a. *The Myth of Persecution: How Early Christians Invented a Story of Martyrdom.* New York: Harper One.

———. 2013b. "Polycarphilia: The Martyrdom of Polycarp and the Origins and Spread of Martyrdom." In *The Rise and Expansion of Christianity in the First Three Centuries of the Common Era,* edited by Clare K. Rothschild and Jens Schröter, 402–17. Wissenschaftliche Untersuchungen zum Neuen Testament 301. Tübingen: Mohr Siebeck.

Munier, Charles, ed. 1974. *Concilia Africae a. 345-a. 525.* Corpus Christianorum. Series Latina 249. Turnhout: Brepols.

Musurillo, Herbert. 1972. *The Acts of the Christian Martyrs.* Oxford: Clarendon Press.

Nautin, Pierre. 1961. *Lettres et écrivains chrétiens des IIe et IIIe siècles.* Patristica 2. Paris: Éditions du Cerf.

Ní Mheallaigh, Karen. 2008. "Pseudo-Documentarism and the Limits of Ancient Fiction." *American Journal of Philology* 129 (3): 403–31.

———. 2014. *Reading Fiction with Lucian: Fakes, Freaks and Hyperreality.* Cambridge: Cambridge University Press.

Nicholson, Oliver. 2009. "Preparation for Martyrdom in the Early Church." In *The Great Persecution: The Proceedings of the Fifth Patristic Conference, Maynooth, 2003,* edited by Vincent D. Twomey and Mark Humphries, 61–90. Dublin: Four Courts Press.

Nicolai, Roberto. 1992. *La storiografia nell'educazione antica.* Biblioteca di Materiali e discussioni per l'analisi dei testi classici 10. Pisa: Giardini.

Noille-Clauzade, Christine. 2010. "Considérations logiques sur de nouveaux styles de fictionalité: Les modes de la fiction au XVIIe siècle." In *La théorie littéraire des mondes possibles,* edited by Françoise Lavocat, 171–88. Paris: CNRS Éditions.

Oddo, Nancy. 2002. "L'invention du roman français au XVIIe siècle: Littérature religieuse et matière romanesque." *Dix-septième siècle* 215 (2): 221–34.

Paige, Nicholas D. 2011. *Before Fiction: The "Ancien Régime" of the Novel.* Philadelphia: University of Pennsylvania Press.

Palme, Bernhardt. 2014a. "Roman Litigation: Reports of Court Proceedings." In *Law and Legal Practice in Egypt from Alexander to the Arab Conquest: A Selection of Papyrological Sources in Translation, with Introductions and Commentary,* edited by James G. Keenan, Joseph Gilbert Manning, and Uri Yiftach-Firanko, 482–502. Cambridge: Cambridge University Press.

———. 2014b. "Die bilinguen Prozessprotokolle und die Reform der Amtsjournale im spätantiken Ägypten." In *Symposion 2013: Vorträge zur griechischen und hellenistischen Rechtsgeschichte (Cambridge MA, 26–29. August, 2013),* edited by Michael Gagarin and Adriaan Lanni, 401–28. Akten der Gesellschaft für griechische und hellenistische Rechtsgeschichte 24. Vienna: Verlag der Österreichischen Akademie der Wissenschaften.

———. 2018. "Libellprozess und Subskriptionsverfahren." In *Symposion 2017: Vorträge zur griechischen und hellenistischen Rechtsgeschichte (Tel Aviv, 20.–23. August 2017),* edited by Eva Cantarella, Michael Gagarin, Gerhard Thür, and Julie Velissaropoulos, 257–75. Akten der Gesellschaft für griechische und hellenistische Rechtsgeschichte 27. Vienna: Verlag der Österreichischen Akademie der Wissenschaften.

Parsons, Peter J. 1983. "Passion of St. Dioscorus." In *The Oxyrhynchus Papyri. 50*. London: British Academy.

Pasquali, Giorgio. 1934. *Storia della tradizione e critica del testo*. Florence: Le Monnier.

Passet, Claude. 1977. *La Passion de Pons de Cimiez (Passio Pontii): Sources et tradition*. Nice: Repro 2000.

Patron, Sylvie. 2015. *La mort du narrateur et autres essais*. Limoges: Lambert-Lucas.

———. 2016. *Le narrateur: Un problème de théorie narrative*. 2nd ed. Limoges: Lambert-Lucas.

Pellegrino, Michele, ed. 1955. *Vita e martirio di San Cipriano / Ponzio*. Verba Seniorum 3. Turin: Edizioni Paoline.

Pelling, Christopher. 1990. "Truth and Fiction in Plutarch's *Lives*." In *Antonine Literature*, edited by D. A. Russell, 19–52. Oxford: Clarendon Press.

Penner, Todd C. 2004. *In Praise of Christian Origins: Stephen and the Hellenists in Lukan Apologetic Historiography*. Emory Studies in Early Christianity. New York: T&T Clark International.

Pervo, Richard I. 2018. "History Told by Losers: Dictys and Dares on the Trojan War." In *Reading and Teaching Ancient Fiction: Jewish, Christian, and Greco-Roman Narratives*, edited by Sara Raup Johnson, Rubén R. Dupertuis, and Chris Shea, 123–136. Writings from the Greco-Roman World Supplement Series 11. Atlanta, GA: SBL Press.

Pezzella, Sosio. 1965. *Gli atti dei martiri: Introduzione a una storia dell'antica agiografia*. Quaderni di SMSR 3. Rome: Edizioni dell'Ateneo.

Philippart, Guy. 1977. *Les légendiers romains et autres manuscrits hagiographiques*. Typologie des sources du Moyen Âge occidental 24–25. Turnhout: Brepols.

Pietersma, Albert, ed. 1984. *The Acts of Phileas, Bishop of Thmuis*. Cahiers d'orientalisme 7. Geneva: Cramer.

Pinheiro, Marília P. Futre, Judith Perkins, and Richard Pervo. 2013. *The Ancient Novel and Early Christian and Jewish Narrative: Fictional Intersections*. Ancient Narrative. Supplementum 16. Eelde: Barkhuis.

Piovanelli, Pierluigi. 2007. "The Miraculous Discovery of the Hidden Manuscript, or the Paratextual Function of the Prologue to the Apocalypse of Paul." In *The Visio Pauli and the Gnostic Apocalypse of Paul*, edited by Jan Bremmer and István Czachesz, 23–49. Studies on Early Christian Apocrypha 9. Leuven: Peeters.

Potter, David S. 1999. *Literary Texts and the Roman Historian*. London: Routledge.

Praet, Danny. 1993. "Semen est sanguis christianorum ( ? ) Een herinschatting van de rol van de christenvervolgingen in de kerstening van het Romeinse Rijk." *Handelingen* 47: 257–68.

Pratsch, Thomas. 2003. "Exploring the Jungle: Hagiographical Literature Between Fact and Fiction." In *Fifty Years of Prosopography: The Later Roman Empire, Byzantium and Beyond*, edited by Averil Cameron, 59–72. Proceedings of the British Academy 118. Oxford: Oxford University Press.

———. 2005. *Der hagiographische Topos: Griechische Heiligenviten in mittelbyzantinischer Zeit*. Millennium-Studien 6. Berlin: de Gruyter.

Quentin, Henri. 1905. "Passio S. Dioscori." *Analecta Bollandiana* 24: 321–42.

———. 1908. *Les martyrologes historiques du Moyen Âge: Étude sur la formation du Martyrologe romain*. Études d'histoire des dogmes et d'ancienne littérature ecclésiastique. Paris: Lecoffre.

———. 1926. *Essais de critique textuelle (ecdotique)*. Paris: Picard.

Quentin, Henri, and E. Tisserant. 1921. "Une version syriaque de la passion de S. Dioscore." *Analecta Bollandiana* 39: 333–44.

Rapp, Claudia. 1998. "Storytelling as Spiritual Communication in Early Greek Hagiography: The Use of Diegesis." *Journal of Early Christian Studies* 6 (3): 431–48.

Rebillard, Éric. 2012. *Christians and Their Many Identities in Late Antiquity, North Africa, 200–450 CE.* Ithaca, NY: Cornell University Press.

———. 2015. "Popular Hatred Against Christians: The Case of North Africa in the Second and Third Centuries." *Archiv für Religionsgeschichte* 16 (1): 283–310.

———, ed. 2017. *Greek and Latin Narratives About the Ancient Martyrs.* Oxford Early Christian Texts. Oxford: Oxford University Press.

Reitzenstein, Richard. 1906. *Hellenistische Wundererzählungen.* Leipzig: Teubner.

———. 1913. *Die Nachrichten über den Tod Cyprians: Ein philologischer Beitrag zur Geschichte der Märtyrerliteratur.* Sitzungsberichte der Heidelberger Akademie der Wissenschaften. Philosophisch-Historische Klasse, 1913, 14. Heidelberg: Winter.

———. 1914. "Ein donatistisches Corpus cyprianischer Schriften." *Nachrichten von der königlichen Gesellschaft der Wissenschaften zu Göttingen. Philologisch-historische Klasse,* 1914: 85–92.

Riggsby, Andrew M. 2006. *Caesar in Gaul and Rome: War in Words.* Austin: University of Texas Press.

Rispoli, Gioia M. 1988. *Lo spazio del verisimile: Il racconto, la storia e il mito.* Naples: D'Auria.

Rizzi, Marco. 2011. "Forme e obiettivi della polemica nel corpus agiografico smirneo." In *Temi e forme della polemica in età cristiana (III–V secolo),* edited by Marcello Marin, 575–86. Auctores nostri: Studi e testi di letteratura cristiana antica 9. Bari: Edipuglia.

Robert, Louis. 1994. *Le martyre de Pionios, prêtre de Smyrne.* Edited by Glen W. Bowersock and Christopher P. Jones. Washington, DC: Dumbarton Oaks Research Library and Collection.

Robinson, J. Armitage. 1891. *Texts and Studies: Contributions to Biblical and Patristic Literature.* Cambridge: Cambridge University Press.

Robinson, Olivia F. 1990–92. "The Repression of Christians in the Pre-Decian Period: A Legal Problem Still." *Irish Jurist* 25/27: 269–92.

Robinson, Peter. 2000. "One Text and the Many Texts." *Digital Scholarship in the Humanities* 15 (1): 5–14.

Ronchey, Silvia. 1987. "*Martyrium Pionii*: Traduzione." In *Atti e passioni dei martiri,* edited by Antoon A. R. Bastiaensen, 155–91. Milan: Mondadori.

———. 1990. *Indagini sul martirio di san Policarpo: Critica storica e fortuna agiografica di un caso giudiziario in Asia Minore.* Nuovi studi storici 6. Rome: Istituto storico Italiano per il medio evo.

———. 2000. "Les procès-verbaux des martyres chrétiens dans les Acta martyrum et leur fortune." *Mélanges de l'École française de Rome. Antiquité* 112 (2): 723–52.

Rosen, Klaus. 1997. "Passio Sanctae Crispinae." *Jahrbuch für Antike und Christentum* 40: 106–25.

Rossi, Alessandro. 2005. "Fabio Vittore: Dal sangue dei martiri nascono i padri? Per una rilettura degli Acta Maximiliani." *Annali di scienze religiose* 10: 181–218.

Ruggiero, Fabio. 1988. "Il problema del numero dei martiri Scilitani." *Cristianesimo nella storia* 9: 135–52.

———. 1991. *Atti dei martiri scilitani.* Rome: Accademia Nazionale dei Lincei.

Ruinart, Thierry. 1689. *Acta primorum martyrum sincera et selecta.* Paris: Muguet.

———. 1859. *Acta primorum martyrum sincera et selecta.* Editio juxta exemplar Veronense novis curis quam emendatissime recusa. Regensburg: Manz.

Rusten, Jeffrey S., and Jason König, eds. 2014. *Heroicus; Gymnasticus; Discourses 1 and 2 / Philostratus.* Loeb Classical Library 521. Cambridge, MA: Harvard University Press.

Sage, Michael M. 1975. *Cyprian.* Cambridge, MA: Philadelphia Patristic Foundation.

Salzman, Michele Renee. 1990. *On Roman Time: The Codex-Calendar of 354 and the Rhythms of Urban Life in Late Antiquity.* Transformations of the Classical Heritage 17. Berkeley: University of California Press.

Sardella, Teresa. 1990. "Strutture temporali e modelli di cultura: Rapporti tra antitradizionalismo storico e modello martiriale nella Passio Perpetuae et Felicitatis." *Augustinianum* 30: 259–78.

Savvidis, Petra. 1992 *Hermann Bonnus, Superintendent von Lübeck (1504–1548): Sein kirchenpolitisch-organisatorisches Wirken und sein praktisch-theologisches Schrifttum.* Veröffentlichungen zur Geschichte der Hansestadt Lübeck. Reihe B 20. Lübeck: Schmidt-Römhild.

Saxer, Victor. 1980. *Morts, martyrs, reliques en Afrique chrétienne aux premiers siècles: Les témoignages de Tertullien, Cyprien et Augustin à la lumière de l'archéologie.* Théologie historique 55. Paris: Beauchesne.

———. 1986. *Bible et hagiographie: Textes et thèmes bibliques dans les Actes des martyrs authentiques des premiers siècles.* Bern: Lang.

———. 1994. "Afrique latine." In *Hagiographies: Histoire internationale de la littérature hagiographique latine et vernaculaire en Occident des origines à 1550,* 1: 25–95. Corpus Christianorum. Turnhout: Brepols.

———. 1995. "La Vita Cypriani de Pontius, 'première biographie chrétienne.'" In *Orbis romanus christianusque ab Diocletiani aetate usque ad Heraclium: Travaux sur l'antiquité tardive rassemblés autour des recherches de Noël Duval,* 237–51. De l'archéologie à l'histoire. Paris: de Boccard.

———. 2002. *Saint Vincent, diacre et martyr: Culte et légendes avant l'An Mil.* Subsidia Hagiographica 83. Brussels: Société des Bollandistes.

Schaeffer, Jean-Marie. 1999. *Pourquoi la fiction.* Poétique. Paris: Éditions du Seuil.

———. 2010. *Why Fiction?* Translated by Dorrit Cohn. Stages. Lincoln: University of Nebraska Press.

Schäfer, Peter, ed. 1981. *Synopse zur Hekhalot-Literatur.* Texte und Studien zum antiken Judentum 2. Tübingen: Mohr.

———. 1986. "Research into Rabbinic Literature: An Attempt to Define the Status Quaestionis." *Journal of Jewish Studies* 37 (2): 139–152.

Schmidt, Peter Lebrecht. 2001. "Die Cyprian-Vita des Presbyters Pontius: Biographie oder laudatio funebris?" In *ScriptOralia Romana: Die römische Literatur zwischen Mündlichkeit und Schriftlichkeit,* edited by Lore Benz, 305–18. ScriptOralia. Reihe A, Altertumswissenschaftliche Reihe 29. Tübingen: Narr.

Schneider, André, ed. 1968. *Le premier livre Ad nationes de Tertullien.* Bibliotheca Helvetica Romana 9. Rome: Institut suisse.

Schubert, Christoph, ed. 2014. *Octavius / Minucius Felix.* Kommentar zu frühchristlichen Apologeten 12. Freiburg im Breisgau: Herder.

Schwartz, Eduard. 1897. "Die Berichte Liber die catilinarische Verschworung." *Hermes* 32: 554–608.

———. 1905. *De Pionio et Polycarpo.* Göttingen: Kaestner.

Scorza Barcellona, Francesco. 2002. "L'agiografia Donatista." In *Africa cristiana: Storia, religione, letteratura,* edited by Marcello Marin and Claudio Moreschini, 125–51. Brescia: Morcelliana.

Seeck, Otto. 1921. "*Secretarium.*" In *Paulys Real-Encyclopädie der classischen Altertumswissenschaft.* 2 A 1: 979–81. Stuttgart: Metzler.

Seidl, E. 1932. "Συνωμοσία." In *Paulys Real-Encyclopädie der classischen Altertumwissenschaft.* 4 A 2: 1445–50. Stuttgart: Metzler.

Selden, Daniel. 2010. "Text Networks." *Ancient Narrative* 8 (1): 1–23.

Selinger, Reinhard. 2002. *The Mid-Third Century Persecutions of Decius and Valerian.* Frankfurt am Main: Lang.

Selmeci Castioni, Barbara. 2012. "Penser la belle image: La représentation du saint comme enjeu du roman moderne." *Littératures classiques* 79 (3): 79–94.

Shaw, Brent D. 2018. "Response to Christopher Jones: The Historicity of the Neronian Persecution." *New Testament Studies* 64 (2): 231–42.

Sherwin-White, A. N. 1952. "The Early Persecutions and Roman Law Again." *Journal of Theological Studies* 3 (2): 199–213.

Slater, William J. 1972. "Asklepiades and Historia." *Greek, Roman and Byzantine Studies* 13: 317–33.

Snyder, Glenn E. 2013. *Acts of Paul: The Formation of a Pauline Corpus.* Wissenschaftliche Untersuchungen zum Neuen Testament. 2. Reihe 352. Tübingen: Mohr Siebeck.

Soler, Joëlle. 2014. "Voyage réel et voyage spirituel dans la première littérature chrétienne de langue latine: La Passion de Marien, Jacques et leurs compagnons." *Rivista di Storia del Cristianesimo* 11 (1): 43–60.

Speyer, Wolfgang. 1970. *Bücherfunde in der Glaubenswerbung der Antike: Mit einem Ausblick auf Mittelalter und Neuzeit.* Hypomnemata 24. Göttingen: Vandenhoeck & Ruprecht.

Spielberg, Lydia M. 2015. "The Rhetoric of Documentary Quotation in Roman Historiography." Ph.D. diss., University of Pennsylvania.

Stelladoro, Maria. 2006. *Euplo, Euplio martire: Dalla tradizione greca manoscritta.* Cinisello Balsamo: San Paolo.

Stephens, Susan A., and John J. Winkler, eds. 1995. *Ancient Greek Novels: The Fragments.* Princeton, NJ: Princeton University Press.

Stott, Katherine M. 2005. "Book-Find Reports in Antiquity: A Re-examination of Wolfgang Speyer with Insights from Biblical Studies." *Ancient History Bulletin* 19 (3–4): 106–30.

———. 2008. *Why Did They Write This Way? Reflections on References to Written Documents in the Hebrew Bible and Ancient Literature.* Library of Hebrew Bible/Old Testament Studies 492. New York: T&T Clark International.

Straeten, Joseph van der. 1961. "Les Actes des martyrs d'Aurélien en Bourgogne: Étude littéraire." *Analecta Bollandiana* 79: 115–44.

Streeter, Joseph. 2006. "Introduction." In *Christian Persecution, Martyrdom, and Orthodoxy* / G. E. M. De Ste. Croix, edited by Michael Whitby and Joseph Streeter, 3–34. Oxford: Oxford University Press.

Sznajder, Lyliane. 2013. "Quelques pistes dans le champ lexical de la fiction en latin." In *Théories et pratiques de la fiction à l'époque impériale*, edited by Christophe Bréchet, Anne Videau, and Ruth Webb, 49–62. Textes, images et monuments de l'Antiquité au haut Moyen Âge 11. Paris: Picard.

Tabbernee, William. 2007. *Fake Prophecy and Polluted Sacraments: Ecclesiastical and Imperial Reactions to Montanism.* Supplements to Vigiliae Christianae 84. Leiden: Brill.

Tarrant, Richard. 2016. *Texts, Editors, and Readers: Methods and Problems in Latin Textual Criticism.* Roman Literature and Its Contexts. Cambridge: Cambridge University Press.

Teitler, Hans Carel. 1985. *Notarii and Exceptores: An Inquiry into Role and Significance of Shorthand Writers in the Imperial and Ecclesiastical Bureaucracy of the Roman Empire (from the Early Principate to c. 450 A.D.).* Dutch Monographs on Ancient History and Archaeology 1. Amsterdam: Gieben.

Teske, Roland, ed. 2005. *The Works of Saint Augustine: A Translation for the Twenty-First Century. 2, Letters. 4, Letters 211–270, 1\*–29\**. New York: New City Press.

Theiner, Augustin, ed. 1864. *Annales ecclesiastici Caesaris Baronii*. Bar-le-Duc: Guérin.

Thomas, Christine M. 1998. "Stories Without Texts and Without Authors: The Problem of Fluidity in Ancient Novelistic Texts and Early Christian Literature." In *Ancient Fiction and Early Christian Narrative*, edited by Ronald F. Hock, Bradley J. Chance, and Judith Perkins, 273–91. Symposium Series / Society of Biblical Literature 6. Atlanta, GA: Scholars Press.

———. 2003. *The Acts of Peter, Gospel Literature, and the Ancient Novel: Rewriting the Past*. Oxford: Oxford University Press.

Thomas, Nicholas L. 2011. *Defending Christ: The Latin Apologists Before Augustine*. Studia Traditionis Theologiae 9. Turnhout: Brepols.

Thomson, H. J. 1949. *Prudentius*. Loeb Classical Library 2. Cambridge, MA: Harvard University Press.

Thür, Gerhard. 2006. "Synomosia." In *Brill's New Pauly*, edited by Hubert Cancik and Helmut Schneider. Leiden: Brill, http://dx.doi.org/10.1163/1574-9347_bnp_e1127460.

Thurn, Hans. 1984. *Die Handschriften der Universitätsbibliothek Würzburg. 3, 1. Die Pergamenthandschriften der ehemaligen Dombibliothek*. Wiesbaden: Harrassowitz.

Tilley, Maureen A. 1996. *Donatist Martyr Stories: The Church in Conflict in Roman North Africa*. Translated Texts for Historians 24. Liverpool: Liverpool University Press.

Timpanaro, Sebastiano. 1963. *La genesi del metodo del Lachmann*. Bibliotechina del saggiatore 18. Florence: Le Monnier.

———. 2005. *The Genesis of Lachmann's Method*. Translated by Glenn W. Most. Chicago: University of Chicago Press.

Trigg, Joseph W. 1984. "Martyrs and Churchmen in Third-Century North Africa." In *Studia Patristica, 15: Papers Presented to the 7th International Conference on Patristic Studies Held in Oxford 1975, 1: Inaugural Lecture, Editiones, Critica, Biblica, Historica, Theologica, Philosophica, Liturgica*, edited by Elizabeth A. Livingston, 242–46. Texte und Untersuchungen zur Geschichte der altchristlichen Literatur 128. Berlin: Akademie-Verlag.

Ullman, B. L. 1942. "History and Tragedy." *Transactions and Proceedings of the American Philological Association* 73: 25–53.

Uytfanghe, Marc Van. 1993. "L'hagiographie: Un genre chrétien ou antique tardif?" *Analecta Bollandiana* 111: 135–88.

Van Beek, Cornelius J. M. J., ed. 1936. *Passio Sanctarum Perpetuae et Felicitatis. 1, Textum graecum et latinum ad fidem codicum mss.* Nijmegen: Dekker & van de Vegt.

Van Hoof, G. 1883. "Acta græca S. Theodori Ducis martyris." *Analecta Bollandiana* 2: 359–67.

Vandoni, Mariangela. 1959. "Dai papiri dell'Università di Milano." *Acme* 12: 189–200.

Vessey, Mark. 2005. "Reading like Angels: Derrida and Augustine on the Book (for a History of Literature)." In *Augustine and Postmodernism: Confessions and Circumfession*, edited by John D. Caputo and Michael J. Scanlon, 173–208. Bloomington: Indiana University Press.

———. 2010. "Writing Before Literature: Derrida's Confessions and the Latin Christian World." In *Derrida and Antiquity*, edited by Miriam Leonard, 289–317. Oxford: Oxford University Press.

Vetter, Paul. 1881. "Über die armenischen Übersetzung der Kirchengeschichte des Eusebius." *Theologische Quartalschrift* 63: 250–76.

Vichi, Anna Maria Giorgetti, and Sergio Mottironi. 1961. *Catalogo dei manoscritti della Biblioteca Vallicelliana. 1.* Indici e cataloghi. Nuova serie 7. Rome: Istituto poligrafico dello Stato.

Walbank, F. W. 1955. "Tragic History: A Reconsideration." *Bulletin of the Institute of Classical Studies* 2 (1): 4–14.

———. 1960. "History and Tragedy." *Historia: Zeitschrift für alte Geschichte* 9 (2): 216–34.

Waltzing, Jean-Pierre, ed. 1931. *Apologétique / Tertullien*. Paris: Les Belles Lettres.

Weidmann, Frederick W. 1999. *Polycarp & John: The Harris Fragments and Their Challenge to the Literary Traditions*. Notre Dame, IN: University of Notre Dame Press.

Weiss, Jean-Pierre. 1990. "Une œuvre de la Renaissance carolingienne: La passion de Pons de Cimiez." In *Hommage à René Braun. 2, Autour de Tertullien*, edited by Jean Granarolo and Michèle Biraud, 203–22. Publications de la faculté des lettres et sciences humaines de Nice 56. Paris: Les Belles Lettres.

West, M. L. 1973. *Textual Criticism and Editorial Technique Applicable to Greek and Latin Texts*. Stuttgart: Teubner.

Wheeldon, M. J. 1989. "True Stories: The Reception of Historiography in Antiquity." In *History as Text: The Writing of Ancient History*, edited by Averil Cameron, 33–63. London: Duckworth.

White, John L. 1984. "New Testament Epistolary Literature in the Framework of Ancient Epistolography." In *Aufstieg und Niedergang der römischen Welt (ANRW). Teil 2. Principat. Band 25. Religion, 2*, edited by Wolfgang Haase and Hildegard Temporini, 1730–65. Berlin: de Gruyter.

Whitmarsh, Tim. 2013. *Beyond the Second Sophistic: Adventures in Greek Postclassicism*. Berkeley: University of California Press.

Wiater, Nicolas. 2018. "Documents and Narrative: Reading the Roman-Carthaginian Treaties in Polybius' Histories." In *Polybius and His Legacy*. Trends in Classics. Supplementary Volumes 60. Berlin: de Gruyter.

Wills, Lawrence M. 2015. "The Differentiation of History and Novel: Controlling the Past, Playing with the Past." In *Early Christian and Jewish Narrative: The Role of Religion in Shaping Narrative Forms*, edited by Ilaria Ramelli and Judith Perkins, 13–29. Wissenschaftliche Untersuchungen zum Neuen Testament 348. Tübingen: Mohr Siebeck.

Wiśniewski, Robert. 2019. *The Beginnings of the Cult of Relics*. Oxford: Oxford University Press.

Wolter, Michael. 1988. "Die anonymen Schriften des Neuen Testaments: Annäherungsversuch an ein literarisches Phänomen." *Zeitschrift für die Neutestamentliche Wissenschaft* 79: 1–16.

Woodman, Anthony J. 1988. *Rhetoric in Classical Historiography: Four Studies*. London: Routledge.

———. 2008. "Cicero on Historiography: De Oratore 2.51–64." *Classical Journal* 104 (1): 23–31.

Zadorojnyi, Alexei V. 2013. "Shuffling Surfaces: Epigraphy, Power, and Integrity in the Graeco-Roman Narratives." In *Inscriptions and Their Uses in Greek and Latin Literature*, edited by Peter Liddel and Polly Low, 365–86. Oxford Studies in Ancient Documents. Oxford: Oxford University Press.

Zahn, Theodor, ed. 1876. *Ignatii et Polycarpi Epistulae martyria fragmenta*. Patrum apostolicorum opera 2. Leipzig: Hinrichs.

Zumthor, Paul. 1972. *Essai de poétique médiévale*. Poétique. Paris: Éditions du Seuil.

———. 1992. *Toward a Medieval Poetics*. Translated by Philip Bennett. Minneapolis: University of Minnesota Press.

Zwierlein, Otto, and Daniel Kölligan. 2014. *Die Urfassungen der Martyria Polycarpi et Pionii und das Corpus Polycarpianum*. Untersuchungen zur antiken Literatur und Geschichte 116. Berlin: de Gruyter.

## ACKNOWLEDGMENTS

The research for this book started when I was asked to prepare a collection of Acts of Christian martyrs that was meant to be a new Musurillo. This endeavor resulted in the publication with Oxford University Press of *Greek and Latin Narratives about the Ancient Martyrs* (2017). Collecting texts with new criteria was always meant to be a first step in my research project. This monograph is its second (and final) step and offers, I hope, new ways of approaching the texts.

I presented aspects of my research in several venues and I want to acknowledge the helpful feedback I received after such presentations. Mark Vessey provided key input when he pointed me toward a text in which Derrida discusses the trembling boundaries between testimony and fiction. James Rives, to whom I also owe a lot for his prolonged, generous hospitality in Durham, where I was stranded by bad weather after a talk, encouraged me to pursue looking into the post-Valerian persecution period as a context of composition for the earliest African martyr narratives at a crucial turn in my project. Audiences at Princeton University, University of Southern California, University of California at Santa Barbara, Oxford University, and Haverford College generously welcomed the first iteration of many of the ideas that ended up in the book. I was lucky to receive very generous readers' reports that helped to clarify many points and reorganize some parts. Afterward, Brent Shaw told me he was one of the readers and we engaged in a very profitable dialogue for which I thank him very much.

Once again Alice Brigance's help has been invaluable. I also want to thank Virginia Burrus for forwarding my book proposal to her co-editors of the series Divinations: Rereading Late Ancient Religion and to Jerry Singerman, the Senior Humanities Editor with University of Pennsylvania Press. I am obliged to Jerry and to Noreen O'Connor-Abel for shepherding the book through the process of editing and production.